Praise for
Books from The Planning Shop

"User-friendly and exhaustive…highly recommended. Abrams' book works because she tirelessly researched the subject. Most how-to books on entrepreneurship aren't worth a dime; among the thousands of small business titles, Abrams' [is an] exception."

— *Forbes*

"There are plenty of decent business-plan guides out there, but Abrams' was a cut above the others I saw. *The Successful Business Plan* won points with me because it was thorough and well organized, with handy worksheets and good quotes. Also, Abrams does a better job than most at explaining the business plan as a planning tool rather than a formulaic exercise.
Well done."

— *Inc.*

"Abrams' book offers a complete approach to creating your plan. Surrounding her explanatory material with commentary from top CEOs, venture capitalists, and business owners, Abrams helps you see your idea through the eyes of potential investors. Her book and your idea deserve each other."

—*Home Office Computing*

"This book stands head and shoulders above all other business plan books, and is the perfect choice for the beginner and the experienced business professional. Rhonda Abrams turns writing a professional, effective business plan into a journey of discovery about your business."

—*BizCountry*

"If you'd like something that goes beyond the mere construction of your plan and is more fun to use, try *The Successful Business Plan: Secrets and Strategies*, by Rhonda Abrams…this book can take the pain out of the process."

—*Small Business School,
PBS television show*

"I would not use any other book for my course on Business Development. *The Successful Business Plan* is the best I've ever seen, read, or used in a classroom environment."

—*Prof. David Gotaskie,
Community College of Allegheny County,
Pittsburgh, PA*

The Owner's Manual
for Small Business

Rhonda Abrams

the**Planning**shop

PALO ALTO, CALIFORNIA

The Owner's Manual for Small Business

©2005 by Rhonda Abrams. Published by The Planning Shop™

ISBN 13: 978-0-9740801-5-4
ISBN: 0-9740801-5-2
Library of Congress Control Number: 2005906052

Project Editor: Mireille Majoor
Cover and interior design: Arthur Wait

Services for our readers

Colleges, business schools, corporate purchasing:

The Planning Shop offers special discounts and supplemental materials for universities, business schools, and corporate training. Contact:

info@PlanningShop.com

or call 650-289-9120

Free business tips and information

To receive Rhonda's free email newsletter on starting and growing a successful business, sign up at:

www.PlanningShop.com

The Planning Shop™
555 Bryant Street, #180
Palo Alto, CA 94301 USA
650-289-9120

Fax: 650-289-9125
Email: info@PlanningShop.com
www.PlanningShop.com

The Planning Shop™ is a division of Rhonda, Inc., a California corporation.

Printed in Canada.

10 9 8 7 6 5 4 3 2

To

John and Barbara Packard

and

Raymond and Etienne Capiaux,

who have believed in me and supported me.

Thank you, dear friends.

Who This Book Is For

This book addresses the entire range of issues facing any business owner or manager—from planning, strategies, leadership, and marketing, to money management, technology, operations, and much more!

Each topic is covered in a concise fashion with advice from one of America's most highly regarded business writers, enabling you to quickly gain the knowledge, skills, and motivation you need to successfully run and grow your business.

This book is for you if:

■ You own a business and want to do everything you can to ensure that you succeed and reach your goals.

■ You're looking for new strategies for growing your business and attracting customers.

■ Your business is facing changes or new challenges and you're seeking insight and inspiration on how best to respond.

■ You're seeking *specific* techniques and skills for managing the critical business tasks you face.

■ You want to make sure you take care of all the nitty-gritty details of business life and stay out of trouble.

■ You're in the process of starting a business and want to make sure you do it right.

■ You're a student in a business class and want to gain insight into the process of owning and running a business.

■ You're at a turning point in your business or career and are seeking ideas and inspiration.

■ You recognize the value of continually learning about business and gaining new insight on how to run and grow a company.

About Rhonda Abrams

A syndicated columnist, best-selling author, and popular public speaker, Rhonda Abrams has spent more than fifteen years advising, mentoring, and consulting with entrepreneurs and small business owners.

Her knowledge of the small business market and her passion for entrepreneurship have made her one of the nation's most recognized advocates for small business.

Rhonda's weekly newspaper column, "Successful Business Strategies," is the nation's most widely read column about entrepreneurship, reaching more than twenty million readers through USATODAY.com, Inc.com, *Costco Connection* magazine, and 130 newspapers.

Rhonda's first book, *The Successful Business Plan: Secrets & Strategies,* was acclaimed by Forbes magazine as one of the two best books for small business and by Inc. magazine as one of the six best books for start-ups. Now in its fourth edition, it is used as the primary text for business plan classes by more than one hundred business schools.

Rhonda's subsequent books include:

■ *Six-Week Start-Up,* helping entrepreneurs launch a business quickly and successfully by taking them week-by-week through the details of starting a business

■ *Wear Clean Underwear,* illuminating how great values make great companies

■ *What Business Should I Start?* guiding would-be entrepreneurs through a thoughtful process to identify the right business for them

■ *Business Plan In A Day,* showing time-pressed entrepreneurs how to quickly develop a compelling, well-written business plan

Books by Rhonda Abrams have been translated into Chinese, Japanese, Korean, Dutch, Portuguese, and Russian.

An experienced entrepreneur, Rhonda has started three companies, including a small business planning consulting firm. Her experience gives her a real-life understanding of the challenges facing entrepreneurs. Currently, she is the founder and CEO of The Planning Shop, which provides entrepreneurs with high-quality information and tools for developing successful businesses.

Rhonda was educated at Harvard University and UCLA. She lives in Palo Alto, California.

Table of Contents

Who This Book Is For vii

About Rhonda Abrams. ix

Introduction xvi

1. Thinking Like an Entrepreneur 1

Feature: Common Traits of Successful Entrepreneurs 2

What Inspires You?. 3

Do You Have What It Takes? 5

Your Chance of Success 7

Your Entrepreneurial Type. 9

From Employee to Entrepreneur 11

It's the Little Things 13

Feature: Status Symbols for the Self-Employed. 14

Facing Our Fears. 15

Learning Courage. 17

Succeeding in Your First Business. 19

Feature: Keys to a "Training-Wheel Business" 20

2. Your Business Concept. 21

Your Business Concept. 23

Feature: Discovering Your Business Concept 24

How Good Is Your Business Idea? 25

Choosing the Right Business 27

Follow Your Passion? 29

Yes, but Is It a Business? 31

3. Turning Dreams into Reality. 33

Turning Dreams into Reality. 35

Goals versus Tasks 37

Commit Yourself to the Turn. 39

Feature: Guidelines for Goals 40

Seizing Opportunities 41

4. Embracing Change 43

Things Are About to Change 45

Feature: Types of Changes Your Company May Face 46

Is It Time to Throw in the Towel? 47

Feature: Change Takes Time 48

Turning Failure into Success 49

Feature: The Promise of Change 50

Get Over It! 51

5. Strategy 53

Focusing on Your Focus 55

Feature: Your Mission Statement 56

Developing Your Strategic Position 57

Finding Your Niche 59

Feature: How Do You Find Your Niche? 60

Paranoia Can Save Your Business 61

Feature: Steps to Diversify Your Business 62

Who's Your Competition? 63

Checking Out the Competition 65

Competing with the Big Guys 67

What Does Winning Mean? 69

The Art of Setting Prices 71

Competing on Price Alone 73

Don't Nickel & Dime Your Customers 75

Feature: Rule of Thumb for Extra Charges: 76

Give It Away to Grow Your Business 77

Preparing Your Businessto Go On without You 79

Develop Your Exit Strategy 81

Feature: A Story about Setting Professional Fees 83

6. Growth 85

Feature: Rhonda's Rules for Growth 86

Committing to Growth 87

How Does Your Business Grow? 89

How Do I Make More Money? 91

Annual Plan for Success 93

Feature: Keys to Annual Planning 95

Feature: One Big New Thing 96

A Virtual Approach to Growth 97

Feature: Is It Time for Your Business to Leave Home? 99

7. Marketing 101

Finding New Customers.. 103
Feature: Marketing Techniques 104
Best Business Name Ever 105
Make the Most of Your Business Card 107
Get the Word Out about Your Business................................ 109
Telling Customers What to Think about You 111
How to Manipulate the Media... 113
Deliver Your Message to Your Customers............................. 115
Advertising That Stays Around 117
Getting Your Ads Right.. 119
Feature: Create a One-Page Sales Sheet 121

8. The Face of Your Business 123

Feature: Networking Basics... 124
Develop Your Elevator Pitch 125
How to Have a Business Lunch 127
Feature: Do's and Don'ts for Business Lunches 128
Powerful Presentations 129
Getting Comfortable When All Eyes Are on You 131
Feature: Don't Get Barbecue Sauce on Your Business Card 132
Dress for Success in Your Business 133
What Kind of Website Is Right for Your Business? 135
Feature: Increasing Website Traffic................................. 137
Gold by Association 139

9. Customers and Sales 141

Who's Your Customer? 143
Getting to Know Your Customers 145
How to Get Your First Customer 147
Make More from Each Customer...................................... 149
Turn One-Timers into Lifetimers 151
Sales Are the Heart of Business 153
Responding to Prospects... 155
Writing Winning Proposals 157
Landing Big Accounts... 159
Sometimes the Best Word Is "No" 161

Making Cold Calls. 163
Dealing with Difficult Customers 165
Getting Rid of Your Best Customers. 167
Encouraging Customer Complaints. 169
Feature: Keys to Successful Sales. 171

10. Leading Your Team 173

Who Do I Want to Work With? 175
Going from Doing to Leading 177
A Field Guide to Advisors. 179
I Get By with a Little Help from My Friends 181
Feature: Partnership Tips. 183
Feature: Working with Friends. 184
All in the Family?. 185
Getting Ready to Hire Others. 187
Feature: Building a Virtual Staff 189
Feature: Are Two Better Than One? 190
Hiring Your First Employee 191
Learning to Be a Boss 193
Attracting, Hiring, and Retaining Great Employees 195
Feature: Who Do You Want on Your Team? 198
Making the Most of Employees. 199
Getting Employees to Use Initiative 201
Avoiding BADD Boss Syndrome 203
Feature: Inexpensive Ways to Reward Employees 205

11. Money and Financing 207

Feature: Money Lingo. 208
The Bottom Line of Business 209
Feature: Money Management Tips 210
Where Do Numbers Come From?. 211
Finding Money for Your Business 213
Start-up Money from Banks? 215
Prepare to Get Your Loan. 217
Show Me the Money?. 219
Using Credit Cards to Finance Your Business 221
Feature: Tax Tips 222

Buy or Lease? 223

Say Charge It! 225

Do I Need to Collect Sales Tax? 227

Feature: Sales Tax Information Resource 228

Spring into Savings 229

12. Details, Details, Details 231

Feature: Nine Ways to Ensure Your Company's Survival .232

Tips and Tricks for Business Life. 233

Overwhelmed by Too Many Choices. 235

How to Get More Hours in a Day. 237

Would It Kill You to See a Lawyer? 239

Feature: All Those Little Government Things 240

Remember the Independent Contractor Deadline 241

Home Office Issues 243

Working from a Distance. 245

Preparing for the Unexpected 247

Go Outside and Play 249

Feature: Vacation Planning Tips 250

Feature: Business Lessons from Baseball 251

Feature: A Dog's View of Business 252

Doing Well by Doing Good 253

Great Faith. Great Doubt. Great Effort. 256

Index 261

Acknowledgments. 268

Introduction

Dear Reader,

Over the years, I've often wished I could find a business consultant in a book—a source I could turn to for ideas, inspiration, or answers. Why, I wondered, didn't my business come with an owner's manual?

After all, virtually everything I have—my computer, my DVD player, even my toaster—came with a manual. But the single most complicated thing I own—my business—came with nothing but a good idea and a lot of motivation.

I decided that since nobody else had developed an Owner's Manual for Small Business, I would create one myself.

Like many entrepreneurs, my personal business odyssey has been a story of growth, change, and excitement. Twenty years ago, I started out with a home-based, one-person consulting business. Over time, my company grew. My clients grew bigger, too, until I was developing business plans for larger and larger companies, even Fortune 100 companies, and had clients all over the country and the world.

In 1994, I saw the promise of the Internet and began an Internet company for small business owners. It was profitable at a time when few dot-com companies made money, and I later sold it.

A few years earlier, I began writing a column about small business for the Gannett News Service. It continues to appear weekly in USAToday.com and over 100 newspapers throughout the U.S. I'm proud to say it's still the most widely distributed small business column in the country. I'm also invited to speak to entrepreneurs' groups throughout the world about how to start and grow businesses.

Today I own a fast-growing publishing company. I deal with the real-life issues facing all entrepreneurs—managing cash flow, making payroll, closing sales, raising money, getting product out the door, and on and on.

To prepare this *Owner's Manual,* I thought about the things I wished someone had told me as I grew my businesses—things I learned the hard way—as well as the questions I am asked most frequently by clients, readers, and entrepreneurs. I wanted to address the toughest issues business owners face, from getting started to exit plans to how to have a successful business lunch.

So turn to this handy *Owner's Manual for Small Business* when you need information, inspiration, or ideas. In the pages that follow, you'll find the advice you'd hear from me if we were meeting face to face—exactly the kind of advice I could have used when I was starting and growing my business.

Good luck with your own venture. I'm pulling for you all the way!

Rhonda Abrams

Thinking Like an Entrepreneur

Common Traits of Successful Entrepreneurs

■ **Ability to develop a clear focus.** You need to understand what makes your business different from your competitors'. Develop a vision and stick with it, rather than moving from one great idea to another. Many entrepreneurs fail because they're always finding their next idea more enticing than their current activities.

■ **Realistic expectations.** If you start a diet expecting to lose ten pounds every week, you'll soon be disappointed and give up. When your goals are more in line with reality, you're much more likely to stick with them and be successful. Very few people "get rich quick."

■ **Willingness to plan.** The most successful business owners are those who develop a clear set of objectives and devise a roadmap for achieving them. They study their market, competition, and operations and are willing to honestly examine the obstacles they are likely to face.

■ **Flexibility and adaptability.** While you need a concrete plan and a clear focus, you must likewise have the flexibility to respond to changing conditions. In business, as in life, all things change, and some things inevitably go wrong.

■ **Ability to overcome the fear of making sales.** At some level, every business owner must be a salesperson. You can't be afraid to cultivate customers, motivate employees, nurture suppliers. You don't have to have this skill when you start a business, but you'll have to develop it to stay in business.

■ **Willingness to work hard.** There's no getting around it; being in business means having to put in the hours to get the job done.

■ **Clear personal goals.** All of us have many competing goals. We want to make lots of money but be home when the kids get out of school. We want to have complete creative control but have a wide array of products and services. These goals are inevitably in conflict. To achieve success, you have to focus on what's really important to you and what is achievable.

■ **Experience.** You needn't have run General Motors to start a used car lot, but you should have some meaningful, related experience, either in your chosen industry or using the type of skills you'll need, before setting off on your own venture.

What Inspires You?

When you think about your business, what do you hope for? To make a lot of money? Use your creativity? Have more flexibility in your life? Do you see yourself working alone or building a company with other employees? Do you hope your company grows very large or do you want it to stay small?

As you build and grow your business, it's critical to understand what motivates you, so you can plan a company that responds to those personal needs. Otherwise, you can easily end up sabotaging a successful company. For instance, I've seen a fashion designer with a great need for creativity who ended up frustrated when her company grew so big she never had time to pick up a pencil. She started to torpedo her own success just so she could get back to the drawing board.

Entrepreneurs are motivated by what I call the Four C's: Creativity, Control, Challenge, and Cash. Of course, we each want all four of these to some degree, but knowing which we want or need most can help us structure our companies to best achieve our goals.

Keep in mind there are sometimes trade-offs between personal goals. Wanting more cash often means having less control; staying at the center of the creative process may mean you need to have a partner or grow slowly.

Which of the Four C's motivates you most?

The Four C's

■ **Creativity.** Entrepreneurs want to leave their mark. Their companies are not only a means of making a living, but a way of creating something that bears their stamp. Creativity comes in many forms, from designing or making a new "thing," to devising a new business process or a new way to make sales, handle customers, or reward employees.

If you have a high need for creativity, make certain you remain involved in the creative process as your company develops. You'll want to shape your business so it's not just an instrument for earning an income but also a means of maintaining your creative stimulation and making a larger contribution to society. But don't overpersonalize your company, especially if it's large. Allow room for others, particularly partners and key personnel, to share in the creative process.

■ **Control.** Most of us start businesses because we want more control over our own lives. Perhaps we want more control over how our good ideas are implemented. Perhaps we want, or need, more control of our

3

work hours or conditions so we can be more involved in family, community, or even golf! Control is a major motivator for most entrepreneurs—usually more important than money. But how much control you need—especially on a day-to-day basis—directly influences how large your company can be.

If you need or want a great deal of control over your time, you'll most likely need to keep your company smaller. In a large company, you'll have less immediate control over many decisions.

If you're a person who needs control, you can still grow your business larger. You'll need to structure communication and reporting systems to ensure that you have sufficient information about and direction over developments to give you personal satisfaction. If you seek outside funding in the form of investors, understand the nature of the control your funders will have, and be certain you are comfortable with these arrangements.

■ **Challenge.** If you're starting or expanding a business, it's clear you like challenge—at least to some degree. You're likely to be a problem solver and risk taker, enjoying the task of figuring out solutions to problems or devising new undertakings. Challenge-hungry entrepreneurs can be some of the most successful businesspeople, but they can also be their own worst enemies—flitting from one thing to another, never focusing long enough to succeed.

If you have a high need for challenge in your business life, it's important to develop positive means to meet this need, especially once your company is established and the initial challenge of starting a company is met. Otherwise, you may find yourself continually starting new projects that divert attention from your company's overall goals. As you plan your company, establish personal goals that not only provide you with sufficient stimulation, but also advance—rather than distract from—the growth of your business. (Or take up sky diving on the side!)

■ **Cash.** Every entrepreneur wants to make money. Perhaps it's just enough money to provide a decent income; perhaps it's so much money you can buy a jet. How much you want or need affects how you'll develop your business. Will you need investors and when? Will you sacrifice control to grow the business quickly?

Usually, control is the primary motivator for entrepreneurs. Control can mean the ability to make decisions, to directly influence the success of the company, or even to have the flexibility of choosing what hours and days to work. Others are motivated by the desire to create something new, whether art or software. My personal top motivator is "challenge," so I've developed a business that is always exposing me to new industries and management problems. Otherwise, I'd be bored. Those who are only motivated by cash often fail.

Do You Have What It Takes?

The cover story of a major business magazine carried the headline: "Do you have what it takes to start a business?" In the story, grinning entrepreneurs answered that question: "You've got to have a maniacal mind-set;" "I don't need an excessive amount of sleep;" "The odds are, most times, you fail."

If being in business means you have to be an obsessive insomniac doomed to failure, then why are these people smiling?

The fact is, that magazine got it wrong: you don't have to be a compulsive workaholic to start a business. Millions of entrepreneurs run successful enterprises, and, thankfully, they're not all obsessed solely with business. Most businesspeople find time for many other aspects to their lives—family, community, hobbies, religion, sports.

The multitude of successful small businesses might not make it to the Top 10, or even Top 100, list of "best companies," but those lists focus almost exclusively on *financial* factors.

But money is not what motivates most entrepreneurs. What do most small business owners care about?

■ **Creating something worthwhile.** This doesn't have to be a cure for cancer. It can be a new tool, a new computer program, a new widget that makes doing a job in your industry easier, or a service that helps people improve their lives.

■ **Using a talent.** Most people aren't going to establish ballet companies because they're amazing dancers, but lots of people start restaurants because they're terrific cooks, go into the accessory business because they love to design jewelry, or make and sell custom cabinets because they're great at woodworking.

■ **Having more time for family.** In today's world, it's hard to balance the desire or need to spend time with your family with most jobs. But by starting your own business, you may have more flexibility, so you can take the afternoon off to chaperone your daughter's Girl Scout troop or take your aging father to the doctor.

■ **Being your own boss.** Many people start businesses because they get tired of seeing their supervisors make stupid decisions or of working in companies where they have little or no influence. Things may not always work out when you are your own boss, but at least you know the mistakes that affect your life are your own.

■ **Creating jobs.** If you want to make the world a better place, one of the things you can do is create good jobs for others. There's justifiable pride in building a business that's big enough to give other people work so they can feed their families, go to school, or pay their rent. And when you treat them fairly and create a positive work environment, you've truly improved the world.

> ## You don't need to be a compulsive workaholic to start a business.

■ **Doing a better job.** Nothing is more frustrating than working for a company that's doing a lousy job. Knowing that you could serve the market better—improve the product, give better service, cut costs, treat employees more fairly—is a great motivator for starting your own company.

■ **Bringing your dog with you to work.** This isn't only about dogs, it's about having more control over your working conditions. It could be the ability to work from home, to wear casual clothes every day, or not to commute long distances. But having my dog with me was definitely one of my motives when I started my business.

In fact, that business magazine was out of touch with the reality of American entrepreneurship. Few entrepreneurs want to—or need to—be obsessive insomniacs to succeed in business. What successful owners of small companies have in common is that they're motivated, self-directed, willing to take measured risks, determined, and optimistic.

If you have what it takes, you may not end up on the cover of a business magazine. But you may end up with the best small company in America: the one that meets your needs and reflects your values.

Your Chance of Success

After giving it careful consideration, you've finally decided to start your own business. But when you excitedly announce your decision at a family gathering, your brother-in-law Sheldon points his finger at you and says in his most ominous voice, "Fifty percent of all businesses fail in the first five years. Get a job."

You've got far better odds of succeeding in business than is commonly believed. That's because the statistics you'll hear about business *failures* almost always mean business *closings*. In many cases, the business hasn't failed, just changed.

For instance, I had my own—successful—consulting practice for many years. Like most sole proprietors, I reported my business income on my personal income tax return, using my own social security number. When I incorporated, the business got its own tax identification number, and I stopped filing a "Schedule C" on my personal tax return. That means my first business probably shows up in statistics as a business "death" even though it was actually getting larger.

To paraphrase Mark Twain, "Rumors of my death are greatly exaggerated."

Overwhelmingly, businesses don't die or fail; the owners close them for reasons unrelated to whether the business is making money.

Take restaurants, for instance. Restaurants have a notoriously high "failure" rate. You'll often hear that 90% of restaurants fail in the first year.

In a study in Columbus, Ohio, Professor H.G. Parsa of Ohio State University tracked new restaurants from 1996–1999. In the first year, 26% closed. Another 19% closed the second year, and 14% the third. Collectively, 59% of new restaurants closed those three years.

> **Businesses typically don't die or fail; owners close them for reasons unrelated to money.**

Now, even though these numbers are much better than the 90% failure rate bandied about, it's not particularly heartening to know that six out of ten restaurants closed in three years.

However, Professor Parsa found that reasons other than economic necessity made the owners decide to close. They cited divorce, poor health, and most importantly, an unwillingness to make the immense time commitment necessary as reasons for shutting their doors.

In other words, they had what Dr. David Birch, former head of a research firm specializing in studying small business data, called the "I Had No Idea" syndrome. Would-be entrepreneurs don't realize just how much is involved with running a business.

After running a business for a year or two, many people discover the effort is more than they anticipated. Suddenly, they're the ones who have to keep the books, find the customers, pay the bills. When the reality sets in, many decide they'd rather return to the relative ease of having a job, and they close up shop.

"Historically about 95% of business endings have been because the owners have chosen to close rather than the financial condition of the company forcing a closing," says Dr. Birch. "While about 500,000 businesses close each year, business failings are only about 50,000 … Once you've hit five years, your odds of survival go way up. Only two to three percent of businesses older than five shut down each year."

The lesson? The best way to get over the first tough years is to be prepared. Find out as much as you can *before* you open your doors. Talk to people who run their own businesses, especially businesses similar to yours, and get a realistic understanding of the time, finances, and emotional resources necessary. Create a business plan. Keep your eyes open—not to the possibility of failure, but to the very real demands of running your own business.

Once you make it over the hurdle of adjusting to the entrepreneurial life, your chances of success are excellent. And Sheldon will be wrong again.

Survival Rates of Businesses

First year:	**85%**
Second:	**70%**
Third:	**62%**
Fourth:	**55%**
Fifth:	**50%**
Sixth:	**47%**
Seventh:	**44%**
Eighth:	**41%**
Ninth:	**38%**
Tenth:	**35%**

Source: Cognetics

Your Entrepreneurial Type

Most business books and experts will tell you it takes a certain type of person to be an entrepreneur. They might say you have to be outgoing, risk-taking, and able to make sales.

It's just not true. Look around: You may know someone who's successful but is a grouch, hates to take a risk, or doesn't get up before noon. They can be an entrepreneur—a successful entrepreneur at that—if they find a business that suits their entrepreneurial type.

What do I mean by "entrepreneurial type"?

When they first consider being in business for themselves, most people think about their interests. But that's just a starting point. Let's say you're interested in antiques. Does that mean you should sell antiques, appraise them, or refinish them? Even if you want to sell antiques, does that mean owning a retail store, selling them on eBay, or finding bargains at flea markets and marking them up for sale to retail stores? Your interest is clear—antiques—but you've got a number of different ways to build a business around that interest.

Based on my experience with thousands of entrepreneurs, I've come up with a number of entrepreneurial types. Here are a few of the most common:

■ **Advisor.** Lots of people would like to be paid just for giving advice; usually it takes a great deal of experience or education to be able to do so. Some kinds of advisors include attorneys, accountants, and financial planners. But many of the best salespeople also consider themselves—and are considered by their customers—to be advisors. For instance, I look to my insurance salesperson to responsibly guide me in my choice and amount of coverage.

■ **Broker.** A broker is a go-between—someone who helps others find the products or services they need. They may charge a percentage of the sales price of the item brokered, a flat fee, or an hourly fee. Real estate agents are perhaps the best-known type of broker, but you could be a broker for almost any kind of product or service (except those with very narrow profit margins). You could, for instance, be an auto, mortgage, business, or even a wine broker. If you've got a strong area of expertise or interest—and enjoy shopping—being a broker is a low-cost way to go into business.

■ **Builder.** One of the largest segments of entrepreneurs are self-employed contractors—carpenters, electricians, plumbers, etc. Whether you're building a whole housing development or laying the floor in one apartment, if you enjoy seeing something created from nothing and you have the necessary skills, being a builder may be for you.

■ **Caretaker.** Our society has a great need to have people and things taken care of, maintained, assisted. That opens up lots of opportunities for those entrepreneurs who are patient and nurturing. If you're a person who can be consistent over time and see yourself as a helping personality, you may be the caretaking entrepreneurial type.

> You can be a successful entrepreneur if you find a business that suits your entrepreneurial type.

■ **Creator.** You may be a person with a vision. Creators include graphic or fashion designers, inventors, and business builders. Creators often need to team up with other entrepreneurs who are strong in sales or operations to help make their vision a financially viable reality.

■ **Owner.** If you've got money to invest, you might be able to put your capital to work for you. Whether you invest in stocks, real estate, vending machines, or businesses, being an active "owner" enables you to leverage your money into additional income without having to show up to work every day.

■ **Seller.** If you're good at sales, you should never have to go hungry. Great salespeople are always in demand. Many of them are self-employed, typically working on commission. If you're good at selling, and willing to work hard, you can earn a lot of money from sales.

So just about anyone can be an entrepreneur—a successful entrepreneur. The key is figuring out what entrepreneurial type suits your personality and your skills.

From Employee to Entrepreneur

This year—as every year—over a million people will start a business in America. And many millions more will start businesses worldwide.

Most will start their companies because they've always wanted to own their own business. Some, however, will become entrepreneurs because they've been laid off from a job.

Whatever brings you to entrepreneurship, you'll quickly find there's a big difference between being someone else's employee and working for yourself. Much of that difference is welcome and wonderful. I certainly think so, since I've been self-employed since 1986. But, frankly, if you've been an employee for a long time—especially for a big corporation—you're going to find some of the changes are tough to get used to.

What kinds of changes can you expect when you go from employee to entrepreneur?

■ **Money.** From now on, every dollar is *your* dollar. Even if you have investors or partners, at the end of the day, money becomes a lot more real. Whether you're spending it or earning it, every dollar has a direct impact on your personal income and well-being. Even if you were a conscientious employee, always watching the company's bottom line, you're going to find you have new respect for money when you're the last one paid, and every dollar spent or unearned could have ended up in your wallet.

Money consciousness is going to take a number of different forms. First, you're going to view expenditures a lot more carefully. For instance, if you worked for a Fortune 500 company, you probably didn't think a great deal about how much you spent on office supplies. But when you have to earn every dollar yourself, and you understand how hard money is to replace, that $29 label maker may seem an unnecessary luxury, especially when you know the same $29 could be used to buy clothes for your kids.

> ## From now on, every dollar is *your* dollar.

■ **Control.** This is definitely a two-edged sword. One of the best things about being your own boss is that you get to make the decisions. You no longer have to follow seemingly senseless corporate mandates. But with control comes responsibility, and you're going to find you have to make oodles of decisions.

There are the big decisions when you first start, such as what kind of business to go into, what kind of financing to look for, where to locate. But the hundreds of smaller choices can be just as intimidating—whether or not to exhibit at a trade show, what kind of insurance to buy, when to hire employees, which tasks are most important, and on and on. It can be exhausting, rather than exhilarating, when so many decisions end up on your desk.

■ **Humility.** Few things instill as much pride as earning your own living. When you do that in your own business, you have the right to be especially proud. But with that pride comes a lot of other stuff too, such as running the errands, stuffing the envelopes, apologizing to obnoxious customers, emptying the garbage. I once heard about a man who was self-employed just one day: when he went to start work and realized there was no one else to order a desk or phones, he quit.

■ **Risk.** Perhaps the biggest change of all is going to be your relationship to risk. When you're an employee, you're concerned with taking care of your career, and it's typically wiser to take fewer risks and thus make fewer mistakes. In your own business, however, taking fewer risks and doing less isn't an option.

If you think these differences seem overwhelming, don't be completely put off by the idea of becoming an entrepreneur. One of the greatest benefits in going from employee to self-employed is that you discover a lot about yourself, including the many talents you never realized you had.

It's the Little Things

Here's a quiz: When you meet someone new, what's the second question you're most likely to be asked? Answer: "What do you do?" It's not just to figure out whether you're a welder or a writer—it's to determine how important you are. For the self-employed, that question can be tough on the ego.

In America, we associate status with our jobs. We feel good about having a fancy office or important job title. Even if we have an entry-level job, if we work with a big company, we often feel a sense of reflected status from the name of our employer.

So when you go from employee to entrepreneur, giving up the trappings of status and success can be tough. And it can be the little things that make you most uncomfortable: standing in line at the post office instead of going to the mail room, buying your own office supplies, answering your own phone.

Even good things can make you feel awkward: giving up ties or pantyhose, going to a child's school in the middle of the day, not having to report to anyone.

Even more frustrating—though you'll get over it—is when you make a lot of money, but no one knows how well you're doing. After all, you still work at home and wear jeans. I had worked for myself for seven years before my friends took me seriously. What changed their impression? I got my first overseas client. Trust me: when someone pays you to go to Australia, you suddenly get respect.

But I knew I was serious long before that. Although I had given up a job where I had an office with a view, assistants, and an expense account, I didn't miss any of it (well, maybe the expense account). Part of the reason is that early on, I took some steps to make myself feel good about being self-employed.

I set up a part of my living room as my "office," printed up business cards, and changed the way I answered my phone (from "Hello" to "Rhonda Abrams speaking"). More importantly, I found a symbol—a status symbol—to remind me of my importance.

For me, it was flowers. My first couple of years in business, I didn't have much money and every penny counted. I lived on cheap spaghetti. But every week, I bought myself flowers for my desk. Somehow, looking at those flowers made me feel like I'd arrived at a "real" office.

Little things matter. You can't afford the assistant, you won't necessarily have a separate room for your office, and if you travel, you're going to take economy instead of business class. But you can find a number of little ways to remind yourself that you're now the owner of a business.

Status Symbols for the Self-Employed

■ **Business cards.** Absolutely! You can't exist without them. They are a must!

■ **A telephone line just for business calls.** This is especially important if you live with others.

■ **Name your company.** Even if you choose "Chris Smith and Associates," you'll feel more like you're in business with a business name. (But keep in mind that if you use any name other than your own, including "and Associates," to be perfectly legal, you may have to file a DBA ("Doing Business As") statement with your local county, city, or state.)

■ **Give yourself a title.** Hey, you really can grow up to be President! In my company, I'm the "Chief Entrepreneur."

■ **Get dressed every day.** No, of course, I didn't think you were going to work nude. But how about getting out of those sweats?

■ **Set up an "office."** Even if your office is just a desk in the corner of the family room, set aside some space used just for your business.

■ **Get your own domain name for email.** It sounds a lot more professional to have an email address such as chris@yourbusiness.com than an email address of chris12345@yahoo.com. It's not very expensive or difficult, and it helps your customers or clients remember you.

■ **Get a gadget.** Hey, we all like our toys. Having a cell phone, a cool computer, or other device can make you feel like you've arrived.

Facing Our Fears

When I started my business in 1986, my two neighbors were terrified at my decision. Both of them worked for a huge bank, and they couldn't understand how I could give up the security of a job for the insecurity of owning my own business. "Aren't you afraid to give up a paycheck?"

Of course I was scared. Starting a business is a big step. As frightening as it is to start a new job, opening up your own shop is even more fearsome. But I knew I had to face my fears if I wanted to change my life.

Fear is a funny thing. Many times, we willingly do things that make us afraid. We line up for horror movies, terrify ourselves on roller coasters, or pay large sums of money to skydive out of planes. Some people enjoy bungee jumping. Talk about scary!

Many of the fears we face in business, we willingly bring on ourselves. The very fact that we are in business for ourselves, rather than staying within the perceived security of a job, is a choice we make.

All too often, we try to run away from our fears, in both our business and our personal lives. Yet, when we try to escape our fears, they often overtake us. If we're afraid of failure, we might not even try. If we're intimidated by success, we may unwittingly avoid those actions that lead to achievement. When we fear change, we stop ourselves from attempting new things.

Fear inevitably leads to procrastination. We all put off doing things that scare us. We fear confrontation, so we avoid dealing with an unhappy customer, counseling an under-performing employee, working things out with a family member. We delay starting a project because we're afraid the client won't like it.

> **All too often, we try to run away from our fears, in both our business and our personal lives.**

But when we allow our fear to stifle us, things only become worse. We now have less time to finish the project, the customer is even unhappier because his complaints weren't dealt with, the employee keeps making mistakes.

Being in business, I've had to learn to battle my fears. Few things in life seem as terrifying as making your first sales call, taking out your first loan, or firing an employee. But there may come a time when you have to do some of these or you won't survive.

Our fears never go away—they just change over time. About a year after I started my consulting company, I asked a friend who had been in business for fifteen years when you get over the fear of never finding another client. His response: "Never." He wasn't exactly right—that fear went away, but I've got new ones.

By now I know I'll always have work. Instead my fears focus more on making the right decisions about which directions to grow my business, whether I'm utilizing or motivating employees in the best way, and the one fear that, indeed, never goes away—can I manage my cash flow well enough to grow my business and pay my bills at the same time?

I've learned that fears, once faced, become less scary. Each time we triumph over a fear, we grow in confidence. We learn that most of the horrible things we fear never come to pass. Even when some of our fears are realized, we find that they're more tolerable than we imagined. We learn we can survive.

The next time you're afraid, ask yourself, "What's the worst thing that can happen? How likely is that?" Then ask yourself, "What happens if I don't do the thing I fear?" Because there are costs—sometimes huge costs—to not facing our fears.

Remember my two neighbors who were afraid to leave their secure jobs? The huge bank for which they worked was acquired. Both of them lost their jobs.

Sometimes the only way to survive is to face our fears—by looking at them straight on and saying, "I can do this even though I'm afraid." Still, I'm not taking up bungee jumping—some fears I'm willing to live with.

Learning Courage

"I'd love to have my own business, but I'm not a risk taker."

I've heard that statement hundreds of times from people who dream of being entrepreneurs. They recognize that at the core of being in business is the ability to take risks. But most leave it at that—thinking you're either born a risk taker or you're not. That's not true. You can actually learn to be braver in both your business and your personal lives.

Taking risks is scary; you'll be afraid. The question is whether you let that fear paralyze you or you learn to deal with it. Conquering fear is a skill, not an art. With determination and practice, you can acquire it over time.

First of all, you have to learn that fear is normal. We look at a woman who's left a high-paying job to start a business, and we think, "Gosh, how come she's not afraid?" The truth is she is almost certainly frightened. Risk takers live with lots of fear, but they deal with their fears rather than turn away from their dreams. I once heard that Frank Sinatra got nauseous before every performance, he suffered so much from stage fright. What would have happened if when he was twenty, he decided he was just too afraid to sing? Remember, courage is not the absence of fear but the willingness to overcome it.

Ask any successful entrepreneur how they felt in business the first few years and they're likely to say, "Scared out of my mind!"

They'll also say they felt exhilarated, liberated, challenged, and more alive than they'd ever been. Because the flip side of fear is the adrenaline, motivation, and even power it gives you (that's why people like to skydive and bungee jump).

You can train yourself to get used to living with a certain degree of fear. The best way is not to jump into a big risk with both feet, but to first challenge yourself with smaller efforts.

> **Conquering fear is a skill, not an art. With determination and practice, you can acquire it over time.**

I've learned a lot about conquering fear from participating in sports. I've gravitated to sports I'm somewhat afraid of—horseback riding, skiing, ice skating. With each, the fear of getting hurt never left me, but as I acquired greater skill in the sport, I also gained greater skill in accepting those fears. The fears became an increasingly small part of the overall experience.

Athletics can also help you get used to falling down and picking yourself up again—a skill you'll definitely need in business. In the

17

sports I play, I fall down a lot. I get bruised regularly, and I've broken a rib horseback riding and cut my head ice skating. But I continued.

You learn you can live with bruises; they go away. And almost no falls are truly life-threatening. The same thing is true in business. You'll make mistakes. They'll bruise your ego or your balance sheet. They'll knock the wind out of you, and you may have to sit it out for awhile. But if you get back in, you'll be stronger, better, more confident.

A ski instructor once told me, "If you're not falling, you're not learning." So one thing I do when I fall—in sports or in business—is ask myself, "What did I learn?" When I make a mistake, I try to reflect on what I learned from that experience.

Famed 49ers football coach Bill Walsh told me, "Some people think it's either win or lose. But every game is followed by another … You're always preparing for the next one … Even in the process of losing … you're improving and refining your skills, and how well you perform when you lose is important in determining whether you will eventually win."

So be gentle on yourself when you take a risk and it doesn't work out quite right. Don't use the word "failure." Very few of us fail entirely. We just fall down, make a mistake.

You'll find it far easier to take more risks if you pick yourself up, learn from each experience, forgive yourself, and move on.

It's also important to remember the risks associated with *not* taking risks. Often we think the safest course is to stay in one place, try to be content with a miserable situation. But that might be the worst course of action of all. We may have misjudged the level of security we truly have. Or even worse, we may slowly eat away at our own sense of worth, our own happiness.

So if you're one of those who think you're not a risk taker, why not challenge yourself? Take a few small, unimportant risks. Allow yourself to make mistakes. Try again. You may surprise yourself and find you're more of a risk taker than you ever imagined.

Succeeding in Your First Business

I'm what's called a "serial entrepreneur." I'm now running my fourth business; I doubt it will be my last. I'm not alone. Many successful entrepreneurs build one company after another, expanding the scope and size of each subsequent company.

If you're new to the entrepreneurial life, it's helpful to know your first business may not be your last. Many first-time entrepreneurs believe they have to be a huge success the very first time they're the boss. They don't. You can become a big success by starting small.

It's natural—and desirable—to have big dreams and big goals. Just remember, you're going to be learning a lot this first time out. You're getting used to dealing with customers, making sales, devising marketing plans, handling finances, adjusting to the risk and responsibility. All of that takes time.

Moreover, as you increase your knowledge of your market, your product or service, and you make additional contacts, you'll almost certainly decide to change many aspects of your business. Eventually, you may choose to close your first business and start another.

Since it's your first business—not your last—why not start with what I call a "training-wheel business?"

By "training-wheel business," I don't mean to be insulting, or to imply that's it a business to be run by kids. I mean choosing a type of business that provides enough support to the first-time entrepreneur so that

when you make the inevitable mistakes, you won't fall so hard.

My own "training-wheel business," for instance, was my management consulting practice. I was a consultant for fourteen years, and if I didn't attract and retain clients, I couldn't keep a roof over my head or food on my table. It was certainly a serious—and fortunately, successful—business.

But consulting is the type of business that is a perfect example of a "training-wheel business." Consulting costs little to start: I needed a computer, business cards, and a phone line. The overhead was low: I worked out of my home and my advertising consisted of attending networking events. All of that meant I had more time to build and grow my business; I had more time to learn.

Making a product? Sell it first at local crafts fairs instead of trying to get it in department stores. Becoming a consultant? Start with small businesses instead of trying to land corporate clients.

If you're new to business, give yourself the opportunity to learn. After all, as I've learned, you'll have plenty of other chances.

Keys to a "Training-Wheel Business"

■ **Low start-up costs.** If you need a lot of equipment, facilities, or staff to start, you'll have to borrow or raise money or use up all your savings in start-up costs. Avoid business concepts that require large up-front expenditures, so you can get into business sooner.

■ **Low overhead.** Low fixed expenses will make it easier to pay your monthly bills. Avoid businesses such as manufacturing and retail, which require inventory, raw materials, high rent, or high labor costs. Instead, choose businesses with low overhead such as independent sales, consulting, and most service businesses.

■ **Proven product or service.** It's hard to sell customers on a new idea or new product. It's a lot easier to get a piece of an existing market than to build a new one—even if you have competition. If your product or service is too new, it takes much longer to build a customer base.

■ **Established marketing channels.** If you have to be creative to reach customers, it's going to cost a lot and take time. It's much easier to sell products or services through proven methods such as trade shows, networking events, and newspaper advertisements.

■ **Simple sales structure.** Many first-time entrepreneurs are attracted by multi-level—or network—marketing programs. These have complicated sales structures, focusing on building "down lines." Avoid these. Instead, look for businesses where you sell directly to the customer/client or with very few layers between the manufacturer and the customer.

■ **A niche.** It's much easier to compete for customers when you specialize. By clearly targeting a specific market—a specific industry or demographic group—you'll make the most of your marketing dollars and can command higher prices.

Your Business Concept

Your Business Concept

Meeting needs is the basis of all business. You can devise a wonderful new machine, but if it doesn't address some real and important need or desire, people won't buy it, and your business will fail. Even Thomas Edison recognized this fact when he said, "Anything that won't sell, I don't want to invent."

The success of a concept often hinges on whether it does something newer or better than anything else. Being newer or better can take many forms:

■ **Offering something new.** This could be a new product, service, feature, or technology.

■ **Offering something better.** This could be an improvement on an existing product or service encompassing more features, lower price, greater reliability, faster speed, increased convenience, or enhanced technology.

■ **Discovering an underserved or new market.** This is a market in which there is greater demand than competitors can currently satisfy, an unserved location, or a small part of an overall market—a niche market—that hasn't yet been dominated by other competitors. Sometimes, markets become underserved when large companies abandon or neglect smaller portions of their current customer base.

■ **Offering a new delivery system or distribution channel.** New technologies, particularly the Internet, allow companies to reach customers more efficiently. This has opened up many new opportunities for businesses to provide products or services less expensively, to a wider geographic area, or with far greater choice.

■ **Increasing integration.** This occurs when a product is both manufactured and sold by the same company, or when a company offers more services or products in one location.

Your basic business concept should be strong in at least one area. If not, you should ask yourself how your company will be truly competitive.

Discovering Your Business Concept

Have you always wanted to be your own boss but don't know what kind of business to start? As you begin to evaluate business concepts, begin by examining:

■ **What you *really* want to do.** Maybe you're one of the lucky ones who knows exactly what business you'd like to start. But just because you've got a passion to do something doesn't mean you should necessarily "follow your bliss." You may, for instance, dream of opening a restaurant or running a bed and breakfast, both very challenging businesses. Before plunging in, take a good, clear, hard look at the realities.

■ **What you've done.** If you need income fast, pursuing a business in which you already have experience will generally be the quickest route. It's also often the most comfortable transition to self-employment. You may already have contacts or potential customers in your address book, know the market and industry well, and have strong referral sources. But look closely at whether you can do this business on your own. And just because you've done something for a long time (and are presumably good at it) doesn't mean you necessarily want to keep doing it any longer.

■ **Your hobbies or interests.** Many people dream of turning their hobbies into their profession. Sometimes that works really well. But I'm not always a big proponent of turning your hobby into your full-time occupation. After all, why take something that's now a source of pleasure and potentially turn it into a source of stress? Remember, doing something to please yourself isn't necessarily the same as doing it to please customers. You may love photography, but will you love it as much after fifty weddings?

■ **Who you know.** Let's face it, lots of people start their businesses because they have a great contact in an industry or business. Perhaps you know someone who needs an independent sales representative for their company or someone in a big corporation who can outsource work to your new consulting business. Also, many people go into business after a potential partner asks them to join the company. Just be cautious. Make certain you like the kind of work you're going into, and whenever you enter into a relationship, put the details in writing.

■ **What you're good at.** Why not use your skills? These may be different than your experience or your hobbies. For instance, you may be the person your neighbors

continued on **page 26**

How Good Is Your Business Idea?

Time for a true confession: my first business idea flopped. When I began working for myself, I started as a "Charitable Giving Consultant." My concept was to assist wealthy individuals and small family foundations with their philanthropic activities. I had the background, I knew people really needed the service, and no one else was doing it. It was a great idea.

Great, but too new. Every time I met with a prospective client, I had to make two sales: first I had to sell them on the concept, then I had to sell them on me.

To my surprise, I discovered I enjoyed doing something entirely different. Even before I got my first charitable giving client (and I got a big one), I met someone who needed a business plan written. Though I had little background in business plan development, I took to it immediately and realized I could make a good living.

That's why I advise people starting a business not to be completely obsessed by devising just the right business idea. It's likely to change anyway. If you're trying to figure out what kind of business to start, keep in mind:

■ **An idea isn't enough.** I've met hundreds of would-be entrepreneurs who are afraid to tell anyone their idea because they fear someone will steal it, and even more who are bitter because they think someone "stole" their idea. Ideas aren't businesses—they're just ideas. I have ideas for dozens of books every year, but that doesn't mean I'm going to be able to write them all, or even that all of them deserve to be written. The key is execution.

Businesses take hard work, persistence, and efficient cash management. Solid business operations beat great business ideas every day of the week. Nobody pays the rent just by coming up with ideas.

■ **You don't need a new idea to be successful.** In fact, most good, profitable businesses are developed from rather mundane ideas. Yes, it may have taken a Levi Strauss to invent blue jeans, but you can have a money-making retail store selling jeans without coming up with anything particularly new or exciting. Most of us don't want huge multinational businesses, we just want solid, profitable companies.

■ **A great new idea can be a handicap.** Here's one of Rhonda's Rules: "It's easier to get a piece of an existing market than to create a new one." Creating a new market is difficult, time-consuming, and expensive. A lot of Internet companies learned that lesson

25

the hard way when they realized customers weren't yet ready to buy online.

It's usually better to be a follower. Remember, the person or company who first invents a new product or service spends a lot of time and money figuring it all out. They work out the kinks, find suppliers, build a market. You can take advantage of their experience by coming in after them, especially if you offer improvements. Of course, in order to operate legally, outright copying cannot be done. You'll find it much easier and cheaper to get established if there's already an "infrastructure"—such as suppliers, distributors, and trade organizations.

■ **Old ideas work.** In fact, some of the best ideas for new businesses are things that have been done before—often for a long, long time. As industries age, big companies come to dominate, and as they do, they often neglect some of their smaller—but still very profitable—customers or market niches. This gives you an opportunity to snap those customers up.

Of course, a really bad idea is deadly. Who thought up the idea of selling furniture over the Internet? Don't people want to see and feel the furniture they're purchasing? No matter how well you run a business, you can't make money selling something people don't want to buy. (But, then again, green ketchup is a big hit. Go figure.)

There's an old saying, "Success is 90% perspiration and only 10% inspiration." I'd say that's giving inspiration too much credit. By the way, does anyone want to buy a stack of old business cards that say: "Rhonda Abrams, Charitable Giving Consultant"?

...discovering your business concept
(continued from **page 24**)

turn to for help installing electronic equipment or decorating their homes. Perhaps there's a business opportunity there if many others in your community need the same type of assistance.

■ **A market opportunity.** Look around: what's missing in your community, industry, or profession that you might be able to provide? There are usually many services or products that still need to be provided. Maybe it's a service available elsewhere but not locally; perhaps you see a big company neglecting or leaving a line of business that you could serve instead.

■ **What you want to learn.** Believe it or not, one good way to learn something is to start a business doing it. Yes, you may need to get some additional training or education, and you won't be able to charge as much as those who know more than you, but you can learn a lot while you're on the job. For instance, you may want to learn more about nature and so decide to organize ecology-based tours.

Choosing the Right Business

Many people dream about starting a business one day but haven't yet taken the plunge. One thing holding them back is that they don't know how to decide if a business is right for them. If you're one of those people, read on.

Over the years, you may have had hundreds of ideas for businesses—or perhaps you've had very few.

Sure, you know there are plenty of possible businesses you could start. After all, family and friends keep suggesting ideas: your sister says you should sell real estate, your exercise partner wants you to open a gym, and your neighbor swears you can make a fortune selling herbal supplements.

But now that you're actually going to put your toe in the entrepreneurial waters, you're stymied. How do you evaluate whether it's a good idea or just so-so? How do you know if it will make money?

Some people think choosing a business is just a matter of trusting gut instinct. But that's not always the best way to judge. After all, you've got a lot at stake. This is a big decision—a much bigger decision than accepting a job. After all, if you take the wrong job, you can always quit and look for another. But starting a business is a huge commitment—it takes a lot of time and determination, and you risk your own money.

Consider these five criteria when evaluating a business idea.

1. **Can succeed as a business.** You probably enjoy doing many things. They might suit your talents and interests; they might even give you a great sense of satisfaction and accomplishment. But if you can't make money doing them, there's a word for these kinds of activities—hobbies. In fact, the Internal Revenue Service refers to businesses that consistently fail to make money as "hobby businesses." (And you don't get to deduct expenses with a hobby business, so watch out!)

2. **Can meet your financial needs and goals.** Different people have different financial situations. One would-be entrepreneur may need to support a family, while another would be happy to make some extra money to supplement existing income. Keep your financial needs in mind when choosing a business regardless of your area of interest.

3. **Can meet your personal needs and goals.** Just as different people have very different financial needs, they also have different personal requirements. One person may be raising children and need a flexible work schedule; another may be able and ready to work twenty-four hours a day, seven days a week to make their dreams a reality. When

27

considering a business, examine how much time you will need to put in to be successful in that endeavor, and make certain it fits with the other demands in your life.

> ## How do you evaluate whether your business idea is a good one? How do you know if it will make money?

4. **Fits your interests and abilities.** What interests you? Animals, accounting, art, architecture? Naturally, you want to find a business that holds your interest. Of course, it's not enough to just be interested in something, you also have to have the skills to be successful. Just be sure to keep your ideas and expectations realistic. I like

driving fast, and I'm a good driver, but that doesn't mean I can become a professional race car driver.

5. **You can get started on it.** When I say "get started," I don't necessarily mean you should go out and get your first customer or ship your first product tomorrow. I'm talking about taking some real steps to put the process of starting your business in motion. This might mean taking some classes to learn essential skills, getting a job in a related business so you can learn about the industry, or starting to develop your business plan. It means doing something with all those thoughts and ideas swirling around in your head.

Remember, millions of Americans own their own businesses. If you're dreaming of one day joining them, take heart in knowing there's a business concept out there that's right for you.

Follow Your Passion?

Ever dream about starting a business where you could pursue your hobby all day? You're not alone. Many books urge career-seekers to "Do What You Love and the Money Will Follow" or "Follow Your Bliss." While this may (or may not) be good advice for people looking for a job, is it a sound idea if you're starting a business?

I don't need to tell you that running a business is different than being an employee. When you own a business, you can never quite escape its problems, payroll, and accounts payable. Do you want to turn your passion into the source of those problems?

Of course, it makes sense to start a business that interests you. No one wants to spend all day doing something completely boring. I'm not advocating for anyone to start a business they dislike. This question is different: should you turn something you already love—fishing, gardening, antique shopping—into a full-time enterprise?

First, examine the pros and cons of turning your hobby into a business:

Advantages

■ You're more motivated.

■ You already know you enjoy it.

■ You build on your existing base of knowledge.

■ You may already have contacts.

■ You may get to be in an environment you like (outdoors, auctions, etc.).

Disadvantages

■ You turn your hobby into work.

■ You lose your source of relaxation and distraction.

■ It may not be a realistic business.

■ Your skills may be insufficient as a professional.

■ Decisions are based on pleasing the customer instead of yourself.

Having to earn money at something inevitably changes the way you feel about it. It's one thing to go fishing or work in your garden to take your mind off your daily life and another thing altogether to take a customer on a fishing trip or design a client's garden. The focus shifts; it's no longer about where you like to fish or what plants you like—it's about keeping the customer happy, on their schedule, and doing it in such a way that you still make money. Remember, even if it's fishing, there's a reason they call it "work."

29

Before jumping into a hobby-related business, be certain to realistically assess the income potential. Hobby- and recreation-related fields tend to attract lots of competitors—many of whom don't need to make a full-time income. When a field contains many people who aren't financially sensitive it tends to reduce the income for all. You may be able to make far more money in a less attractive business. Freelance newspaper writers, for example, generally earn a pittance, because so many people want to see their name in print. Those who write far-less-glamorous technical manuals can actually earn a living.

> **Having to earn money at something inevitably changes the way you feel about it.**

There are two times in your life when following your passion—whether in business or otherwise—is most advised: when you're young and when you're older. If you dream of a life near the slopes, be a ski instructor in your twenties. That's when you typically have the greatest physical capability, the fewest financial responsibilities, and the most years ahead to do something more "serious."

Likewise, when you're a little older—your kids are out of college, you have some money saved, and you're not totally dependent on income for your livelihood—then you're better able to deal with the financial reality of a business that follows your passion.

Of course, for some people—those who are truly passionate about something, truly skilled, or just lucky—doing what you love can lead to an extremely satisfying life. Last summer, our guide on a river in the Australian rain forest said he had given up his day job, bought a boat, and decided to lead tours. For years, he was on the same river, answering the same questions from tourists, but he still loved every minute of it.

Can you turn your passion into a business? Perhaps. But don't forget the other side: you can become passionate about your business. I've met many entrepreneurs who would never have imagined that one day they'd care deeply about granite or dental hygiene or employee recruitment. And they go fishing on the weekend.

Yes, but Is It a Business?

A friend took me to dinner to pick my brain about her new business. She was excited: she had a great idea, had lined up a strategic partner, and was raring to go. She had visions of raising millions of dollars and going on the Internet. I felt terrible telling her that while, indeed, it was a great idea, it was nevertheless a lousy business.

What were the problems—and there were many of them—with my friend's idea?

First, like many novice entrepreneurs, her idea was too grandiose. She had too many services, serving too diverse a market, to be able to develop any one aspect successfully. The single biggest problem facing entrepreneurs is a lack of focus. It's a big enough challenge to stay focused on even a narrowly defined market with a clearly delineated product; when you take on too much, especially in the early days of a company, you almost guarantee defeat. My friend's business could have easily, and better, been broken up into two or three businesses, any one of which might have succeeded, but she was committed to serving the whole market.

Many entrepreneurs, of course, fall to the other extreme: their business idea is *so* narrowly defined that it's actually the basis for just one product or even one feature of a product rather than a whole business. This is particularly true in two categories: consumer products and technology. Let's say, for example, that you have a great recipe for a new kind of sauce. One sauce, no matter how terrific, might not be enough to build a

whole company around; you might need to come up with a line of sauces.

When your business idea is too limited, you may not be able to grow big enough to survive. Even if you are successful, you're vulnerable if a larger company later decides to mimic your idea. The good news—and this is particularly true in technology or if you can develop a cult-like following of customers—is that your company can become an excellent candidate to be acquired by another that wants to include your product as part of their offerings. You won't be your own boss, but you might get a pile of cash.

> ## The single biggest problem facing entrepreneurs is lack of focus.

The next biggest problem in my friend's business plan was she hadn't considered the real costs of delivering her proposed services. One of Rhonda's Rules is "Things take longer and cost more than planned." To be successful, my friend's company depended on achieving lower costs than her competitors. She thought she could do this just because she was operating on the Internet. Get real! Internet businesses are just like land-based companies: you still need customer service, employees, and substantial marketing efforts. If you're depending on cost savings for a competitive advantage, thoroughly research and prove that such savings can actually be achieved and sustained.

Finally, my friend's biggest problem was my friend. She's stubborn, unwilling to listen, insistent on getting and keeping control. (So why is she my friend? I'll have to discuss that another time....) It's not enough to have a great idea, or even great operations; a company needs leadership and management. You can't build a business without building a team. You have to work *with* people, not just have them work *for* you.

It's not always easy to scale back your vision or your need to be in charge. But if you want to grow a company, not just make yourself a job, you've got to consider whether your good idea can really be a good business.

Turning Dreams into Reality

Turning Dreams into Reality

How do you make your dreams come true? What makes the difference between those who just dream and those who make their entrepreneurial dreams come true?

The other day I realized that I'm quite a dreamer. Almost every day, I spend some time imagining what my future might look like. But, while I'm a frequent visitor to the future, I don't take up permanent residence there. I try to use my hopes and dreams as a target to shoot for, a guide for my path in my everyday business life.

That's one of the first things you have to recognize about your dreams: they can be an escape from your current reality or a foundation for a new reality. You cannot change—your life or your business—unless you can imagine a new reality.

If you let your dreams take over—if you act on them without examining them—your fantasies can distract you from more achievable goals.

For instance, if you dream of having a bigger house, faster car, or more luxurious lifestyle (and who doesn't?), it's easy to be seduced by get-rich-quick schemes. These drain your money and time away from more achievable goals, such as going back to school or getting a better job.

If you want to make your dreams come true, it's necessary to develop what I call the "discipline of dreams." You have to be able to clarify your dreams, evaluate them, and move them from the stage of imagination to action.

Dreams can be an escape from reality or a foundation for a new reality.

Let's define a "dream scale"—from the least achievable stage of dreaming to the most achievable:

- **Fantasy.** Concepts which are impossible to achieve or highly unrealistic. It's not surprising that guys on late-night infomercials for make-millions-in-your-spare-time schemes are typically photographed sitting on yachts in tropical locations; these hucksters know they're selling a fantasy. Don't get me wrong: I understand that it can be useful to have fantasies that make life more bearable, especially when you're otherwise happy with your life or not in a position to change. Just don't act on them and don't sign up for that multilevel marketing scheme!

- **Dream.** Concepts which are potentially achievable but where only the positive aspects are seen. Many people have their own idea of their dream business; my neighbors want to own a charming bed and breakfast in a quaint New England seaport. Is this a fantasy? Not exactly. After all, some people *do* run delightful B&Bs on Cape Cod. The reality, however, is that it's very difficult.

■ **Vision.** Concepts which are achievable and at a stage where the downsides and difficulties come into focus. At the vision stage, you're willing to challenge your assumptions (and the claims of those who promise to make your dreams come true). You're not afraid to understand the costs, limitations, and work required, as well as your chances of success. For those who are just dreamers, this feels like "popping the balloon." For those who are going to be successful, this feels like the beginning.

■ **Goals.** A specific, realistic objective. At the goal stage, you start to give yourself clear, practical targets for achieving your vision. You understand how much you can—and cannot—achieve, and you begin to put numbers and dates to your ambitions.

■ **Plans.** A step-by-step outline of how you are going to achieve your goals. This is where you determine how to make your vision a reality. You list action items, milestones, and activities. And then you go to work!

I believe in dreams. In my company, I always start our annual planning sessions the same way—by brainstorming wild ideas and discussing big goals for our future. But that's only the first hour of a three-to-five-day process. We spend the rest of the time discussing and prioritizing our goals, then devising a detailed plan for achieving them. If we didn't, our aspirations would still be dreams. Instead, we're busy making our dreams come true.

Goals versus Tasks

If you're like me, you have a "To Do" list that goes on and on: calls to make, emails to send, contacts to connect with, and a ton of things to write or do.

I get such a good feeling from checking items off my list that it's tempting to focus on things I can do easily, things that are quick rather than important. Usually, I manage to attend to the most urgent items.

At the end of the day, or the week, I look over my list and see I've done a lot, but all too often I still feel a lack of accomplishment. And I think if only I'd worked longer, harder, or figured out how to survive with only two hours' sleep, I'd finally take care of everything.

The problem is, in day-to-day life, it's natural to focus on *tasks* rather than *goals*. We look at what we have to do right now rather than examining where we are really heading and what we need to do to reach that goal.

When was the last time you sat down and asked yourself: "What are my top three goals for the next six months, the next year, five years from now? What are the one to three most important things I can do to reach those goals?" And once you've set those goals, how do you remind yourself of them in the press of daily business? How do you keep focused on long-term goals rather than spending all your time on short-term tasks?

Since goals are usually overwhelming ("Be financially secure within ten years; be profitable by the end of the year; find a strategic partner"), you have to break them down into more manageable tasks. That's the only way you'll ever achieve them. But our daily To Do list usually consists only of stuff we *have* to do, not stuff we *should* do—the stuff that really makes a difference.

> ## Usually, we take care of BUSYNESS rather than taking care of BUSINESS.

I know you're saying, "Rhonda, there aren't enough hours in the day. I can't get through all the items on my To Do list now. I work and work and work, and I've still got a pile on my desk to plow through." Well, you've got my permission to let some things slide.

Let's face it: you're not going to accomplish everything you want in a day. You're not going to get everything done. Some stuff is going to fall through the cracks. Is it going to be the important things or the unimportant things? Usually, we take care of *busyness* rather than taking care of *business*.

There are some things you can do to help yourself: stop taking on new projects, especially those that are not directly related to your top goals. It's easy to see an opportunity and feel you have to grab it now. That's not true. Usually, more opportunities come along.

We have to learn to give the priorities we've already chosen a chance to succeed. Taking on too much at one time is like having quintuplets: you wouldn't choose to give any up, but none of them are going to get quite the attention they deserve.

Something that's helped me stay focused on my top priority was to put physical reminders where I could see them. I made a little sign listing my top goal that I kept on my desk. And I even put technology to work: I turned my screensaver into a message board reminding me of my top goal. Whenever I stopped typing for a while, took a call, or walked away from my desk, the reminder scrolled across my screen.

What is the single most important thing you can accomplish in the next six months in your business—the one thing that can really make a difference between cruising ahead versus just staying afloat? How will you make sure it stays on your To Do list? If you stay focused on goals, rather than on tasks, you, too, may reach your goal this year. I'm pulling for you.

Commit Yourself to the Turn

When I was first learning to ski many years ago, a ski instructor gave me some advice about how to successfully navigate changing direction: "Commit yourself to the turn."

The same advice is true in business. Whenever you want to go in a new direction, you have to follow the same advice: "Commit yourself to the turn."

Skiing is all about turns. As a beginner, you make big turns across the entire width of the ski run. If you're like me—a little cautious and timid in a new sport—you go slowly as you make these turns. As a result, there's a moment in each turn in which you realize you're facing straight downhill. That's when you get scared.

Now here's the interesting part: if you stay committed—if you don't let fear get the best of you—your body moves you around, safely completing the turn. If you waver, thinking, "Oh my gosh, I don't want to go straight down," then you stop turning and actually end up facing downhill—what you wanted to avoid.

Business, too, is all about making turns. When you start a company, you have an idea of where you want to go, but you can quickly find you have to change your plan—sometimes slightly, sometimes a great deal. As you continue in business, you discover there are times that call for you to make dramatic turns: perhaps new competition enters the market, your profit margins

erode, or new technologies create vast differences in how you conduct business. You have to go in a new direction.

You may be a little timid as you set off on a new course, or you may rush quickly into it. Whatever your confidence level at the beginning, as you get into your turn—as you start to face and deal with the consequences of the choices you've made—that's when you get scared.

And that's when you have to commit yourself to the turn. When you are developing a new direction for your company—a new project, expansion, new technologies—you have to follow through with enough support, resources, and especially time, to give it a reasonable chance of success.

If you are working with others, especially employees, it's particularly important that you stay committed. Employees take their lead from you, the leader. If you waver in your resolution to your new project, employees will feel uncertain about their future and will hesitate to make the necessary changes and sacrifices to help ensure success. You have to believe. You have to stay the course.

That doesn't mean you can't examine and

readjust the details of the choices you've made. You can and should. But be careful: I've seen many companies that either pull the plug on a project too soon, or, more often, commit only half-heartedly to new undertakings. Both approaches lead to failure: Ending a project too soon means you haven't given it enough time to prove whether it can succeed; half-hearted commitments inevitably lead to failure.

When you don't commit yourself to the turn, you're going to end up facing straight downhill.

As you make a change in your business life, indeed in any part of your life, follow through sufficiently to give it a chance to succeed. Give your new direction enough energy and commitment to create the momentum to carry you through the inevitable rough spots. Commit yourself to the turn.

Guidelines for Goals

Tips for a productive goal-setting process:

■ **Make certain the goals are well defined, quantifiable, and time bounded.** Example: "For the next three months, I'll call twelve new prospects a day and go to all my daughter's after school activities." This gives you a good yardstick by which to measure progress and helps you set priorities for how you spend your time.

■ **Be realistic given the many demands on your energies.** Example: "For the next three months, I'll call eight new prospects a week and go to my daughter's soccer games."

■ **Translate those goals into achievable *short-term* objectives.** Example: "This week, I'll call eight new prospects and go to my daughter's soccer game Tuesday."

■ **Put the most emphasis on goals within your control rather than those determined by the actions of others.** Example: "I'll make eight cold calls this week" instead of "I'll get three new customers."

■ **List when you will re-evaluate your goals, measure progress, and set new objectives.** Example: "I will examine these goals on June 30 and set goals for July."

■ **Put limits on selected goals.** Some goals will be outside your complete control

continued on **page 42**

Seizing Opportunities

When it comes to figuring out how to succeed, many business owners remind me of the man in this joke…

A flood threatens a town, forcing everyone to evacuate. But Joe thinks, "I'm a devout man; God will save me" and stays put. As the waters start rising, Joe's neighbor comes by: "Joe, come with me; we've got to go." But Joe declines, "I'm a devout man; God will save me."

The waters keep rising. Joe scrambles to his second floor. A firefighter in a rowboat floats by Joe's window. "Get in the boat or you'll drown," the firefighter says. Joe again declines, "I'm a devout man; God will save me."

Finally, the flood waters are so high that Joe is forced up on his roof. A police helicopter comes by and throws down a rope. "It's your last chance, climb up or you'll drown," the policeman yells. "No, I'm a devout man; God will save me."

Soon Joe drowns. He arrives in Heaven and challenges God, "I'm a devout man; why didn't you help me?"

"What do you mean?" God replies. "I did help; I sent a neighbor, a firefighter, and a helicopter."

Many of us are like Joe—we wait for something to rescue us while missing opportunities to help ourselves. Whether in our business or personal lives, we hope for a lifeline—a new customer, rave reviews of our product, or a great relationship—to just show up.

Alas, life isn't like that. While we wait for success to fall in our laps, real life keeps trudging along. But like Joe, if we want things to be different, we must learn to recognize opportunities and seize them; we have to do *something*.

> **We keep waiting for something to rescue us while missing opportunities to help ourselves.**

Let's face it: if you want your business or your life to change, you have to be an active participant in your own transformation.

But where do you start? How do you learn to recognize an opportunity when it's being thrown your way?

■ **Make a plan.** Form a vision of what you want to achieve and then develop a plan to make that vision a reality. You can't judge whether an opportunity is one to seize or let pass unless you have a context for understanding whether it fits into your goals.

Developing a plan gives you a framework for decision making.

■ **Get accustomed to making choices.** Moving forward means seizing some opportunities but allowing others to pass by. Entrepreneurs have many great ideas on how to improve their businesses, and life will present you with many tempting prospects. You can't act on every good idea.

■ **Recognize that the "perfect" solution is never going to come along.** Often we fail to act because we're waiting for the perfect opportunity or the perfect timing. Life doesn't offer perfection, it offers chances.

Looking for perfection is a way of avoiding making choices.

■ **Get out of your "comfort zone."** Sure you're comfortable doing what you're doing, but if it's not bringing you the results you want, you're going to have to change. And change is always uncomfortable.

■ **Make a commitment.** Get used to saying no. Get used to saying yes. But whatever you do, do it with commitment and conviction.

Like Joe, we have to learn how to recognize opportunities and then grab on.

...guidelines for goals
(continued from **page 40**)

("I will increase sales by 25%"), so it's important to put limits on how long you will focus on such goals. "If I can't sell this new product after calling ten of my current customers, I'll put my efforts into a different product."

■ **Reward yourself when you accomplish your goals.** Rewards keep you motivated to set and reach other goals, and as an entrepreneur, there's usually no one else to acknowledge your achievements but you. So if you land a big sale or make all your calls for the month, give yourself a reward.

Embracing Change

Things Are About to Change

You've finally got it right. Your product is almost perfect. You've got loyal customers, and your sales are clicking. Your employees show up enthusiastically and do their jobs well. Your suppliers are steady. Everything's great! Know what this means? It's time to start worrying.

It's not that I'm a pessimist, not at all. It's just that the one certainty I have about business life (as in all life) is that things change.

Knowing that things will change is good to remember in the midst of bad times, but you've got to keep it in mind during good times, too. If you're overly complacent, happily believing you've figured everything out, then you're unprepared for the changes that are inevitably just around the corner.

Some companies, especially those dealing with technology, have change at the very core of their existence. But even if your business is selling something as apparently unchanging as chocolate chip cookies, change is inevitable.

Take Levi's. The basic Levi's jean has hardly altered in over 150 years (except for the removal of a metal rivet from the crotch, which caused unpleasant side effects for miners warming themselves next to camp fires. Ouch!). But Levi Strauss & Company changed dramatically during that time. Its market went from miners to minors in the 1950s, and expanded to the entire world by the 1970s. Levi's went from being a purveyor of work clothes to the world's largest fashion manufacturer, and when the business world adopted "Dress Down Friday," they went back to providing work clothes through their Dockers division.

It's even more important for a small company to be able to embrace change. After all, one of the key advantages a smaller business has over a huge corporation is its ability to quickly respond to new opportunities. But you have to prepare your company for a world of constant change.

The first challenge is to understand what kinds of change improve your company's ability to survive, and what types of change threaten its very identity. In one of my favorite business books, *Built to Last,* authors James C. Collins and Jerry I. Porras show how the best companies identify their "core ideologies," which remain constant over the years. They differentiate those ideologies from "noncore practices" which can adapt, evolve, or disappear over time.

Collins and Porras cite the department store Nordstrom as an example. Nordstrom's core ideology is "Service to the customer above all else." If they lose sight of that ideology, Nordstrom would cease to be Nordstrom.

But the fact that they have a piano player in each store is a "noncore practice" which they could change if times demanded.

For change to be effective, you have to encourage a change-oriented attitude at every level of your company. People are generally more comfortable with old problems than with new solutions, and it's natural for employees to be threatened by change. But you can help reduce those fears.

The best way to create a change-welcoming workplace is to start by hiring people who seem flexible. Look for attitude, not just skills, as part of your hiring process. Next, get everyone thinking about change all the time, and make it a normal part of business conversation. Informally, and in scheduled meetings, ask employees to discuss the kinds of changes they anticipate facing in their specific areas of responsibility. Remember, employees are often in a better position to foresee changes than you are.

To help get a focus on change, I recommend delineating the specific types of change your company may face and addressing each separately.

Just remember what someone once said, "Even if you're on the right track, if you just sit there, you'll get run over."

Types of Changes Your Company May Face

Market changes. Nature and number of customers, customers' buying habits and patterns, demographic and sociological shifts

Industry changes. Distribution channels, vendors, availability of capital, key economic concerns

Competitive changes. Nature and number of competitors, new entries, new types of competition for your category

Technological changes. Hardware and software products and services that could positively or negatively affect your product or service's marketability, as well as technology you could adopt to improve operations

Sales and marketing changes. Marketing approaches and vehicles, sales channels, sales force, advertising and promotion

Management changes. Availability of adequate staff, management patterns, pay schemes and levels, benefits, recognition programs

Operations changes. Production/manufacturing or delivery/fulfillment methods

Is It Time to Throw in the Towel?

Every time one of my projects flops, I ask myself: "What did I learn? What should I do differently next time?" This helps me snatch a bit of victory from defeat. And, I hope, it keeps me from repeating the same blunder over and over.

When something is going badly—really badly—it's a good idea to throw in the towel sooner rather than later. I'm not a card player, but I've heard that if you're dealt a bad hand in poker, you should toss it in early. The more you put in the pot, the harder it will be for you to fold and the more you'll likely lose.

Every undertaking needs a reasonable chance to develop, of course. New businesses, for instance, usually take from two to five years to become profitable. If we're too quick to quit, we'll never make a go of anything. But there's a difference between prudent patience and being unwilling to face unpleasant facts. Next time you're having one of those 3 a.m. heart-to-heart sessions with yourself, wondering whether it's time to get out of something, ask yourself these questions:

What direction have things been going? If you're in a downturn now, is it a momentary glitch in an otherwise positive picture or one more in a long series of defeats?

Are you learning, improving? Sometimes, a specific situation may not be a huge success but the increased knowledge or skills you're developing are worth the effort.

What is your "opportunity cost?" What could you be doing with your life, your time, your money, instead? Are you passing up other chances to succeed by sticking with this?

What effect is this situation having on you, your family, and friends? You may be willing to forge ahead but at what price to your own and others' well-being? Are you really doing others a favor by keeping them connected to a declining situation, or could they move on to other opportunities as well?

Finally, take a good hard look in the mirror and ask yourself whether there's truly a reasonable chance, not just a last-ditch hope, that things are going to get better. Can you ever get things to work or are you just avoiding change? Sometimes it's time to make the tough choice, hard as it is, to get out.

There's an old Bulgarian proverb that says, "If you wish to drown, don't torture yourself in shallow water." I hope I've finally learned, when I'm in a doomed situation, to at least give it a quick death. And then I can face the future bravely and move on.

47

Change Takes Time

I once saw a handwritten note over a jar for tips: "If you fear change, leave it here."

We all fear change. Yet we all want to change—our habits, our appearance, our income. Most of us want others to change—our spouses, our children, our employees. Sometimes, no matter how much we want change, no matter how hard we try, we just can't seem to make it work.

One problem is that we want change to happen overnight. We go on extreme diets or change business direction suddenly. We want to be able to push a button—like a Star Trek transporter—and immediately get from one place in our life to another: "Beam me up, Scotty."

Change is a *process,* not an immediate outcome, a journey rather than a destination. The most difficult stage of change is when you've come part way but haven't left old ways entirely behind. Experts say it takes at least a year for a change to become a habit. So be patient with yourself and others. Change takes time.

When you plan on making a change—or want a change to happen in others—recognize that you'll go through stages:

1. **Contemplate.** You start thinking about your goals, but they still seem unachievable.

2. **Reframe.** You start saying, "This is going to happen; I can make this work."

3. **Plan.** You convert desires into specific, realistic actions you can take.

4. **Commit.** You make a real commitment to your goals and plans.

5. **Try and fail.** You begin to make changes but you're inconsistent; you fall back into old patterns.

6. **Recommit.** You remind yourself of your goals, your plan, and your belief that you are capable of success. You start again.

7. **Habit.** You consistently change your behavior.

Turning Failure into Success

I'm often asked by business students, "What's the key to being a successful entrepreneur?"

I have a clear, but surprising, answer: "Change how you think about failure."

In business, the stress is always on success. Seminars promote "Small Business Success." Magazines run stories on "Secrets of Success." Even I'm guilty—my first book was titled *The Successful Business Plan.*

Failure is the "F word" of business—it's not polite to mention it. After all, failure is what happens to other people, right? But what about when *we* fail? We either try to forget the experience quickly, or we wallow in self-doubt and recrimination.

But if you're in business, sooner or later, you're going to have failures. I certainly have. I've had big deals that have fallen apart, partnerships end, even a business I needed to close. But sometimes, these "failures" have turned out to be fortunate; they've forced me to re-examine my goals, decisions, methods. Then, I've been able to choose to take a different—better—path.

I'm not alone. Most successful people (there's that word "success" again) will tell you that some of the most important, most beneficial, events in their lives were things they viewed as "failures" at the time. But they used their failures to learn new attitudes and skills, to move on to new opportunities, and to get perspective on their lives.

Failure does not lie in an event itself; it lies in how we see that event, and what is learned from it.

Of course, some failures have a major economic impact on your life, such as bankruptcies or divorces. But even these significant, very painful, events can be seen as a chance to start on a new path, over time.

Here's how the best entrepreneurs deal with failure:

■ **Redefine it.** I asked a large company how they dealt with employees' failures. "We don't have failures," I was told. "We have learning experiences." I live in Silicon Valley, California, and one reason this area breeds innovation and new companies is that when someone has started a company that later fails, they're not considered a failure. Instead, they're considered to be an *experienced* entrepreneur.

■ **Analyze it.** Football coach Bill Walsh said most people view games as either win or lose instead of focusing on what they learn while losing. That's how they'll eventually become winners. A venture capitalist friend of mine said he only invested in entrepreneurs who had started at least one failed company. He wanted them to have learned hard lessons before he gave them his money. If—when—you fail, take a close look at the causes. After each and every setback, big or small, take a clear, cold look at what happened.

■ **Depersonalize it.** Stop kicking yourself; everybody fails. Steve Jobs is a billionaire, running two successful companies simultaneously (Apple and Pixar), but do you remember his NeXT Computer? It failed. And he was once fired from the very company he founded (Apple). Analyze your mistakes, but you won't learn anything if you're too busy beating up on yourself.

■ **Change it.** Okay, so now you know what you did wrong. Here's the hard part—you actually have to change your behavior. Did you take on too many projects at once? Push too hard to make a sale? Start a new venture without enough research? When you find yourself in a similar situation, stop. Remind yourself of what you learned and actively try to change your behavior. Be patient and forgiving because change takes time.

■ **Get over it.** Move on. Don't dwell on your successes or on your failures. You've got a life to live, and each day is precious. So, like the old song says, "Pick yourself up, brush yourself off, and start all over again."

The Promise of Change

Few things are as hopeful as opening day of the baseball season. Every year, I welcome opening day as a symbol of getting a fresh start, a clean slate.

Opening day of the baseball season is a new year that's truly new. The box score reads 0-0. All things are possible. It doesn't matter how you did before, or what other people think of you. For instance, on opening day 2002 *Sporting News* and *Baseball Digest* predicted the Anaheim Angels would come in dead last in their division. That year, they won the World Series.

I don't like many of the sports metaphors used for business, but if any sport is analogous to business, it's baseball. That's because:

■ **You make errors.**
■ **You've got many chances to try again (162 games).**
■ **There's no set time limit.**
■ **Strategy is more important than sheer size or strength.**
■ **The rich guys aren't always the most successful (in spite of what Yankees fans think).**
■ **Most importantly, if you bat .400, you're in the Hall of Fame!**

Get Over It!

My friend Ann, a psychotherapist, recently shared with me her two-step program for mental health: "Get over it. And stay over it." I've found Ann's program serves equally as a terrific prescription for better business health.

Ann's advice sounds flippant, but it's not. In every life—and every business—bad stuff happens. We all encounter our share of defeats and disappointments, disloyalty and deceit.

When bad things happen, we have to deal with them. But there's a difference between dealing with something and wallowing in it.

Most of us know someone to whom we'd like to shout Ann's advice: an employee who harps on situations resolved long ago, kids who keep whining even though you've told them "no" ten times, a spouse who brings up old spats like a broken record.

"Get over it!" we'd like to yell. "And stay over it!"

Yet, we, too, may find ourselves stuck on old issues. If we tried making a big change—introducing a new product, opening a new location—and failed, we may be paralyzed and afraid to try anything new again. If we entered into an important relationship—with a partner, supplier, spouse—and were cheated or mistreated, we may find ourselves mistrusting everyone. It's easy to nurse old hurts.

But old hurts block new ideas, new chances for success or happiness. When we're stuck in the past, we can't move forward. To improve our businesses, and our lives, we have to find a way to forge ahead. So no matter what failure or setback we encountered, we have to learn how to get over it. Once we do, we have to teach ourselves how to stay over it.

> **When we're stuck in the past, we can't move forward.**

That's not easy. So how do we follow Ann's two-step program?

■ **Get over it.** To get over something, first you have to deal with it. You can't just pretend it never happened. Repression, as I'm sure my friend Ann the psychotherapist could tell you, isn't the answer.

Real problems have real consequences, and they have to be resolved.

Business failures or setbacks typically leave us with financial, credit, or legal messes needing to be cleaned up. It may take a while to get those straightened out, but doing so is part of the process of getting over it. Neglecting them is a sure way to stay mired in the original defeat.

Getting over it also means trying to figure out what happened and why. It's easier to move forward when you see what you've learned from a bad situation, what you'd do differently next time, what you can do to make it better now. Perhaps you need to apologize to those you've wronged or forgive those who've hurt you. And, if necessary, say your goodbyes.

■ **Stay over it.** This is where it really gets tough. In the short term, even when you've been very badly hurt, it's easy to tell yourself that you're over it—for a day, a week, or a month or two. But how do you put it behind you permanently?

Yes, I know, some things are impossible to forget. Failures, losses, disloyalty—you can't just pretend they never happened, and you wouldn't want to. It's important to remember your past, what you've learned, what you'll change.

But remembering isn't the same thing as holding a continual pity party. Old hurts are like scabs—they heal best when you stop picking at them. When you find yourself thinking about old disappointments—feeling angry, afraid, or sorry for yourself—make yourself stop. We all have internal conversations with ourselves. Now's the time to remember Ann's two-step program and tell yourself firmly, "Stay over it."

"Get over it—and stay over it." I'm not sure I'd advise you to use those words the next time your mate, child, or employee complains. But it's a good message to give yourself—again and again. Because once you're over those old defeats, you've got a better chance for new victories.

Strategy

Focusing on Your Focus

Whenever someone asks me to name the biggest problem for small business owners, my answer comes as a surprise. I don't recite the expected litany of typical responses: paperwork, taxes, finding good employees. No, I reply with one word: Focus.

In a small business, there are so many different things to do, and so few people to do them, that an entrepreneur has to continually juggle priorities. It's very different than working in a big company, where there are specialists for every product line, market segment, and area of operation.

At one of my workshops, one small business owner told me that throughout her work day, she thought of herself as having different job titles: Marketing Director, Chief Financial Officer, Director of Operations, shipping clerk, and so on. And she was an artist!

Handling so many tasks at once is exhausting. You're constantly pulled in different directions. You've got a To Do list for each area of your business that could take up all your time. It's very easy to end up feeling that you're not succeeding very well in any of them.

Compounding the problem is that many of us are, in essence, running more than one business at once. Not out of choice, but of necessity.

For instance, a landscape designer might prefer to spend most of his time designing new

gardens, which is business #1. But serving an entirely "one-time" clientele can mean expensive marketing (continually having to acquire new clients) and might not provide sufficient stable income. So, he might wisely decide to also offer ongoing garden maintenance—business #2. Since he doesn't live in a sunbelt state, his business is seasonal. So he also offers snow removal—business #3. Eventually, some of his customers ask him to install and remove their outside Christmas decorations. Since that's more predictable than snow removal, he adds and starts marketing that service. Business #4.

Adding each of these "businesses" makes sense, but it can make an entrepreneur schizophrenic. After all, our hypothetical landscape designer really wants to be creating inviting gardens, yet he spends part of his time fixing electric lights on reindeer on rooftops.

While I'm not dealing with twinkling Santa Clauses, I face the same dilemma. I own and run a publishing company. That's my primary source of income. Business #1. But I'm also a speaker for conventions and conferences. Business #2. Taking up a lot of my time is writing books. Business #3. And you thought all I did was lie in a lounge chair by a pool, sipping a tropical drink, effortlessly typing out 700 words of expertly crafted business insight for my weekly newspaper column. Business #4.

I'm a big believer in finding a niche and sticking to it. As a business strategy, being highly focused makes it far easier to succeed.

But, you don't want to have *all* your eggs in one business basket. If you're too dependent on one client, or even one product line, you're very vulnerable if there's a change in that market.

What's an entrepreneur to do?

■ **Make certain you have an overall concept of your business that logically covers the different aspects.** For instance, the landscaper actually runs a company designing and maintaining outside spaces of clients' buildings.

■ **Develop separate business and marketing plans for each "business line."**

■ **Create separate To Do lists for each line, so you can see where each of them stands.**

■ **Don't be too hard on yourself.** Remember, it really is hard to run so many businesses at once.

Your Mission Statement

"If you don't know where you're going, how will you know when you're lost?"

A Mission Statement is a written document that makes clear what your company does, and where it is going, and enables everyone involved in your company to share and understand the mission.

A Mission Statement doesn't have to be long. Sometimes a relatively brief one sums things up best. By selecting a very small number of items, you send the message that these are your company's highest priorities.

The key elements of a Mission Statement:

■ **A brief description of what you do (especially important for new businesses as an anchor)**
■ **A vision of what you want to become**
■ **The philosophies and values that will characterize your actions**

continued on **page 58**

Developing Your Strategic Position

During my first few years as a management consultant, I helped business owners learn to improve their operations and marketing. I helped entrepreneurs learn how to increase their profit margins and design more effective brochures. In other words, I helped them with the nuts and bolts of running a company. Over time, I realized that nuts and bolts aren't enough.

In today's increasingly competitive and constantly changing business environment, it's not enough to know *how* to run a business. You have to have a clear understanding of *what* business you're really running. You need to find a way to meaningfully differentiate yourself from the competition and create a bond between you and your customers. What you need is a clearly defined strategic position.

Today, defining a strategic position is as important for the proverbial "mom and pop" small business as it is for a high technology company. I learned this from one of my very first clients, a florist. Although this business was located in a neighborhood storefront and might be perceived as just another "bucket shop"—a place where people pick up a dozen flowers on their way home from work—in fact, they specialized in exquisitely designed arrangements for high-society weddings and events, often importing unique flowers from Europe or the tropics. On any given day, however, you might walk into their shop and not be able

to find so much as a dozen roses or daisies. They didn't try to be all things to all people.

This type of positioning better equipped my clients to deal with increased competition as both supermarkets and discount warehouse stores began selling cut flowers. They were clearly different from their competitors.

A strategic position differentiates you from others. It shows you have something to offer that's unique, special, and difficult or impossible to replicate. When defining your company's strategic position, look at:

■ Industry trends and developments

■ Competitive opportunities and openings

■ Changes brought through new technologies

■ Your strengths and interests

After a few years in business, I had to struggle with defining my own strategic position. I had been doing a wide variety of management consulting, taking whatever came along. But just hanging up a shingle and saying, "I'm a management consultant" was like the florist who says, "I sell flowers." Yeah, me and who else?

So I started clarifying my company's position. By coincidence, I had attracted a number of law firms who needed advice on improving their marketing. I came along at just the right time to meet the new trend in the legal industry of more actively courting potential clients. After working with a few law firms, I realized I could easily develop a strategic position, a specialty, in marketing law firms. Eureka!

There was just one hitch: I was bored out of my mind. Even though there was an excellent fit with industry trends, market needs, competitive openings, and my skills, the work just wasn't a good fit with my interests. Instead, I chose to differentiate my practice on the basis of the nature of the service I offered—business plan development—rather than the market segment.

Your company's strategic position can be based on your market niche, type of product or service, quality of customer service, pricing, convenience, or anything else that will significantly distinguish you in a meaningful way from the others out there who offer similar services or products. There's no one "right" position, and your positioning will change and evolve over time. But defining your strategic position is a critical way to answer that nagging question, "What business are you in?"

…your mission statement
(continued from **page 56**)

- ■ **Key strategies for reaching your goals**
- ■ **What distinguishes you from your competition**

A Mission Statement only achieves value when management and employees use it as a touchstone. Share your Mission Statement with all those who have a stake in your company: employees, customers, shareholders, even suppliers and distributors. You want them all to know what you're trying to achieve. Of course, nothing proprietary should be included in a Mission Statement.

Keep in mind that your Mission Statement can evolve over time. As conditions change in your industry, the economy, or your management style and beliefs, you can go back and re-examine and revise your mission.

Finding Your Niche

We're all familiar with the concept of specialists. If you discover you have a heart disease, for instance, you're going to make an appointment with a cardiologist. After all, you want a doctor who has specific knowledge and experience with your particular problem and concerns. But have you ever thought about becoming a specialist yourself—finding a specific niche for your business to serve?

Imagine, for instance, that you wanted to start a housecleaning service. In most communities, there are hundreds of housecleaners. You'd have lots of competition.

But what if you specialized? What if you only used natural or non-toxic products? Then, you might name your business something like "Healthy House Non-Toxic Cleaners." You'd advertise in publications or join organizations serving customers who are particularly concerned about keeping their homes safe—perhaps parents of young children or animal owners. Assuming there were enough such potential customers in your community, you'd have an instant way to set yourself apart from the competition.

When thinking about choosing a specialization or niche market, be sure it's:

■ **Sizable.** Your market segment should be distinct, but not so small that there won't be enough customers to make a profit.

■ **Reachable.** There should be publications, organizations, or events for your specific market so you can let them know you exist.

■ **Self-defining.** Your potential market should have, or feel they have, special needs. After all, that's why they want a specialist.

■ **Sustainable.** Select a niche that can support your business long-term, where you won't quickly deplete the customer supply. Avoid specialties highly affected by changes in the economy, and be sure it's something you won't get bored with quickly.

Finding a specialty is one of the most powerful ways to set yourself apart from competitors and focus your marketing efforts. You'll find another benefit, too: specialists typically charge higher prices. For instance, according to the American Society of Travel Agents, travel agents who specialize in a particular market segment made an average of 11% more than general travel agents.

You and I already know your business is special—why not become even more special? Find yourself a niche and then let the world know all about it!

How Do You Find Your Niche?

■ **Industry or business type.** Few things give you as much credibility with potential clients as having served similar clients before. People in every industry believe their industry is unique. So when you specialize in an industry, potential customers are reassured by the fact that you're already familiar with many of the unique aspects of their line of work. If you specialize in an industry, however, you may have to broaden the geographic area you serve.

■ **Demographic group.** Ever hear of hair salons just for children? How about computer classes for seniors? Or financial investing for women? Targeting a specific demographic group gives you an immediately recognizable way to attract customers and make them feel welcome. Of course, when you target a demographic group, you need to become familiar with the issues important to that group, their sensitivities, and buying habits.

■ **Unique knowledge.** Like the cardiologist, you can choose to emphasize areas in which you have in-depth education or experience. You need the training and understanding to handle the unique needs of your customers. Many niches based on unique knowledge, however, can be developed on the job. A graphic design firm, for instance, might specialize in preparing annual reports for publicly traded companies. There are many federal rules that must be followed in annual reports, but you could immerse yourself in those without taking classes.

■ **Style.** As with the example of housecleaners who use only non-toxic cleaning supplies, choosing a specific style of service or product is another way to specialize. You could, for instance, have a furniture store offering only all-wood furniture or a restaurant serving only organic food. Consumers can easily see what sets these businesses apart from their competitors.

■ **Geographic.** Choosing to narrow in on a geographic area is an obvious way to specialize, and many entrepreneurs focus on this as their niche. However, as a niche, geography often is not enough of a competitive advantage. Ask yourself, 'Is location enough of an advantage on its own to make customers choose me over my competition?'

Paranoia Can Save Your Business

In most aspects of life, I'm a fairly trusting person, but there's one thing that makes me totally mistrustful: being overly dependent on *one* big customer or *one* sales channel. I don't want my future financial security controlled by someone else, and neither should you.

This dread of being reliant on one source of income doesn't really qualify as "paranoia." Paranoia, after all is an *unreasonable* fear; I'm being completely *reasonable*. I've seen businesses collapse when their one big customer suddenly vanished.

As a consultant, when I worked with a company, one of the first things I looked at was whether they put all their income eggs in one basket. They often did: one customer accounted for 80% of their sales, one trade show accounted for 90% of their leads, or one distributor handled 100% of their accounts. I quickly helped them realize they needed to diversify and helped them devise a strategy to accomplish this.

Yet a few years ago, I realized I was in the same boat. I own a publishing company—The Planning Shop—and, fortunately, our books sell very well in bookstores. But we relied on one distributor to get our books on bookstore shelves. A few years ago, that one sales channel accounted for over 90% of my income stream.

So imagine my paranoia when my distributor was acquired by a large corporation. What if they changed financial terms? Their service declined? They stopped distributing our books? What would that mean to me? I didn't start my own business only to place my economic future in the hands of a big corporation hundreds of miles away. If I wanted that, I could have stayed an employee, right?

> **"Just because you're paranoid doesn't mean they're not out to get you."**

That paranoia woke me up. I realized I needed a second sales channel. Since the other 10% of our income came from sales to business schools that use our books in their classes, I targeted the academic market. I promoted my office manager to the position of full-time academic marketing director, and we developed an aggressive marketing plan. Of course, this was expensive—and risky. But it was far less risky than continuing to depend on just one source for my income.

Within two years, however, our decision to develop a second channel paid off. We more than doubled our overall sales, and the academic market became a substantial source of our income.

It's natural to drift into becoming overly dependent on one customer or sales channel. After all, as entrepreneurs:

■ **We specialize.** Becoming a specialist in an area means being able to compete better and charge higher prices. For a small company, it's beneficial to focus on a niche.

■ **We maximize our profits.** By concentrating our sales efforts in a single channel, we substantially reduce our marketing costs while increasing their effectiveness.

■ **We give great customer service.** We want to make certain our one big customer is completely satisfied, so we devote most of our efforts to servicing that account.

■ **We get lazy.** Hey, we're making enough money; why should we change?

So we have to pay attention to the need for a second—or third—income stream.

Fortunately, I've discovered that a little bit of paranoia—but just a little—can be a useful thing. After all, as the saying goes, "Just because you're paranoid doesn't mean they're not out to get you."

Steps to Diversify Your Business

1. Get a solid foundation. One of Rhonda's Rules is "Build one business a time." It's almost impossible to develop a second sales channel until you've successfully developed your first.

2. Identify current secondary sources of sales. It's likely you get some or your sales—or inquiries—from one type of customer without doing much marketing.

3. Develop a plan. Cultivating a new sales channel is very much like starting a new business. Research the market, interview prospective customers, create a budget, develop a plan.

4. Focus on just one new channel at a time. Don't try too many new things at once; success is more likely if you focus your efforts.

5. Renew your enthusiasm. Remember the energy you had when you first started your company? Stretch your wings again.

Who's Your Competition?

If I asked you who your competition is, you're likely to mention the company down the street or across town that sells the same product or service as you. When I ask you how you're different from your competition, you'll tell me that you're faster, cheaper, or better than your cross-town rival.

But today competition comes in a lot more forms than just the guy down the block. If you want to compete effectively, you have to understand how you compare in more ways than just your prices.

A big part of the change in the competitive arena is the **Internet.** You may be the only company in town that sells purple doorknobs; before the Internet, you could have cornered the local purple doorknob market. Today, however, customers flocking to buy those doorknobs hop on the Internet and start checking suppliers all over the country.

Services aren't immune from the power of Internet competition. Sure, if you're a dentist, it's impossible for a patient to have a tooth pulled on the Internet, but if you're a graphic designer, it's not that difficult for a client to have a brochure designed by a cross-country competitor. In an age of Internet competition, you have to distinguish yourself with more intense customer service, unusual offerings, or the power of your personality or talent.

The Internet doesn't just give you a million new competitors, it creates a new type of competitor: **Information.** After surfing the web, customers may walk into your store knowing the wholesale cost of your doorknobs. Just ask a new car dealer. Car shoppers walk into showrooms armed with a stack of computer printouts detailing the wholesale cost of every option. How will you cope with a more informed customer who may be willing to put up with the inconvenience of mail order if you don't cut your profit margins?

You're lucky, even though it may not seem that way, if all you're competing against is the Internet and your land-based competitor in town. An overlooked competitor and the hardest one to beat is **Inertia.** In most cases, customers have the option *not* to buy at all. Let me emphasize that it's not enough for you to know the customer needs your product or service. The customer must truly believe they need *you.* If you're a plumber, a person with an overflowing sewer isn't going to be doing a lot of comparison shopping. But most customers don't have that type of pressing, pungent need.

Customers don't do what they should do; they do what they have to do or want to do.

How will you compete against inertia? How will you make customers recognize they truly need or badly want your product or service?

> It's not enough for *you* to know the customer needs your product. The customer must believe *they need you.*

If you're taking on the competition, you also have to understand all the **other ways for customers to spend their money.** If a customer walks into your jewelry store shopping for diamond earrings, they may walk out without purchasing—not because your earrings cost more than ones they can get at another store or on the Internet but because they realized they'd rather buy an electronic gadget or take a vacation. You have to understand the context of a customer's

purchase. What makes your product or service more valuable than the other tugs on a customer's pocketbook?

When thinking about your competitors, don't just consider those companies or options that compete with you currently. Also consider who might compete with you in the near future. It's not enough to take comfort in the fact that other companies have overlooked a particular product or service. Once you show you can be successful, who will want to take a piece of that market from you?

In the end, the best way to beat the competition is to have each and every customer so satisfied with the quality and value of your product or service that they couldn't imagine going anywhere else. When customers are so enthusiastic that they sing your praises to their friends and colleagues, it's tough for others to compete. So, today, as you work with your clients and customers, remember you're not just creating one satisfied customer, you're actually beating the pants off the competition.

Checking Out the Competition

"Let's go shopping!" While those are three of my favorite words, this spree is very limited: we're just going to check out what the competition is up to.

In general, I'm not a big believer in spending much time or energy worrying about what the other guy—or gal—is doing. Over the years, I've learned that success depends much more on what you do than on what your competitors are doing.

Yes, big businesses spend millions of dollars fighting over each percentage point of market share (just think Coke versus Pepsi; Ford versus GM). But for a small company, that's not very productive.

But that doesn't mean you can just ignore the competition. From time to time, you should check out who's out there, what they're offering, and what they're charging.

If you approach this competitive analysis exercise as an opportunity to learn—and not just get mad at that *#%&##!* who steals some of your customers—you may find ways to enhance your products or services, or at least improve your marketing.

Competition comes in three major forms:

1. Alternatives and inertia. These are all the other ways a customer can spend their time and money. I can remodel my kitchen or go on a vacation, have a pedicure or buy a blouse. As a small business, you don't have the marketing dollars to compete against this kind of nebulous competition.

2. The big guys. The Wal-Marts, Home Depots, Lawyers 'R' Us—national companies or franchises with huge marketing budgets. Don't just dismiss these as being inferior because they're big—a lot of these companies have adopted some of the customer service practices that used to be the hallmark of small business.

3. Direct competitors. The ones who keep you up at night. They're other small companies like yours: close to customers, ambitious, and trying to reach the same target market. In most markets, there's enough business to go around, but you'd better know what your direct competition is doing.

The easiest way to begin your competitive analysis is from the comfort of your computer. Just jump on the Internet. Here's the plan of attack:

1. Websites of direct competitors. Drill down way beyond the home page. Be sure to read the "About Us" section and any press information, as well as descriptions of their products or services.

Here are some of the things to look for on your competitors' sites:
• Descriptions of products/services

- Prices
- Client/customer lists—testimonials
- Staff—to see their qualifications and what size company they have
- Their strengths
- How they position themselves—what words they use to describe themselves
- Which segment of the market they appear to be targeting

2. Next, try this trick to find which websites link to your competitors' websites. Go to Google, **www.google.com,** and in their search bar, type in the word "link," followed by a colon, then a space, then the full URL of the website. If I wanted to see who was linking to my website, I'd type "link: www.planningshop.com". You might then want to contact some of the websites that link to your competitors and ask them to link to you as well.

3. You can also see if any of your competitors have been written about in the press recently. Check their names at the Google News directory. Go to **news.google.com.**

4. Going back to the Google home page, do searches on the names of your competitors and the generic description of your product/service category and location (if appropriate). Use alternative phrases as well. In other words, if you want to find out who's competing with you in the landscaping business in Phoenix, also try phrases like "lawn care" and "Arizona." Go also to the Yahoo directory, **www.yahoo.com.**

5. If you target specific industries as customers, check out the websites of those industry associations. Search for listings of exhibitors at past trade shows (you might need to check under "events" or "conventions"). That will give you an idea of whether your competitors are actively marketing to the same industry.

6. If you're willing to spend a bit of money, and your competitors are pretty well established, you can get a Dun & Bradstreet report on them. Go to **www. dnb.com.**

Finally, not all competitive analysis can be done online. Check to see if your competitors advertise in the phone directory. Perhaps you might phone or visit a competitor to see what they offer and how much they charge. Don't request proposals or bids—just ask for a simple brochure or have a quick discussion on the phone. Better yet, join a local chapter of your trade association and get to know your competitors personally. Then you can sit down and discuss what they're doing face to face.

In the best of all possible worlds, the fact that you have competition should cause you to constantly improve your products and services. That way, you'll make more money—and can really go shopping!

Competing with the Big Guys

Are they building a Wal-Mart in your community? Has a Starbucks opened down the street? How about another Home Depot or Lowes? Are your customers now buying off the Internet instead of from you? Does this mean you're doomed? What can you do to compete with the big guys?

In virtually every retail segment—and many service industries as well—megacompanies are edging out small businesses. More money is being made by fewer players. From 1997–2002 retail sales increased by over three-quarters of a trillion dollars, while the number of companies decreased by almost 100,000 (U.S. Census Bureau figures).

Don't close up shop just yet! While it's certainly difficult to survive in today's retail environment, it's not at all hopeless, and many small companies are managing to thrive. Here's what the survivors are doing:

■ **Compete on your terms, not theirs.** The single most important thing to recognize is that you're never going to be able to win playing the big boys' game. You won't be the low-price leader; they will. So don't try.

■ **Differentiate.** You know that you're different from the big competition, but your customers might not be so discerning. You have to offer a mix of products and services that are clearly distinct from the big competitors'. Convenience or service alone are unlikely to be a sufficient differentiator. One office supply store added more and more gift items as they recognized they couldn't compete on price with the office supply superstores.

■ **Do something.** Recognize that you're going to have to make some changes—in product selection, services, employee training, marketing, and more. If you just sit there, you're going to get run over.

> **You have the advantage of being able to adapt to new trends and market developments much more quickly.**

■ **Outsmart them.** Big companies move slowly; you have the advantage of being able to adapt to new trends and market developments much more quickly. Stay abreast of industry and market trends. Keep informed. You can't just take care of day-to-day business; you have to plan a strategy for even the smallest company.

■ **Link special services to purchases.** It's incredibly frustrating to provide great pre-sale advice, but then have the customer make the actual purchase at a cheaper store or website. Look for ways to offer desirable or unique services as an add-on benefit as part of, or after, the purchase. When I purchased my barbecue grill at a local hardware store, they included free delivery and assembly—services I would have had to pay extra for at the hardware superstore. One local bookstore hosts special events with leading authors—free to those who purchase books.

■ **Use inexpensive marketing approaches.** Big companies have to spend a fortune on marketing. Keep your marketing costs low by using approaches such as trade shows, public relations, and customer retention and referral programs.

■ **Have terrific employees.** Small companies can be at a distinct advantage in providing employees with a better place to work than most superstores. In addition to offering better wages and benefits, small employers offer more communication and recognition as well as less workplace politics and bureaucracy. Say thank you—a lot. Offer unique benefits that show you value your employees—I give employees paid "well days" so they can take off when something really good happens—a new love, a fun outing with their child, a gorgeous day to go to the beach.

■ **Improve employee training.** Megastores often provide better training—at least in sales techniques—to their workers. Small companies often neglect to train their workers adequately. Make sure they know the products and know how to interact positively with customers.

■ **If you can't beat them, join them.** Some superstores, such as Home Depot, contract out services (such as roofing or kitchen remodeling), often using local subcontractors. Perhaps you can get a piece of this action, but don't allow your whole business to become dependent on this source.

■ **Band together.** There's been a remarkable resurgence in local downtown areas as businesses have joined together in business improvement districts (BIDs) or Mainstreet USA programs. Likewise, independent bookstores formed "Booksense" to offer joint programs and marketing, helping them compete against bookstore chains and Amazon. There's definitely strength in numbers.

What Does Winning Mean?

In all aspects of life—but especially business and sports—you hear a lot about winners and losers. But what, exactly, does it mean to win? Do you have to beat others to be a champion, or is achieving personal excellence sufficient?

I've spent a lot of time thinking about the role of competition in business, especially smaller business. Conventional business theory—the kind you read in business school textbooks—is that a business needs to be focused on beating its competition. Coca-Cola spends a lot of time worrying about Pepsi—and vice versa. But if you're not running a multinational, multimillion-dollar company, is such a focus necessary? Or even healthy? I don't think so.

During the dot-com "bubble" when new technology companies received millions of dollars in financing, business analysts and venture capitalists emphasized how critical it was to get big fast—to beat the competition in capturing a market. This is called "first mover advantage." Fledgling companies spent truckloads of money on expensive ads (remember those sock puppets?) because common wisdom was that only a few companies in each business category would survive. The key was growing faster—not necessarily better—than the other guy.

Virtually none of the companies that followed that "beat-the-other-guy" path are around today.

Meanwhile, many of the companies that paid little attention to being first or biggest, but instead tended to running their own business well, are still around. They didn't get a lot of money from venture capitalists, so they didn't have the pressure to grow large quickly for a speedy return on investment. Rather, they focused on coming up with products or services that actually made money, serving their customers well, and running their operations to keep costs down. You may not know the names of these companies because they didn't do a lot to attract attention; they just took care of business. They still do.

> You can define excellence in your own business, indeed in your own life, without focusing on beating the competition.

Even big companies may be better off spending less energy worrying about the competition and looking to internal excellence. A company I admire a great deal—3M—has as one of its stated goals to invent products that change the basis for competition. In other words, they don't want to beat their competitors; they want to create a whole new playing field. Think of some of the products that have resulted from this kind of thinking: Post-Its, masking tape, Scotch-Guard, and literally thousands more.

It's human nature to compare ourselves to others. Studies of happiness indicate that our perception of our own well-being is determined in large part by how we think we stack up to others around us.

It is natural to respect winners, especially those who have worked hard to achieve their success. My eyes well up when I see a proud medal winner standing atop the platform. But our society often becomes obsessed with winning rather than with excellence.

Ancient Olympians competed only as individuals, not as members of teams. The concept behind the ancient games was that of individual achievement through competition,

but the goal was to achieve arête or "excellence," not just winning. Competition, then, was to bring out excellence—not to define it.

You can define excellence in your own business, indeed in your own life, without focusing on beating the competition. Look at what you excel at—your company's "core competencies"—and strive to be the best you can be at those.

At the 1996 Olympics in Atlanta, my niece Adeena was a medal presenter. She told me that some of the happiest, proudest athletes she met were not the ones who won the medals but those who were just so thrilled to have made it to the Olympics. Their years of effort had led them to be able to be there, to participate, to be in the game.

Success comes to those who strive for excellence and achievement rather than those who spend their energy trying to defeat the other guy or gal. Excel at your own game, and the competition will have to worry about you.

The Art of Setting Prices

The other day I saw a small purse for sale in a department store, priced at more than $100. In another store I found a virtually identical purse—without the designer's name—for less than $20. How do people come up with these prices?

While prices baffle us as buyers, we're often just as likely to be confused as sellers. How do you set a price for your products or services? The reality is that pricing is an art, certainly not a science.

Once upon a time—when the business world was dominated by manufactured stuff—prices had a somewhat more rational basis. You took the cost of raw materials and added labor costs, overhead, marketing, and then a percentage as profit.

That was basic pricing theory. But it doesn't work so well in today's small companies. Even if we're manufacturing products, most of us would have difficulty figuring our costs on a per-item basis.

But setting prices is a particularly vexing problem when what you sell isn't a physical product. The business world today is dominated by companies that sell things other than "stuff:" services, software, knowledge. How do you get clients to properly value your work when what you sell is expertise, and expertise isn't something that can be touched or counted?

How do you set prices? How do you know that you're actually charging enough to be profitable and not leaving money on the table when customers would pay more? How do you know when you're charging too much, losing customers or clients to others?

Setting prices is a complex process, a mix of many factors:

■ **Market rates.** Clearly, the most important thing to consider is what the going rate is for similar products or services. While I might think a book I write is worth $200, few people are willing to spend that kind of money on a book. To determine market rates, talk to your trade association, ask suppliers, talk to others in the industry, go shopping.

■ **Exclusivity.** If you're the only company providing a necessary product or service, you can charge more. That's where finding a niche can lead to higher prices. For instance, I saw a janitorial service specializing in serving banks. That's a smart niche because they need bonded, trustworthy janitors and can charge higher prices as a result.

■ **Quality.** Quality does command higher prices, but it's often difficult for a consumer to judge. How can a potential customer know that one type of fruit preserve is higher quality than another or that one attorney is better qualified than another? That's why "sampling" can be an effective way of marketing, whether it's giving out free tastes of your jam at the farmer's market or an hour's free consultation.

■ **Trustworthiness.** There's value in buying something you trust—whether it's a hamburger, a novel from a known author, or a lawyer's services. Trustworthiness increases as a result of personal experience, referrals, brand name, testimonials, years in business, and a strong previous client list.

■ **Convenience.** We understand that buying something at the corner store may cost more than if we drive to a big box store across town. The same is true for any product or service. A plumber who can attend to a problem immediately, or a computer consultant who comes to a client's home, can command higher prices.

■ **Cost to reach market.** If a market is difficult to reach—or it takes a long time to make each sale, then you'll have to charge more. If you have to advertise to reach your market, you'll need to recoup those costs. If it takes a year to work through the procurement department of a major corporation, you should be able to charge more to account for that time and effort.

■ **Development time.** You can usually charge more for things that take a long time to develop, create, or build. Since you have a greater investment in staff time, and overhead, it's generally fair to increase your

prices to account for that development time. However, your customers may not always fully appreciate the time it took for you to produce that product, so you may encounter price resistance.

■ **Small market, big prices.** If a relatively small number of people want your product, you should be able to charge more than if many people want that product, since costs must be spread to the few who want and value that product. That's one of the reasons that a more complex version of a product—whether software, automobiles, or personal electronics—may cost considerably more than the basic version.

■ **Capacity.** How busy are you? If you've got more work than you can handle, you can probably raise prices. If you're sitting there idle, lower your prices or find something else to sell.

■ **Perceived value.** This is where design, packaging, and marketing come in to play. Apple Computer realized that good design can increase the value (as well as the usability) of what might otherwise be mundane products (computers, MP3 players). A professional-looking website and marketing materials can increase your perceived value.

In the end, pricing is always more of an art than a science. And the proper price still comes down to two primary factors: what the market will pay and what you need to make a profit.

Competing on Price Alone

An old joke: A store owner purchases pencils for ten cents a piece, then turns around and sells them for only a nickel. Noticing this bizarre behavior, his partner asks, "How do you expect us to stay in business that way?" The man replies, "Volume!"

Surprisingly, many novice entrepreneurs choose a similar strategy. They think they can succeed merely by pricing their products or services cheaper than the competition. Low prices, they assume, will generate sufficient sales to more than make up for smaller profits. Like the store owner in the joke, these entrepreneurs rationalize, "What I lose in margins, I'll make up in volume."

Competing on price is risky. Yes, some big businesses—and perhaps your local discount drycleaner—seem to thrive on low prices. But low prices mean narrow profit margins. Narrow profit margins mean less cash. With a small financial cushion, you're vulnerable with every slight increase in costs. The landlord raises your rent 5 percent? That may be your entire year's profit.

Then what happens? You'll have to find ways to reduce costs even further. The first thing you'll be tempted to do is reduce wages and benefits. Watch out! This means you won't be able to attract good employees. The ones you have will be less likely to be productive or loyal. You'll be busy keeping an eye on them, and they'll be keeping an eye on the clock.

The next thing you'll do is cut your marketing efforts. However, businesses that compete primarily on the basis of price almost always depend on high levels of marketing to keep customers coming in the door.

The customers who do come to such businesses are fickle. Low-price shoppers are loyal to price, not to you. So if the competition decides to squeeze you out with even lower prices, a lot of your hard-won customers will be gone in an instant.

> **Low-price shoppers are loyal to price, not to you.**

While price should never be the cornerstone of your strategy, it certainly cannot be ignored. So how can a small company, which may not qualify for the supplier discounts or achieve the economies of scale available to a larger business, still maintain competitive pricing?

■ **Carve out a niche.** If you "own" a market, you have more room to set prices. If there are 100 mechanics in your city, you'll face constant price competition. But if you're the only mechanic specializing in Volvos, you'll face much less price pressure.

■ **Work smarter, not cheaper.** Let's face it, a lot of your competition is just plain dumb. Improve profits through innovative practices. Southwest Airlines, for instance, first saved money by issuing reusable plastic boarding passes instead of paper passes, and then they were the first to use electronic ticketing. Southwest maximized profits by getting their planes back in the air an average of twenty minutes after landing instead of the two hours it took other airlines. By being smarter, Southwest became the most consistently profitable airline in the industry.

■ **Focus on value, not price.** Value is a term used to mean the combination of price and quality. When you shop for a winter coat, you may be willing to pay higher prices to get quality that will last many years. Likewise, a client may be willing to pay a higher price for your printing services if you can deliver the job faster with fewer errors than your competition. Excellence and service are competitive advantages that let you justify higher prices.

■ **Target the right customers.** Not all customers are willing to pay more, even for better quality. So make certain you aim your marketing efforts at customers who will respond to the differences you offer and can pay a slightly higher price for that value.

■ **Build loyalty to you, not your price.** Even if you use special pricing (discounts, introductory offers, sales) to attract customers, go to work immediately developing a relationship that keeps customers coming back when the price goes up.

Don't let yourself get caught in a continual battle to be the "low-price leader." You may win that battle but lose the war or your business. Remember, you've got a lot more to offer than just a low price.

Don't Nickel & Dime Your Customers

When I first went into business, I sat down with a lawyer to review my legal and tax responsibilities. When we finished, he gave me some advice I've remembered to this day. "Rhonda," he counseled, "don't nickel and dime your clients. Clients willingly pay thousands of dollars in hourly fees without complaint, but if I bill them $2 in long distance calls, they'll get upset. It's small items that alienate clients."

He was right. We all hate being "nickled and dimed." You're often more likely to lose a customer over a small extra charge than a big fee. When I was a consultant, I never charged clients for items such as photocopying or long distance calls. Other consultants added those charges routinely, but I preferred to treat them as part of my cost of doing business. Over the years, it probably cost me very little and kept my clients from being aggravated.

Customers generally react negatively to all charges that seem like part of the supplier's normal cost of doing business. I might spend $3,000 on fees for a graphic artist to design marketing materials and feel that's an appropriate fee. I certainly understand when she passes along the printing costs. But if I see a $3 item on my bill to reimburse her for calls to the print shop, I'm going to feel she's unprofessional.

My reaction to extra charges is also going to be influenced by how much I'm able to understand the fee itself and whether it's out of line. As a consumer of legal services, I'm not in a position to judge the difference between a fee of $150 per hour and $250 per hour; I just want to find the best lawyer at an affordable price. But if I also get charged for photocopying documents, I'll know I'm being overcharged if I'm billed twenty-five cents per page. I'll then feel like I'm being overcharged for professional services as well.

> **Extra fees often leave a sour taste with a customer.**

Be cautious any time you add a charge where there is no perceived value to the customer. If I spend a few dollars more per yard on carpet, I understand I'm buying higher quality and recognize that value. But what value do I perceive in the extra cost the carpet company charges me just for moving my couch a few feet? Sure, I know there is a real expense for the carpet company in having employees spend time moving even a small amount of furniture, but I still react negatively to an "extra" fee that likely applies to 99% of all their customers.

I understand why companies add these kinds of fees. After all, competing carpet companies are asking less for their carpet and later tacking on all kinds of extra charges. How do you compete if you don't add those same types of additional fees? It's easy to feel you must play the same game.

Part of the answer is to make it clear to your customers that you are including all the extra services *free*—and that's a really strong marketing word to use. For instance, when I was shopping for a new barbecue, I paid a few dollars more to buy one from a local hardware store, rather than the big home improvement company, because my local store provided assembly and delivery *free*.

When you do assume the costs for items that your competitors charge for, feel free

to list those items on the bill followed by the word, "Complimentary." That lets the customer know you could charge but don't. That builds good will and customer loyalty.

This isn't to say you should never add any extra charges to a base price, just that it's important to use judgment every time you add another line to your bill. But always let the customer know about additional fees *before* they make the purchase.

Remember, extra fees often leave a sour taste with a customer and these fees are usually encountered at the end of a transaction. Is that really the last impression you want to leave with an otherwise satisfied customer? If so, you're likely to lose future business and referrals from that customer. Instead, try to make the last interaction with a customer the most pleasant; so go ahead and move that sofa for free.

Rule of Thumb for Extra Charges:

1. Absorb all normal, nominal, predictable costs.

2. Charge your customer for unusual or significant expenses.

Give It Away to Grow Your Business

Warning: This is not about **making** money. That's right, in a business book, I'm going to discuss why some things you do should **not** bring you income—at least not immediately.

It's time to think about ways to give your products or services away *free*.

This isn't just about doing good for others—although that's definitely a prime motive. The fact is, donating or giving away your products or services is also a very effective way to build your business. And when you involve your employees in these efforts, it's also a good method of building company morale and loyalty.

Surprisingly, few of us know how to give. Often, we don't know *what* we should give, especially when we're in a service rather than product business and *when* we should give. For the owner of a retail sporting goods shop, it's relatively easy to donate equipment to a local little league team. But if you're an accountant, what types of services make sense as a donation? And when a stranger asks for free tax advice at the baseball game, you're going to get heartburn from more than just the hot dogs.

■ **Donating products or services to worthy causes.** Attorneys are generally required (by bar associations) to provide some legal services free, or "pro bono publico," which means "for the good of the public." But all of us can—and should—help our communities by donating some of our time or products to help others. My publishing company, for instance, regularly donates books to youth entrepreneurship programs.

If you are in a service business, you can donate some of your time. You can help community organizations by providing them with some of your time and expertise. Or, you can donate some of your services to needy individuals. You can also donate your services in the form of gift certificates to be auctioned off for local charities.

You can also get your company involved in donating products or services that are not directly related to your business. One company, for instance, decided to "adopt" a local elementary school. The company donated funds to the school and encouraged their employees to donate books to the school library. The company also allowed employees paid time off to tutor students.

Charitable activities increase employee loyalty, as employees are more committed to their employers when they share broader values than just increasing the bottom line.

A word of caution, however: many scam artists prey on small businesses by posing as charitable organizations. Be sure you check out the validity of any charity you choose.

77

You can check out charities at the Better Business Bureau (**www.bbb.org**). And *never* give a credit card number over the phone, even to well-known causes.

■ **Lower your prices.** Sometimes you don't have to give everything away absolutely free; you can just lower your prices. There are a number of instances when you might choose to do this: to serve a community group, for lower-income customers, or to attract or keep a desired customer. Some companies have a formal "sliding scale" with discounts for certain types of customers or situations. I do this myself. I earn part of my income by speaking at conventions, conferences, and workshops. However, I generally voluntarily reduce my speaking fees for non-profit entrepreneurial organizations.

■ **Sampling.** We've all been in supermarkets where they give away free samples of food. Those companies hope that once you taste their product, you'll want to buy more. You can do the same in your business, in essence, by giving potential customers a "taste" free—even if you are in a service business.

For instance, if you're an accountant, you could offer potential clients a free review of last year's tax returns as a way of sampling your services. A dentist could offer one free teeth cleaning. This kind of sampling attracts new customers and allows them to get acquainted with you and your services.

Sampling is an especially helpful technique if you're introducing something that is very innovative or unusual. After all, even things we now consider commonplace were once hard for customers to understand. For instance, when Post-It notes were introduced, the only way 3M (the company that makes Post-It) could get customers to try these brand-new "sticky notes," was to give away millions of samples.

■ **Help others succeed.** In the process of building my business, I was fortunate to have many people who helped me. Even casual acquaintances gave me assistance. They introduced me to key contacts, provided free expert advice, shared resources, gave me technical assistance. It's amazing how much help I got along my way. Now, I try to do the same for others. I realize it's part of what it takes to build a community of successful entrepreneurs, and it's my way of repaying all those people who helped me.

So another way you can give is by providing assistance to other entrepreneurs. Sometimes it's as simple as introducing an aspiring businessperson to a potential customer, helping someone find a supplier, or showing a novice in your business how to get something done. These informal donations don't seem like charity, but they help give back to others and strengthen our entrepreneurial and civic communities.

Preparing Your Business to Go On without You

What happens to your business if something happens to you? I faced that issue when I had to have surgery. Even though my surgery was routine, the prospect of going "under the knife" forced me to prepare for the security and continuity of my business in case something happened to me.

For many entrepreneurs, their business is their most valuable asset. Yet they do little to make sure their company and its value are sustained if they're out of commission. Even if you're unavailable for a relatively short period of time, can your business keep going without you?

On the most basic level, make certain your company can continue if you're merely indisposed. You don't want to lose money, orders, or worse, just because no one else has the authority to pay a bill or has the password to access your email.

Ideally, it would be best if you didn't lose customers—and your customers didn't lose access to the products or services you provide—while you're out of circulation. You can take steps to cover your business even if you are a solo entrepreneur.

To prepare for a more serious situation, you'll need the help of an attorney. It's not easy to think about, but should you become incapacitated or die, you don't want your company to fall apart while your family is forced to figure out the legal situation. And they certainly don't want to be thinking about such issues at a time like that.

Let's start with things you can address without an attorney to handle short-term difficulties:

■ **Check-signing authority.** Have an extra signatory on your bank and payroll accounts. I use my accountant; CPAs and attorneys legally have a fiduciary responsibility to protect your assets, so they're generally trustworthy. It could also be a spouse, partner, or other person you trust completely.

■ **Minor expenses.** To make it easy to handle day-to-day purchases, get a credit card for the person who's going to handle your administrative matters in your absence. You can set a low credit limit or even limit the credit card to certain types of purchases if you feel you need protection.

■ **Passwords.** Can anyone else manage your website or critical data, such as your email, computer documents, and bank accounts? Make sure someone trustworthy knows where to find your passwords.

■ **Basic knowledge of your business affairs.** If you don't have an administrative employee, does anyone in your family know how to locate your tax records, find your accounts receivable, or use your software program? Do they know who your attorney or accountant is? Make a list of such details and show a family member.

■ **Getting the work done.** Can you find someone to fulfill your actual work obligations while you're out of commission? If you have employees, train at least one of them. If not, find a colleague in the same line of work and agree to be each other's "understudies."

Those matters you can handle on your own. But it's probably best—especially if your business has substantial value—to sit down with an attorney and discuss long-term issues:

■ **Will.** If you die without a will, the government does *not* get your assets, but the law determines which of your relatives will inherit. A will makes certain the person you wish to receive your assets actually does.

■ **Revocable living trust.** Even with a will, your assets—including your company—may get tied up in probate court. By transferring your assets into a revocable living trust, you can ensure that a capable person (whomever you choose as trustee) can immediately start administering your company.

■ **Tax planning.** You can minimize any estate taxes on your business and avoid disruption to your company with a little advance tax planning.

■ **Life insurance.** Finally, if you'd like your employees to be able to purchase the business (or one of your heirs to buy out another), there are methods to purchase life insurance policies to make this possible at relatively minor cost. Ask your insurance agent and/or attorney.

You owe it to yourself, your heirs, and your employees to take a few precautions to ensure the well-being of your company if something happens to you.

Develop Your Exit Strategy

When you're building a business, you don't spend a lot of time pondering how you're eventually going to get out of it. Oh, maybe you think one day you're going to make enough money to retire, but while you can envision yourself golfing or gardening, what's happened to your company? You need an "exit plan."

An exit plan is a long-term strategy for transferring ownership of your company to others.

"Whoa, Rhonda," I imagine you saying. "I hardly know what I'm going to be doing next month. Why should I figure out what I'm going to do with my company ten or twenty years from now?"

First of all, your exit might not be so far away. It used to be when someone started a business, their intent was to build a company, make money, and perhaps leave the enterprise to their children. Today, many entrepreneurs hope to start a business, grow it to a certain size, and then sell it to a larger company.

If you're looking for an investor in your company, you have to spell out an exit: investors want to know how they're going to get their money back. For most investors, it's not enough to get a share of profits; they eventually want their investment turned to cash.

If there is more than one partner in the business, having a clear exit strategy reduces the friction that comes from unspoken exit assumptions. I've seen a situation where one founder dreamed of building a company worth millions of dollars to be sold in a few years, while the other hoped to build a modest business she could run for the rest of her life. They never shared these different exit goals, and it's not surprising they quickly clashed over every expenditure and strategic decision.

> **An exit strategy can help direct your company's short-term and long-term growth.**

Even if you own the company yourself and hope to have it last through the ages, an exit plan helps direct its growth. If, for instance, you would like to be acquired by a larger company, you might target your product development and marketing efforts in ways that complement rather than compete with that company. An exit plan may even help you choose the name of your company: "Rhonda, Inc." may be more difficult to sell than "Small Business Advice, Inc."

There are a number of ways you can exit your company or at least be able to convert some of the value of your company to cash:

■ **Sell.** This is often the simplest way to get value out. All types of companies can be sold, not just retail or manufacturing enterprises. Typically, professional businesses, such as doctors' and dentists' practices, are bought into by new partners. Even a one-person consulting business may be sold.

■ **Be acquired.** Your company may be a good fit for a larger company. Perhaps they want your customer list or the part of the market you have cornered. Perhaps your company offers certain capabilities or technologies that add value to the larger company.

■ **Merge.** This is similar to being acquired, but the assets of the two merging companies form a new entity. You would probably still own stock in the resulting, merged company.

■ **Go public.** When you issue shares in your company that are traded in a stock market, this is referred to as "going public" or issuing an IPO—Initial Public Offering. This doesn't necessarily mean you depart from management of the company, but you now have a way to get money for your ownership interest by selling some of your personal shares of stock.

■ **Have family members take over.** When Levi Strauss started selling blue jeans, he probably didn't envision having a family-owned company bearing his name still going strong 150 years later. But even if you know you'd like this to happen, you need a plan. Your family members might not want to run, or be capable of running, the company. After all, Levi Strauss didn't have any children; he was lucky his nephew took over.

■ **Employee buy-out.** An excellent way to keep your company together and to retain the jobs you've created is to structure a way for either key management or employees as a whole to buy the company. An ESOP— Employee Stock Ownership Plan—can help them finance the purchase and give you the cash you need.

■ **Go out of business.** This is the simplest end (assuming you have no debts or major employee commitments), but you also get the least financial reward. But sometimes you just want to close up shop and get on with the rest of your life.

A Story about Setting Professional Fees

There once was a manufacturing company in a big city. This manufacturing plant was totally dependent on one piece of equipment to produce their goods. Suddenly, one day, that machine stopped! The entire assembly line came to a halt. Workers stood around with nothing to do. The company began losing thousands of dollars every hour the machine was down.

No one in the company could figure out what was wrong with the machine. So the company owner, in desperation, called an outside expert consultant for emergency help.

The consultant rushed to the manufacturing plant. Calmly, he walked all around the machine, looking closely at the gears and mechanism. Then, he stopped. He rummaged around in his bag, pulled out one small part, and replaced that part on the machine. *Voila!* The machine started up! The assembly line began rolling. Employees went back to work. The company began to make money once again.

One week later, however, the company owner received the consultant's bill. It was for $10,000! The owner was outraged. After all, even though the consultant got the machine working, he was only there for five minutes and used only one small part. How could the consultant justify charging so much money for so little work?

Thinking he'd outsmart the consultant, the business owner came up with an idea. He asked the consultant for an *itemized* bill. Without hesitation, the consultant obliged:

- **Part to fix machine:** $5.00
- **Knowing which part to fix:** $9,995.00

Growth

Rhonda's Rules for Growth

■ **Know what business you're in.** This is harder than it sounds. Most companies have never clearly articulated their strategic position in the marketplace. Why do customers buy from you? What are your core competencies?

■ **Take care of your bread-and-butter business.** Before you consider new directions, clearly define the business activities that bring in the money to pay the bills. Never jeopardize these activities, even if they're not particularly exciting.

■ **Don't bet all your money on one horse.** Many businesses depend on one or two customers or distribution channels to bring in the bulk of revenue. Be careful! Being overly dependent on one or two revenue streams is perilous. You never know what can happen.

■ **Clearly define your target market.** Analyze the characteristics of your customer base so you understand exactly who buys from you. Having a clear target market—for both your current and future business offerings—enables you to be much more effective and efficient in your product development and marketing efforts.

■ **Build one business at a time.** Most entrepreneurs see opportunities to grow in many directions. Concentrate on only one new direction—product line, target market, distribution channel—at a time.

■ **Choose a strategy you can afford.** Growing a business takes money: for marketing activities, new staff, inventory, and more. How will you fund that growth? Through your own revenues? Then growth will be slower. By taking out loans? Then you'll have greater financial obligations. By finding an investor? Then you have to give up part of your company's ownership. Figure out the kind of financing you're willing to live with, and choose your growth strategy accordingly.

■ **"Make sure the dog will eat the dog food."** That's a quote from Eugene Kleiner, the pioneering venture capitalist. What Eugene meant was that no matter how good your ideas appear to be, you have to make certain you've got a product or service that customers really want. Before sinking a fortune in a new endeavor, conduct some test marketing to make certain customers respond.

Committing to Growth

You're sitting there running your business, day in and day out. Things are going along relatively smoothly. Sure, some days are better than others; some months are better than others. But overall, you're fairly satisfied. If it ain't broke, don't fix it—right? Not necessarily. It's time to grow your business.

Growth is hard. Really hard. It means changing roles—taking on more responsibilities in your own company. It means expanding in new directions—taking on more risks and, often, more debt. So why grow?

First, recognize that if you don't grow, your business will inevitably shrink. As someone once said, "If you just sit there, you'll get run over." There are three primary reasons why:

1. Natural loss of customers. Every year you'll lose some customers no matter how good a job you're doing. After all, some customers move away or their needs change. Nobody's client base stays the same forever.

2. New competition. Inevitably, you'll face new competitors or new types of competition. If you've got a healthy market, new competitors will enter to get a piece of the action. Even in a troubled market, some new, creative competitors may see opportunities. And we all know about the increasing competitive threats from the Internet and globalization.

3. Increasing costs. You don't need me to tell you that prices keep rising on just about everything, especially with high gas prices affecting all shipped goods. Increasing prices mean shrinking profit margins even when your sales remain stable.

Being aware of those negative pressures should keep you on your toes at whatever stage of business you're in. But there are certain times in the life of a business when it's particularly important to sit down and consider growth.

> **Start working now to increase the value of your company.**

When do you know you're at one of those critical growth turning points?

■ **You're four to seven years from retirement.** What's going to happen to your income when you decide to leave your business? Perhaps you've been saving money and investing wisely in retirement plans or real estate. Good for you. In that case, it won't matter if you just close up shop and walk away.

Most entrepreneurs, however, continually reinvest their profits in their businesses. Their business is, in effect, their retirement plan. So if they're not able to turn their business into cash when they retire, they'll have to keep on working.

Instead, start planning now to build your business so it has significant value—and the ability to be sold—when you're ready to retire. Achieving growth takes a few years, so start working on growth soon.

■ **You want to sell your company within the next few years.** Even if you're not ready to retire, you may want to sell your company in the near future. If so, you need to start growing your business now.

Most entrepreneurs vastly overestimate the actual worth of their companies. You may believe you can sell it to your employees or a competitor, but the reality is that a very small company commands a very small price—if it's able to find a buyer at all.

Once again, you need to start working now to increase the value of your company and it's attractiveness to a buyer. Remember, it takes time to achieve significant growth.

■ **Your industry is consolidating.** In rapidly consolidating industries—think hardware stores or banking—it's difficult to stay very small. In those industries, big companies become huge companies. They do so by acquiring medium-sized companies and

fast-growing smaller companies. What's left behind—struggling—are the very small companies with little or no annual growth. Your only strategy for survival may be to grow large enough to either compete or be acquired.

■ **You're bored.** When an owner is bored with their company, bad things start to happen. Why? The owner begins to neglect the business, focus only on personal interests, or go off in unrelated directions. Growth—focused, planned growth—provides a meaningful challenge, resparking the owner's interest without jeopardizing the well-being of the company.

■ **Your best employees are bored.** Stagnant companies lead to stagnant employees. Growth offers employees an opportunity to learn new skills and stay fresh, as well as make more money. To retain your best employees, they need an opportunity for growth.

My company is growing, so I know that growth presents a major challenge. But there are times in the life of any company when it must grow in order to survive and thrive.

Take heart: growth not only results in increased income or a higher sales price for your company. The process of growing is also exhilarating and exciting—making it more interesting to go to work every day.

How Does Your Business Grow?

A few years ago, I received a call from an entrepreneur—Matt—who wanted to grow his business. He was seeking help with a business plan for growth.

Matt owns a small towing company, and over three years he built his business from one tow truck to five. Matt was rightfully proud of his success, but he wanted his company to get even bigger. Before he started sinking money into expansion, Matt realized he needed a plan for growth.

Smart guy! Matt was ahead of most entrepreneurs in recognizing that there are many ways to grow a company.

At first, most businesses grow fairly naturally. For instance, Matt's company grew just by adding trucks as demand increased. But at some point in the life of a company, growth can go in a number of different directions. Just like Matt and his towing company, you've got a number of growth strategy options:

■ **Do what you're doing now, only more of it.** This is what we usually think of when we talk about "growth." In Matt's case, he could add more tow trucks. But just because you've been doing one thing successfully doesn't mean the market can necessarily support expansion. Before Matt sinks money into those shiny new yellow trucks, he'd better look at two things: the market and the competition. Is there really enough business in his community for more tow trucks? Obviously, when Matt started, plenty of cars were breaking down and there was more demand than could be met by other companies. If there is still a two-hour wait for a tow, he can probably continue to expand this way.

> **Finding ways to serve your *existing* customers better is a great way to grow.**

Beware! If you grow this way, at some point you're going to tick off your competitors. Right now, Matt is a little guy—the big tow companies don't pay him much notice. As Matt's company gets bigger and starts to compete with larger, richer competitors, they're going to come after him. They can afford to step up advertising, cut prices, increase service, or take other measures to cut Matt's business and profits just when he needs to make truck payments.

■ **Add new markets for the same product or services.** Another option for Matt is to expand to new markets for his existing services. The obvious place for Matt to examine would be neighboring communities that he could serve fairly easily from his present location. Perhaps Matt just needs to widen his advertising reach or add a local phone number for an adjoining community. Over time, he might need to add a second location to serve those areas better.

Expanding geographically is only one way to add additional markets. You could instead choose to target new industries, new demographic groups, or types of customers. For instance, if your computer training company now mostly targets young adults, you could consider adding marketing efforts and classes for seniors. Or, if you now serve a corporate market, you could expand to consumers.

■ Extend your product or service line.

Finding ways to serve your *existing* customers better is a great way to grow. Since you've already spent the money to acquire customers, by adding products or services to sell them, you can substantially increase your profit margins.

Think of these "add-on" sales as growth that is deeper, not wider. You could do this by purchasing a company that provides a complementary service—instant line extension—or you can grow new products or services in-house.

Matt immediately thought of one service his primary existing customer base, auto

dealerships, needed. It was a service that these dealers had mentioned they wanted and couldn't easily find. Matt realized he could quickly add that service with little extra expense. To determine what other types of services he might add to serve his existing clientele, Matt arranged to meet with each of his major customers.

■ Create new markets or increase the size of the market.

Most of the time, companies compete for a share of an existing market—a piece of an existing pie. But sometimes you can actually expand the market—make the pie bigger. For instance, when Apple first made computers easier to use, it created a huge new market for technology.

But trying to create a new market is risky, costly, and tough. Most small companies do not have the resources to create new markets or enlarge existing markets. What, for instance, could Matt do to increase total demand for towing services in his community? Open a Fiat dealership?

Taking the time to think through his growth options saved Matt a lot of money and got him on the right growth track. Before Matt added one truck, or even one tank of gas, he found ways to grow his business with relatively little risk. It just takes a little planning.

How Do I Make More Money?

"How do I make more money?" If I looked at all the questions I'm asked about growing a business, most come down to just this one: How do I make more money?

Novice entrepreneurs think there's some special trick that will enable them to get rich overnight. Experienced businesspeople know no such magic exists, but they'd still like to learn strategies to increase their cash flow.

What really works if you want to make more money?

1. Make more sales. "Duh!" I can hear you saying. Anyone can tell you that to make more money you have to make more sales. But it's important to remember this basic truth. No matter how brilliant your product, marketing, or strategy, if they don't lead directly to sales, you won't have more money in your bank account.

2. Work harder. This isn't a guarantee of growth. If what you're now doing isn't successful, then doing more of it isn't going to help. If, on the other hand, what you're doing *is* working, then you've got to put in more hours, make more sales calls, manufacture more products if you want to earn more.

3. Change. If what you're doing isn't working, figure out why. Are you selling the wrong product or service? Charging too much? Not doing the right marketing? Sit down and analyze what's not working. Be tough on yourself. Then, force yourself to change.

4. Target different customers. Are you targeting the most profitable customers? Are there other market segments that are easier to reach or that will make bigger purchases than your current customers? Evaluate whether other markets could produce higher income.

5. Product-ize your service. If you're now selling a service, then what you are actually selling is your time and there's a limit on how much you can make. Instead, can you outline a cookie-cutter approach so you can hire others to do it, too? Is there a way to turn a one-time service into an ongoing purchasing program—sort of a subscription service? Are there associated products you can sell along with your service?

6. Sell the same customer more things. The most expensive thing to acquire is a customer. Once you have a client, can you provide them with related products or services? Can you get more "wallet share"— that portion of your customer's budget they spend on related products and services? For instance, most hairdressers capture only a fraction of what customers spend on beauty-related products and services. By offering a range of other services and products, a hairdresser can gain a higher percentage of each customer's total beauty purchases.

7. Sell higher-priced items. This, too, seems pretty obvious. But many businesspeople overlook the fact that it takes virtually the same effort to make a big sale as a small one. Can you find a way to change your product or service offerings so that you're selling products or services with higher ticket prices?

8. Hire help. This is especially important if you're a one-person shop. It's hard to grow alone. When you work solo, it means you have to do everything. If you're good at making sales, get out there and make sales, and hire a part-time administrative assistant to do the paperwork. If you're good at delivering your service, then hire someone to go out and make sales. Maximize your earning potential by using your own time in the most productive way.

9. Use technology. Technology, when used well, can enable you to be a much more effective marketer. Do you have your customer list—and prospects—in a usable database? Can you send them regular emails? Do you have a website? Can customers place orders on your website? How can technology speed the work you have to do—administrative tasks, finances, production—so you have more time to make more money?

10. Make a plan. Before you go off in all directions, make a thoughtful plan about how to grow your business. The harsh truth is you won't get rich overnight, so it's important to know that you're heading in the right direction. Think through your options, your budget, and your goals, then decide on a course of action. Stick to it. The money will follow.

Annual Plan for Success

Want to grow your business? The single most important thing you can do is to create an annual business plan.

Every September my company develops an annual plan for the coming year. As a result we have a clear sense of where we're going and how we should spend money. We have specific goals and objectives, and we can measure our progress. Most importantly, our company is growing dramatically.

Developing an annual plan can be a fairly formal process—like the one we do at The Planning Shop. We start gathering information for our plan weeks in advance, hire an industry consultant, and spend a few full days in planning sessions.

But an annual planning process can also be much simpler, especially in a very small business. Set aside a few hours or a day to work exclusively on your goals and objectives for the coming year. Get away from your office or store. Include everyone who's critical to the growth of your company in your planning process.

The steps to a successful annual planning process go from setting overall goals to developing a specific plan of action:

■ **Evaluate the past.** Before going in new directions, see what's worked for you and what hasn't. In particular, identify which activities have been the most successful in terms of *profit,* not just income.

■ **List your goals.** Write down *all* your goals: how much money you want to make, products or services you want to add, new marketing approaches, changes in operations. Include personal goals that affect your work life.

> ## You can't reach a goal you haven't set.

■ **Get specific and add numbers.** Turn general goals into very specific, quantifiable objectives. Let's say one of your goals is to increase your business next year. Decide whether that means more customers, more income per customer, or both. Describe the exact type of customers you want. Then with each goal, add a specific *number*: the number of customers, average dollar sale per customer, total sales for each product line or sales channel. Numerical goals are very powerful motivators.

■ **Develop steps.** Identify the steps necessary to achieve objectives. For instance, to attract more customers, you'll need to increase marketing. List the ways you'll do this: advertising, trade shows, direct mail, cold calls. Then, add numerical targets for each step. How many trade shows will you attend? How many ads will you run?

■ **Estimate costs.** Put a dollar figure next to each step. If you don't know exact costs (and you won't), write down your best estimate. Everything you do has a financial cost; it's important to understand those costs as you develop your plan.

■ **Estimate time expenditure.** Activities don't just take money, they take time. Estimate how much time each step might take. For instance, writing a newspaper ad may take two hours, while exhibiting at a trade show may take forty hours' preparation and five days for the show and travel.

■ **Decide on responsibilities.** Determine who will be responsible for each step and how many people are needed. This means that each goal/step has someone who is in charge of following through.

■ **Prioritize.** By now, you've got a To Do list that would take more money, more time, and more people than you have. So prioritize your goals and steps. Start with your bread-and-butter business—the things that keep your doors open. Next, choose those with the highest probability of success. Eliminate some goals entirely rather than attempting them all half-way.

■ **Conduct a reality check.** Look over your list. Does it fit with how you and your employees truly behave? If your plan seems overly ambitious, it probably is. Go back and reprioritize.

■ **Get consensus.** Discuss the plan with all affected parties. Do they agree it's realistic? Are they willing to commit to it? Getting everyone on board improves the chance you'll actually achieve your goals.

■ **Set deadlines.** Put target dates beside each step to create real-life deadlines.

■ **Write it all down.** You now have an action plan with goals, deadlines, and job assignments.

An annual plan is a great roadmap for success. Remember one of Rhonda's Rules: You can't reach a goal you haven't set.

Keys to Annual Planning

As you develop your annual plan, examine the following:

■ **Strategic position/Company vision.** What's going on in your industry, community, or the economy? How have your competitors changed? Do you need to rethink some of the fundamental aspects of your business to respond to changing conditions or new technology?

■ **Goals.** List your goals for the year in order of priority. Include quantifiable, numerical objectives whenever possible. Evaluate which will have the greatest impact on your business. Be realistic about the time and money involved.

■ **Product/Service development.** Evaluate the products or services you offer. Track how well each sells, your profit margin, and the customer base for each line. Do you need to phase out certain products or add new services? Would different products attract a more stable customer base? What steps can you take to improve the quality of the products/services you sell?

■ **Personal development.** Many people start businesses because they are good at something, but as pressures increase, they don't have time to take classes or read books to improve their skills. Continually improving your own skills is critical for every business owner.

■ **Budget.** Develop a budget every year. Begin by listing fixed expenses, then list variable expenses and expenses for expansion and growth. Project a reasonable, *conservative* income based primarily on past performance and secondly on marketing plans. This gives you a reasonable basis for decision making.

■ **Marketing.** What are the specific activities you're going to continue or undertake to secure the necessary income and build customer loyalty? Develop a specific marketing plan and budget for the year.

■ **Getting organized.** Don't just plan to become better organized. Instead, develop efficient *systems* to keep on top of your administrative paperwork. Institute financial management procedures so you always know your financial situation and get better control of your money.

You have a greater chance of succeeding in your goals if you're realistic about what you have the time and ability to do. And don't depend on overly optimistic income projections to offset expenditures: that's how the government works and look where that's got us.

One Big New Thing

Is your business relatively healthy, but you still feel stuck? Have you made about the same amount of money for the last few years, but you'd like to make more? Perhaps you're a little bored with your day-to-day business and want a new challenge?

If you need to get your business un-stuck, then sit down and ask yourself, "What's **one big new thing** I can do to significantly increase my income this year?"

Don't think of ten big things, or fifty small things, you could do to grow your business. Concentrate on only *one* thing, but make sure it's a *big* thing. It has to be something that can potentially make you a meaningful amount of money within a year. Ideally, it will also make you more excited about your business.

I'm a big believer that long-term business success comes from thoughtful planning and properly executing the day-to-day fundamentals of running your company. So don't drop everything to pursue your new goal. Don't jeopardize your bread-and-butter business.

But to make significant changes, you often have to establish what authors James Collins and Jerry Porras (in their book *Built to Last*) called a BHAG—or Big, Hairy, Audacious Goal. A BHAG should:

- **Be a stretch for you**
- **Be achievable**
- **Include a deadline**
- **Have a measurable outcome**

There are a number of big new things you could pursue, including a new:

- **Client or customer, such as landing the account of a large corporation**
- **Target market, such as focusing on an additional demographic group or an industry you don't currently serve**
- **Product or service, especially one that's an extension of your current offerings**
- **Modification to a product or service, so it can be sold to a broader market**
- **Distribution channel, to give you an additional way to reach customers**
- **Operational efficiency, so you can significantly reduce your expenses and increase your profits**

A Virtual Approach to Growth

Have you ever failed to land a prospective client because they thought your company was just too small or that you couldn't serve the scope of their needs? Well, there's a way to add size, depth, and strength to your company without adding even one employee—by forming a "virtual company."

For instance, in a brochure from a consulting company I know, there is a section in which they describe "The Team." Listed are an impressive group of people, each with top credentials and expertise. Looking closely, however, you'll see that only two of these consultants are actually employed by the consulting company. Instead, the two company founders have formed an alliance with a group of experts.

Now, this consulting company isn't trying to be deceptive. Below the name of each team member is clearly printed the name of their own individual businesses. Nevertheless, by listing these experts together as a team, the consulting firm creates a very positive impression. Clients have a full range of top specialists at their disposal.

Creating a "virtual" company—or a marketing alliance—enables you to:

■ **Do joint marketing.** It's less expensive—and more effective—to combine marketing lists and create combined marketing materials. You can also reach a larger pool of potential clients.

■ **Offer clients a wider range of services.** Sure, you may believe that you can serve all of your clients' needs, but the client may not feel the same way. Many clients prefer to hire specialists rather than generalists. By offering clients a team of specialists, you're more likely to get—and keep—a client's business.

> If you choose your partners well, you'll get the chance to work with people you respect, enjoy, and can learn from.

■ **Reduce clients' apprehension.** Many clients are reluctant to hire one-person or very small companies. They're fearful that they could be stranded if something happens to the one key person.

■ **Present a more impressive image.** Together with your alliance partners, you're going to have a longer list of former clients,

97

a broader range of experience, awards, and other references than you would have on your own.

There's another benefit: if you choose your partners well, you'll get the chance to work with people you respect, enjoy, and can learn from. That's better than always going it alone.

But one of the biggest barriers to putting together a virtual company is recognizing you may have to give up some part of a client's business to someone else. Are you willing to get a small piece of a big pie rather than all of a very small pie—or no pie at all?

Let's say you're a graphic designer who specializes in designing websites. Currently, you also do some of the technical programming for your clients, but that's not really your specialty and you're limited in the scope of technical functions you can include in your designs. By coming together in a virtual company with a more skilled website programmer, you're far more competitive when making proposals to prospective clients. But you may end up giving up a piece of the total monthly fees.

Many types of business owners can benefit from forming a virtual company with other small companies or individual consultants and then offering their services in an integrated package. These alliances can range from the relatively formal—with a combined website and marketing materials—to the very casual, perhaps working together for a proposal to one client.

Remember, virtual companies are not legal entities. There are no rules—one member of the alliance can bill the client and then subcontract to the other members, or each individual member can bill separately. The key is to stay flexible so you can meet the client's needs.

When you're planning to put together a "virtual company," look for partners that fit your own style of communication and maintain the same level of quality. And, as always, only do business with those you trust and respect.

Remember, you can't be everything to all clients, and you can't do everything yourself. As the old saying goes, "The whole is greater than the sum of its parts."

Is It Time for Your Business to Leave Home?

Is your business getting too big for your back room? Do you find yourself scrambling to pick up the kids' toys (or even the kids) before a client arrives? Is the gardening equipment left outside because the garage is filled with inventory? Maybe it's time to ask your home-based business to move out.

If you're thinking about moving out, consider four major factors: physical, psychological, family, and financial.

■ **Physical.** Your business may grow so large that your home can no longer contain it. You may need to manufacture some items, hire more employees, or see clients more frequently in your own office. You may run into not only physical limitations but zoning prohibitions as well. Or your family may just want the family room back.

■ **Psychological.** Let's face it, some people thrive on the solitude of working alone, while others miss the "water cooler" effect. Some people find that working at home improves their concentration, while others find they're always taking care of home tasks during their business work day. A friend told me her home was never cleaner than when she worked at home because she always did household chores before work. She had to get an office.

■ **Family.** Family considerations may dictate whether you can work at home or not. You may need to be home with children after school or take care of an elderly parent. On the other hand, it may be impossible to get any work done with your kids around, or your spouse may hate the fact that you've turned the family room into your office.

■ **Financial.** Moving to a "real" office or workspace costs money. Besides rent, you have to cover utilities, cleaning, furniture, and a wide variety of unexpected extra expenses. You may face increased insurance, and your costs for transportation, food, and clothing will probably go up. More importantly, many of these costs are *fixed*: you have to pay them every month regardless of income. Home-based business owners are used to a lot of flexibility in their expenditures, so you have to adjust to "overhead."

Marketing

Finding New Customers

"More customers! More sales!" Virtually every business owner wants to know how to increase their sales volume. It's time for a refresher course in the best way to drum up new business: marketing.

If you're new to business, marketing can seem overwhelming. If you've been in business for years, marketing can seem like drudgery. It's time to regain some of the enthusiasm, energy, and creativity you had when you first opened shop. Remember all those networking meetings you used to attend but haven't had time for in years?

Whether new or long-established, every business relies on marketing for its ongoing success. When it comes to marketing activities, it's frustrating that there's no magic bullet—no single or one-time activity—that brings all the customers you need to your door. Marketing must be an *ongoing* activity utilizing a number of simultaneous, complementary approaches.

Typically, what happens with most entrepreneurs is that they pay a lot of attention to marketing when they first start their businesses. Once they reach a satisfactory level of sales or develop a sufficient client list, they let marketing slide. That's a recipe for long-term decline. There's always a certain amount of natural attrition in any business's customer base. As well, new competitors will attract some customers away. You have to keep on marketing just to retain a constant level of income.

Marketing efforts can also become stale. If you keep using the same approaches—same ads, same trade shows, same promotions—they can lose effectiveness over time.

It's time to try something new. If you've only gone to networking groups, try advertising in the local newspaper. If you've only advertised in the newspaper, perhaps it's time to join networking groups.

Before you go out and spend a lot of money, sit down and plot out at least a mini-marketing plan. Make sure your marketing activities are a good fit for your type of business. Come up with a budget. Just as importantly, remember that potential customers need repeated exposure to your name and message before they will notice and remember you. So, don't blow your entire marketing budget on one mailing.

Marketing Techniques

■ **Advertising.** Advertising often brings quick results, especially if you're announcing a special sale. Advertising works best when you maintain an ongoing advertising program because ads keep your name in front of customers.

■ **Business cards.** Your business card can be more than just a way to convey basic information; it can serve as an effective, inexpensive marketing medium.

■ **Direct mail.** Direct mail can be effective—but also expensive. When I first went into business, I sent out a 500-piece mailing to a purchased list of customers. I only landed one client, but it was a big one! Direct mail must be repeated at least quarterly to be effective.

■ **Events.** Hosting events at your place of business, especially if you're in retail, is a good way to attract customers. Partner with local organizations—perhaps in a fundraiser—to find new prospects.

■ **Networking.** When I started my consulting business, I built my client list primarily by joining local entrepreneurial and industry organizations. I also had a lot of lunches with potential referral sources. Get out there!

■ **Public relations.** It can be a big boon to your business when the media run a story mentioning your business. However, developing an ongoing PR program takes time and resources.

■ **Referrals.** Everyone wants word-of-mouth advertising, but this takes time. The best way to generate referrals is by ongoing networking, but you can also institute a reward program to encourage customers to recommend you to their friends.

■ **Specialty advertising products.** You can imprint your company name on just about any item—mugs, pens, calendars, mousepads, t-shirts. Customers perceive these as gifts and rarely toss them. This keeps your name in front of them.

■ **Trade shows.** By exhibiting at trade shows, you reach a highly targeted customer base and interact with prospects face to face. Keys to success: choose your trade shows wisely, prepare good marketing materials to distribute, and immediately follow up with the prospects you meet.

■ **Website.** A website won't generate sales immediately. But a website helps support your other sales efforts and gives your business credibility.

Best Business Name Ever

I collect cute business names: "All You Knead" (a bakery), "The Barking Lot" (a dog groomer), "Shear Ecstasy" (a hair salon). A clever business name can be an excellent marketing tool, making your company immediately memorable.

But a cute or memorable name isn't necessarily a requirement for or guarantee of success. There's nothing particularly memorable about the names *Microsoft, Safeway,* or *The Walt Disney Company,* but those companies have certainly been huge successes.

Coming up with a business name can be one of the most creative aspects of starting a business or introducing a new product, but it can also be one of the most frustrating. Big companies spend hundreds of thousands of dollars researching names and sometimes even they fall flat on their faces.

In small companies, *you* are the brand, and the best name for your company may be your own, perhaps with a descriptive phrase to clarify what you do. My first business was called "Abrams Business Strategies," since I developed business and marketing plans. But a name that is too closely identified with one person may limit the growth—or eventual sale—of your company.

Before you name your muffler business "I'm Exhausting," consider the following factors that contribute to making a name effective:

■ **Conveys the correct information.** Make sure that your potential customers are *not* confused about what you do. This can be harder than it seems: "ABC Mediation Services" may provide both mediation and arbitration, a distinction potential customers may understand. A very clear company name, "Prepaid Legal Services," immediately tells customers what to expect (but watch out if your services later change—see below).

■ **Won't get dated quickly.** Avoid names too closely identified with recent trends or which limit the types of products or services you'll offer. You are likely to change the scope of your products or services over time.

■ **Conveys the right feeling.** Ideally, choose a name with positive connotations. For instance, a day spa named "Haven" or "Oasis" transmits the sense that the customer is going to escape the stresses of life.

■ **Easy to spell.** This is particularly important when you need customers to remember your Internet address or when clients will have to spell your company's name often.

■ **Easy to pronounce.** People have a hard time remembering names they can't say easily. That's why on the back of their chocolate bar wrappers, Ghiradelli printed instructions on how to pronounce the name.

■ **Is memorable.** This isn't always possible, of course, or even necessary. A company with a straightforward name, "Des Moines Chiropractic Clinic" may develop a better business than a company with a cute name. Names don't determine success.

> Coming up with a business name can be one of the most creative aspects of starting a business or introducing a new product, but it can also be one of the most frustrating.

■ **Is pleasing to the ear.** If you have a sufficient advertising budget, you can make even a "bad" name work. For instance, most of us remember the tagline, "With a name like Smuckers, it has to be good." But generally,

a pleasant-sounding name is preferable to an awkward one.

■ **You can get the domain name.** It's best if your website has the same name as your business or something closely related. Before finalizing your name, check to see what Internet domain names are available.

■ **Doesn't violate trademarks.** You don't want to spend thousands of dollars building your brand only to discover that someone else has the trademark rights. Do a quick trademark search online at the U.S. Patent & Trademark Office, **www.uspto.gov.** If necessary, check with an attorney.

In the end, however, one of the most important considerations is whether *you* like the name and feel comfortable with it. After all, you're going to be seeing it and saying it a lot.

Most importantly, don't get stuck looking for the perfect name. This will slow down the launch of your business or new product. At some point, you just need to make a choice.

Make the Most of Your Business Card

What's the most important marketing item you have? Here's a hint: it's small, inexpensive, and you probably haven't given it much thought. It's your business card.

Most of us think of business cards as just a reference document: a means of conveying basic information people need in order to contact us. We rarely design our business cards with the idea that they will be marketing tools.

Looking at your business cards as a marketing device opens up a new way of thinking about those small pieces of cardboard. Why not have different business cards for different occasions? Perhaps you'll want one for networking events or trade shows and a slightly different one for clients or customers.

It's time to take a fresh look at your business card. Does it help people remember you? To be motivated to do business with you? Does it convey what you do? At the very least, is the information clear?

Here's a business card refresher:

■ **What to include.** Once upon a time, people only put their name, company name, address, and one phone number on a business card. Then came fax numbers, email addresses, cell phone numbers, and websites.

All that information isn't absolutely necessary. Including too much data forces you to use tiny type. Not only will you be meeting many baby boomers with aging eyes, but you'll often hand out your card at Chamber of Commerce mixers in poorly lit hotel ballrooms; tiny typeface is going to be very hard to read.

> **Looking at your business cards as a marketing device opens up a new way of thinking about those small pieces of cardboard.**

Moreover, all that detail means you'll likely omit information that's more important: what you actually do. Add one brief line describing your business, especially if you have a specialty: "general contractor specializing in home remodels," "travel agency focusing exclusively on European leisure travel." If you have more than one specialty, have more than one card.

To make room for that marketing line, you may have to get rid of other data, especially for cards you use at networking events. Do you really still need your fax number? Can you eliminate your full street address?

■ **Color.** Adding color makes a big impact, and it's not that expensive. In a stack of cards, black-and-white cards seem flat. Color is especially good for logos. Be careful to make certain your information remains clearly readable. Light-colored ink on dark paper, and pale ink on any paper, are hard to read. Choose colors that are appropriate to your line of business. A lawyer probably wouldn't want pink on their card—a florist or childcare center might.

■ **Logo.** If you have a logo, use it! Logos make your business card stand out. If you don't yet have a logo, consider designing one or using typeface in such a way as to make a "logotype." Even adding a graphic element such as a bold line, triangle, or circle adds visual interest and helps people remember you. You can hire a graphic designer to create a logo for you, or use a low-cost logo-creating service.

■ **Reverse.** I once had beautiful cards with just my logo against a black background on the reverse. People were frustrated when they couldn't jot down something they wanted to remember about me on that side of the card. That doesn't mean the back of your card has to remain blank. Use it to print more information about your business or even to offer a discount. Just remember, once someone has put your card in a file or a drawer, they'll probably never see the reverse side again.

■ **Printing your cards.** Local copy shops, such as Kinko's, are fast and relatively inexpensive. They also have designers who can help you lay out your card. Ask them to create a "ten-up" layout for business cards with crop marks and give you the electronic file. You can then create cards or make changes whenever you need to.

There are also online printing companies, which are typically quite inexpensive for business cards. With an online printer, you either upload your own design or choose from their selection. However, you'll be limited in your choices of card stock, colors, and such.

Your business card is a representation of you and your company. A little planning helps you make the most of that small piece of marketing real estate.

Get the Word Out about Your Business

I asked a successful business owner what kind of marketing he did and how customers heard about his business.

"Word-of-mouth," he replied. "I get most of my customers from word-of-mouth advertising."

He's not alone; most successful companies depend on referrals from past customers. When you want an accountant or architect, a plumber or painter, don't you ask a friend or fellow entrepreneur for a name? But how can you create word-of-mouth advertising for your business?

The best way to develop word-of-mouth advertising is to run a terrific business for many, many years. After a decade or so, you're sure to have a large number of former clients who think you're terrific. That's great, but what do you do in the meantime?

Here are a few techniques to help spread word-of-mouth advertising:

■ **Stay in touch.** Keep your name and contact information in front of past customers. Create a mailing list—preferably an electronic database—and contact your past customer list regularly. How often? Every other month is a good schedule, but no less than twice a year.

The Internet makes staying in touch easier. You can send individual emails if you have a small number of past customers.

Or create a regular email newsletter with content your customers will find useful. Of course, always get permission (or "opt-in") before sending bulk mailings. (You can register to receive my free business tips email newsletter at **www.planningshop.com.**)

■ **Keep your name in front of past customers.** Specialty advertising products—pens, mugs, calendars, and the like—keep your name in front of a customer for a long time.

Most people think of advertising only as a means of attracting new customers, but it's also very effective in reminding your past, satisfied customers about you. This increases the likelihood they'll remember you the next time they or a friend need your product or service.

■ **Participate in professional organizations.** If you've only thought of people who belong to your professional or industry association as competitors, you're missing the boat.

Professional or industry colleagues are frequently an excellent source of referrals. They'll often refer customers if they can't meet a specific request or need or when their own workload is too great. Some will want to work collaboratively with you on projects.

■ **Ask customers for referrals.** You can entice current customers to refer friends to you by offering incentives, such as discounts or gifts for each new customer they send your way. But incentives are often unnecessary. Instead, remind customers you'd really appreciate it if they'd refer their friends to you. Then surprise them with a gift when they do. I recently referred someone to my veterinarian, and when I got a $25 gift certificate in the mail, I was delighted! It seemed more like a gift than a bribe.

> Most people think of advertising only as a means of attracting new customers, but it's also very effective in reminding your past customers about you.

■ **Testimonials.** One form of "referrals" is testimonials from past customers you use in your marketing materials or on your website. The fact that other customers let you use their names adds credibility and trust.

■ **Get active in community groups.** Helping your community is not just good citizenship, it's good business. People who've met you at a bake sale for the Girl Scouts or who've seen your company's name listed as a sponsor of the Earth Day Walk-a-Thon are more likely to do business with you.

■ **Exhibit at trade shows.** Trade shows are not only a great way to meet many potential new customers at once. These events aslo make it easy for past customers to see you and spend time with you in a comfortable setting.

■ **Delight your customers.** When you do something that not only satisfies a customer but delights and surprises them, they'll remember you. If your car repair shop washes your car before returning it, or your butcher adds a bone for your dog, you're not only going to come back, you're going to tell your friends. And you'll be part of their word-of-mouth advertising campaign.

Telling Customers What to Think about You

Here's a quiz. Can you name the companies associated with the following taglines? "Just Do It!" "You Deserve a Break Today!" "It's the real thing." "We try harder."

You probably guessed all four. That's because an effective tagline or slogan becomes so closely identified with a business you often don't even need to mention the company's name. Of course, these companies—Nike, McDonalds, Coke, Avis—spent tens of millions of dollars promoting these phrases.

But it doesn't take a multimillion-dollar advertising budget to make a tagline effective. In fact, an effective tagline is one of the cheapest forms of marketing available.

If you've got a big budget, you can hire a marketing or advertising firm to come up with a tagline for your company. Or, you can get some of your creative employees, friends, or family members to help you devise a tagline for your company.

The keys to an effective tagline are:

■ **It's short and easy to remember.**

■ **It's consistent with your company's strategic position.**

■ **You use it repeatedly and prominently.**

■ **It conveys something you want potential customers to remember or feel.**

■ **It's short and easy to remember.** This seems obvious but once you start working on your tagline, trust me, you're going to be tempted to make it longer and more complicated than it should be. A tagline must say something about your company, but it can't say *everything*. Once you think you've settled on a tagline, see if you can edit it down or find a way to make it even more concise. If it's too long, customers won't remember it.

> **A tagline doesn't have to be memorable to everyone to be effective—it just has to be memorable to those you want as customers.**

■ **It's consistent with your company's strategic position.** This is perhaps the most important element of a good tagline—it tells customers what's special about you and how to distinguish you from competitors. Avis' "We Try Harder" was clever because it

111

took a disadvantage (the fact that they were not the market leader) and turned it into an advantage—they do more, care more than their bigger rival. The Avis slogan makes it almost seem like competitors are slacking off on the job.

If you serve a specific or niche market, you might want to focus your tagline on that. "Legal services for the real estate industry" may seem boring to your friends, but it could be very effective if you're an attorney specializing in handling real estate deals. Remember, a tagline doesn't have to be memorable to everyone to be effective—it just has to be memorable to those you want as customers or referral sources.

■ **You use it repeatedly and prominently.** Once you've chosen a tagline, use it all the time! Naturally, you should use it in your marketing materials (brochures, flyers, newsletters), on your website, and in every bit of advertising you do. But you should use it everywhere you can, on your business cards and on the bottom of every email. This is where having a tagline becomes really inexpensive—it's a little ad attached to everything you do.

■ **It conveys something you want potential customers to feel.** Why is "Just Do It" such an effective tagline for Nike? Because it gives a sense that Nike is there supporting their customers' athletic aspirations; it helps customers feel that Nike is on their side. When a tagline conveys a feeling, it helps increase the bond between you and your customers.

Many businesses never develop a tagline, and you certainly don't have to have one for success. However, an effective tagline helps you clarify what makes your business special in just a few words. It makes your business and name more memorable to customers.

How to Manipulate the Media

"Alert the media!" Wouldn't it be nice if you could get free publicity for your business? Imagine what it would do for your business if newspapers, magazines, or TV and radio stations ran stories praising your amazing products or outstanding service. We'd all like good publicity for our companies, but how do we get reporters and editors to notice us?

Every week, journalists receive loads of press releases and emails announcing new products or pitching stories. With so much competition for reporters' attention, how do you make your story stand out?

First, it's easiest for a reporter if you do a lot of the work. Most people in the media are overworked. The more you're able to make your story easy for them—in the sense that the details are all there—the better your chances of getting publicity.

Most importantly, you've got to have something the readers, listeners, or viewers of a media outlet find interesting. Sure, you think it's important you've promoted Ann Wong to vice president, but why would others care?

What you need is a "hook." A hook is an aspect of your story that hooks readers in—the thing that makes your news compelling. Some stories, of course, are naturally compelling: a closely contested election, a hot sports contest, a really cool new consumer product. But most of us who run small businesses don't have stories that are naturally gripping.

Instead, find an angle to give to reporters showing your story is timely, amusing, informative. One easy way is to tie your story to outside events that generate their own publicity, such as holidays, local celebrations, sporting events, or new legislation. Reporters always need timely tie-ins.

> **Reporters need reliable sources they can turn to quickly. Become one of those sources.**

Other tips to help get your name in the news:

■ **Be creative.** Reporters are tired of the same old stories. The offbeat and unusual grab attention. Sometimes just a little twist on a story is enough; for instance, an accountant who sends out a list of the Ten Worst Tax Deductions instead of the Ten Best.

■ **Be visual.** Television, in particular, needs visually stimulating stories, but having a good photo opportunity also increases your chance of making it into the newspaper. Find ways to make your story visual, like the pet store that sponsors an Easter parade with pets in bonnets. They're on TV every year.

■ **Work with others.** Leverage the power of other organizations to gain visibility. Often, these organizations have their own public relations staff or existing relationships with reporters, increasing the chance of getting coverage.

■ **Use statistics.** Media outlets love numbers. If you provide objective, trustworthy information related to your industry or market, you've got a better chance of having your story covered. You're likely to get more coverage if you include colorful graphic representations of the statistics.

■ **Become the expert.** Reporters need reliable sources they can turn to quickly. If you're an expert in your field, stay in touch with key journalists who report on your industry so they know to give you a call when they need a quote or source.

■ **Be available.** No one can cover or quote you if they can't reach you. Include all your phone numbers and contact information in your press release. Don't send out a press release and then leave on vacation.

■ **Follow up.** Reporters get hundreds of press releases a week. They're not necessarily going to read yours. Make a follow-up phone call, or two, and send an email to bring attention to your story.

■ **Respect deadlines.** Don't call reporters when they're on deadline, typically in the late afternoon for daily journalists. Mid-morning is usually the best time.

■ **Do your homework.** Get to know which media outlets (TV and radio stations, newspapers, Internet sites, trade publications) cover your industry or the type of story you're likely to have. Develop a database of such journalists, and keep in touch with them. If possible, get to know them personally.

Finally, keep trying—over and over! The companies that get the most coverage are those that regularly and repeatedly stay in touch with reporters. A one-time press release is far less likely to get you coverage than an ongoing public relations campaign. You're going to have to be a little bit of a (very polite) pest, contacting reporters fairly often. Just don't tell anyone I said so.

Deliver Your Message to Your Customers

Your kitchen pipes burst, and you need help fast. You used a great plumber two years ago, but you threw away his card when your three-year-old poured strawberry jam in your kitchen drawer. When you look in the phone directory, no names seem familiar, so you end up calling a stranger.

You and your plumber both lost out because he failed to keep in touch with you. If the plumber had a direct mail program—sending printed mailings to you throughout the year—you'd remember his name when you needed him. And his business would grow.

Most small businesses feel direct mail is out of their range, fearing both the costs and the hassle. You have to pay for printing, design, and postage. You may have instead decided to contact potential customers through email, figuring that's a lot cheaper.

Well, it's time to think about direct mail.

With email, you're competing against many other advertisers—and spammers—and it's likely your message may not get through email filters. Direct mail—a physical piece of paper—leaves a stronger, more lasting impression than an email. Sure, many people routinely toss junk mail in the trash, but many others actually read and keep the advertising they receive.

With a little planning, you can develop a cost-effective, successful direct mail campaign. The keys to direct mail success:

■ **Your mailing list.** Choose the recipients of your mailing carefully. The best names are those of your current and past customers. That's why it's critically important to maintain a customer database.

> **If you consider what a customer spends with you over many years, you may find direct mail is a bargain.**

If you send bills to your customers, it's easy to build an address list. But if you don't currently capture your customers' contact information, encourage them to give you their names and addresses by prominently displaying a sign-up sheet for your mailing list or conducting a drawing for prizes as an incentive for customers to give you their data.

You can buy names from companies specializing in selling prospect lists or you can purchase lists of subscribers to magazines serving your target market. When buying lists, make certain the characteristics of the people on the list match those of your potential customers in terms of demographics, geography, income, and interests. Perhaps you can swap your mailing list with businesses that serve similar clientele in your area.

Take time and care when developing your mailing list. By eliminating names that are less likely to be responsive, you greatly reduce costs.

■ **Your message.** Your direct mail piece must be motivating. Think through what you want to tell potential customers, what you want to sell them, and what you want them to do. Provide an incentive such as a discount or gift with purchase. Add a deadline, but make sure it's far enough in the future so you have time to have the mailing piece printed and sent. Make certain everything is simple and clear.

One way to save money is to ask your suppliers if they have preprinted direct mail pieces you can use, and to add your company name and contact information. Large companies and big manufacturers often produce such collateral material (and sometimes make co-op money available) for small vendors. Ask suppliers if they will help underwrite the costs of a mailing if you feature their products.

■ **Your ongoing program.** Like any form of marketing, direct mail takes many repeat exposures to be successful. You can't think of direct mail as an "I tried it once" proposition. Expect to send direct mail pieces to your key target market five to six times a year. It's better to send repeat mailings to a limited number of highly qualified prospects than to send a mass mailing once.

Common wisdom is that direct mail response rates are very small—1 or 2 percent. But a carefully executed direct mail campaign can achieve higher returns. Moreover, it's a mistake to judge the effectiveness of direct mail on the response to any one individual mailing. Instead, consider the lifetime value of each new customer you attract—or referral you get—as a result of your direct mail activities. If you consider what a customer spends with you over many years, you may find direct mail is a bargain.

Advertising That Stays Around

Look around your desk. How many advertisements do you have at your fingertips? None? Look again.

You probably have quite a few ads; you just don't think of them that way.

For instance, on and in my desk, I've got "ads" for three software companies, my dog's veterinarian, a shipping service, the local Humane Society, the San Francisco Giants (go Giants!), an online bookstore, a consulting company, two computer makers, an office supply manufacturer, and a bunch of publishing companies.

No, I'm not the world's biggest collector of advertisements. Instead, the ads I have around are in the form of pens, keychains, letter openers, calendars, mousepads, tote bags, calculators, mugs, and a lot of stuff just to play with. Each of these items are imprinted with the name of a company.

All these things represent one of the most powerful, most affordable, and most overlooked forms of marketing—specialty advertising or promotional products.

Over the years, I've learned a lot about specialty ads from my sister, Janice Hill of Jacksonville, Oregon, who's been a top salesperson of imprinted promotional products for over twenty years.

"Small businesses have a limited amount of money to spend on advertising," explains Janice. "They need to make their ad dollars work hard. When you give a customer a mug or a calendar, they don't think about it as advertising, they consider it a gift, yet they have your name on their desk or the wall all year round."

> **Specialty advertising is one of the most powerful, most affordable, and most overlooked forms of marketing.**

One of the great advantages of this kind of marketing is that your customers see your name repeatedly. Studies show it takes multiple exposures to an ad before a person notices it. How many radio advertisements can you afford? Compare that to the cost of calendars or pens. "If someone wants a pizza, and they have a magnet with the name of your pizza restaurant on their refrigerator, they're going to call you," says Janice. "It's easy for them to find your number without looking in the phone book—where they also see your competitors."

Promotional products can also make other forms of advertising more effective. Offering a free gift for new customers when you advertise in the newspaper or sending a small item in your direct mail piece can make customers pay more attention.

Interestingly, the largest percent of promotional items sold are what the industry calls "wearables:" t-shirts, hats, windbreakers, and so on. Many of these are given not to customers, but to employees, as a reward for reaching certain goals (such as safety), to promote an internal company campaign or message, or most importantly, to reinforce the company's image and logo.

To get the most out of your specialty ads, keep these things in mind:

1. Target your market. Is your audience male or female? Do they spend most of their time in the office, home, or car? Understanding your market helps you choose items customers will use and see repeatedly.

2. Choose items that are different and interesting. Many people get the same thing over and over again, such as pens. If you find something that is both useful and somewhat unusual, there's a greater chance your customer will keep it and use it.

3. Choose a gift related to your business and appropriate for your customers. A keychain and calendar may work for a mechanic; an accountant might want to give calculators or BIG erasers.

4. Simple messages are better. On most promotional products, you don't have a lot of space for your imprint. Keep your message simple. Of course you want to feature your company name. You may also want to provide some contact info—website or phone number—and one simple message at most.

5. Don't choose a product solely on price. Your goal is to have customers keep and use your specialty ad. Customers will keep higher quality, more thoughtful items longer, thus increasing the effectiveness of your ad.

I buy a lot of imprinted promotional products from my sister for my company, and I've learned that specialty ads work. It doesn't hurt that Janice gives me the family discount. But specialty ads can be an effective marketing tool for you, even if your sister isn't in the business.

Getting Your Ads Right

"We're moving online!! Blowout sale at our store location. Phone orders welcome." That's what the advertisement said.

But here's what the ad did not say:

- **What the company sold**
- **Where the store was located**
- **The address of their new website**

Few things are more frustrating to a customer—and more wasteful for a business—than when vital information is left out of an advertisement, flyer, or brochure. Yet I'm surprised at how often basic details are overlooked. And it's not just small businesses that make these fundamental mistakes.

For instance, I could have told you Kmart was going to be in trouble long before they entered bankruptcy. Why? A few years ago, I saw a patio set that interested me advertised by Kmart in a glossy, four-color insert in my regional Sunday newspaper. Not knowing where the nearest Kmart was located—and since no addresses were printed on the ad—I called the 800 number on the insert. Imagine my frustration when Kmart didn't answer their phone on Sundays! All those Sunday inserts and no way to get information. Needless to say, I bought my patio furniture somewhere else.

Details! Details!

One of the most common reasons for omitting necessary details is that the person writing the ad takes basic information for granted. After all, you already know what city you're in or what your area code is, so you forget that it's not obvious to the reader.

> **Few things are more frustrating to a customer than when vital information is left out of an ad, flyer, or brochure.**

It's easy to forget details, so before you print an ad or brochure, check to see that you have included:

1. Name of your company!

2. The nature of your product or service. Unless you own Macy's or Microsoft, don't assume readers automatically know what your business sells. Even if you send your ad only to existing customers, many people remember a business by what it sells—not its name. ("The drycleaners at Main and Second streets," "That cute clothing store downtown.")

3. Where you're located. Include the city and state (perhaps even the country if doing business internationally or online). This is critical if you're in retail, but even if your customers don't come to your store or office, including a location helps customers relate to your business.

4. Hours and days you're open or hours and days of the sale.

5. Website address. You do have a website, don't you?

6. Phone number with area code. If you're not going to be available to answer calls, record a message with vital information. Include country code if you do business internationally.

7. Email address. This can be omitted if you're never going to answer emails.

8. Special terms or limitations, if any. In other words, are the discounts not applicable to certain types of items or services, or does the offer expire after a certain date?

Those are the basics. Once you've got those covered, what can you do to make your ads more effective in getting sales?

1. Create an eye-catching headline. The first thing you have to do is get attention. A headline doesn't have to be incredibly clever—"Fifty percent off" gets my attention.

2. Tell the benefits. Let potential customers know immediately why they should be interested in doing business with you. This can be something as simple as "Lowest price for your auto insurance."

3. Provide lots of information. Ads chock-full of specific products or services are often surprisingly effective.

4. Include a call to action. Customers often respond to a direct appeal for action, such as "Hurry—Supplies are limited," or "Call today to book your appointment!"

Finally, before you go to print, have your ad read by at least two other people. And ask them to tell you what's missing!

Create a One-Page Sales Sheet

It's easy to develop a one-page product or service sales sheet. This is a detailed description of just one product or service that fits on a page. You'll find many uses for a one-page sales sheet: as handouts at trade shows, leave-behinds for sales appointments, packing inserts, and to send in response to phone or email requests. You can upload a PDF of the sales sheet to your website.

Here's how you can make your own one-page sales sheet:

1. **Write up your text.** Keep your copy short and to the point. Start with a one-paragraph description of your product or service. Provide the basics: what it is, what it does, and why your customer should buy it. Focus on your product's benefits, not just its features. Use bullet points. Choose powerful, descriptive—but truthful—adjectives.

2. **If appropriate, include prices.** One-page sales sheets are intended to be sales tools, so you typically want to include prices. However, in some cases, your prices may vary by customer or season. If so, maintain a separate price list.

3. **Add a photo, graphic, or something visual.** Ideally, this would be a picture of your product. If your product or service can't be photographed or isn't particularly photogenic, use a chart or graph that illustrates benefits or cost savings.

4. **Consider design elements.** Divide your page into columns; short spans of text are easier to read and more visually appealing than long ones. Use a maximum of two typefaces. Leave enough white space. Text and graphics pop when they have some breathing room. Use color and boldface type sparingly; if you try to add emphasis to everything, nothing stands out.

5. **Finally, include a call-to-action.** Tell people where and how they can order or buy your product or service. Provide a phone number and website address for further information. If you have a limited-time or special offer, make sure that information is clearly visible. Encourage readers to act soon.

The Face
of Your Business

Networking Basics

■ **Attend.** You can't meet people sitting in your office. I know how difficult it is to drag yourself to some of these events, and they may seem like a waste of time. But you never know which event may bring you the big customer. Remember, you've got to kiss a lot of frogs before you find a prince.

■ **Take business cards and a pen even to a purely social function.** If you're going to a business mixer or trade event, take plenty of cards.

■ **Wear a name tag.** Sure, those stick-on labels proclaiming, "Hello, My Name Is…" seem silly, but people will have an easier time remembering your name if they see it as well as hear it.

■ **Approach people.** Even if you've been a wallflower all your life, now's the time to get over it. A good way to meet people is in the drinks line or next to the buffet table. If it's a business event, it's perfectly appropriate to start a conversation with, "Hi, I'm …." If it's social, you can make a positive comment about the food, the room, or the host. You don't have to be brilliant.

■ **Have your elevator pitch ready.** In even the most social setting, you're likely to be asked what you do for a living. Modify your elevator pitch (see page 125) to be most appropriate for the group.

■ **Give people your business card.** You don't have to wait for someone to ask, especially at a business gathering. It's perfectly appropriate to hand someone your business card as you introduce yourself.

■ **Ask others for their business card.** If someone doesn't offer you a card, and you think you may want to follow up, just ask, "Do you have a card?" If they don't, whip out that pen you brought and write the info on the back of one of yours.

■ **Actively listen.** The tendency, especially if you're nervous, is to want to either stand back and say nothing at all or to immediately start talking about yourself. Instead, ask questions of others and then really listen. Use your time to establish rapport rather than trying to make a sales pitch.

■ **Move on.** Don't stay with the same people for the whole event. Mingling means moving around. You can excuse yourself to go get another drink, or just end a conversation with "It's been great talking with you. Let's have lunch sometime."

■ **Follow up.** You've gone to the event. You've made the contact. You have their business card. Now make the call.

Develop Your Elevator Pitch

"What do you do?" In modern life, we're asked that question all the time. In business, you'll be asked what you do at networking events, when meeting prospective clients, or approaching potential investors. Yet even though we know the question is coming, it's amazing how often we fumble for the answer.

That's why you need to have your "elevator pitch" ready.

An elevator pitch is the short description you give about your company in the time it would take to ride up an elevator (and not an elevator in a skyscraper, either!). An elevator pitch is clear, concise, and to-the-point. As importantly, especially when delivered to potential investors, your pitch shows you understand the core aspects of your business. (If you don't know what it is you really do, you'll still be fumbling for words as you pass the fifteenth floor.)

It's not easy to develop an elevator pitch. It takes quite a bit of thinking and practicing to decide which points to include. Even more frustrating, because an elevator pitch must be short, you have to decide what aspects of your business to omit. Often these can be things you're really excited about—a new technology, a great location, the fact you get to travel a lot—but if they're not central to the core or success of your business, then they don't belong in an elevator pitch.

Your elevator pitch should touch—very briefly—on three items.

■ **The products or services you sell**
■ **What market you serve (demographic, geographic, or industry)**
■ **Your strategic position/competitive advantage**

If you're in an easy-to-understand business, your elevator pitch theoretically could be very short: "I sell real estate." However, that doesn't distinguish you from the thousands of other realtors out there. A more memorable pitch gives listeners a reason to remember you: "I sell homes in the North County area, specializing in first-time buyers."

> **Your grandma should be able to understand your business well enough to describe it to someone else.**

The biggest mistake most people make when answering the question "What do you do?" is that they take that question too literally and start describing exactly what they *do*. For instance, at one networking meeting when each attendee was asked to introduce themselves, a woman who sold advertising described in detail what she did: came to the client's office, picked up their ad copy, went to the printer, sent back proofs, and so on.

While this may sound silly, entrepreneurs with more complicated businesses use this approach all the time. Living in Silicon Valley, I've heard dozens of elevator pitches for new businesses that describe a company's technology in painful detail without ever once stating the company's market, business model, or competitive advantage.

Your elevator pitch must not only be short, it must be clear. Unless you're in a highly technical field, your neighbor or grandma should be able to understand your business well enough to describe it to someone else. After all, you want grandma out there marketing for you too, don't you? If people you meet don't quickly understand the nature of your business, they'll never be able to send clients your way.

Make sure your employees and other key individuals (investors, referral sources) are fluent in your company's elevator pitch. After all, they are likely to be in a position to describe your company many times.

It's often a good idea to use an analogy as part of your elevator pitch, especially if you're in a new or difficult-to-grasp field. "We're the Yahoo for teens" says that you're creating an Internet portal for teenagers.

An elevator pitch doesn't have to be given in an actual elevator. You'll find you use it often—introducing yourself at networking meetings, in emails to prospective customers, running into an old friend at a ballgame.

So sit down and figure out your elevator pitch. Practice it over and over. (You could even try it in an elevator.) Then you'll be prepared the next time someone asks you, "What do you do?"

How to Have a Business Lunch

Having lunch is an essential business skill. I'm not talking about sitting at your desk eating a burrito, but about business lunches where you entertain prospective or current customers. Though comedians may joke about "three-martini lunches," social events are an important part of your business.

Don't feel embarrassed if you are uncomfortable with the idea of talking to a prospective client over a grilled chicken breast. Many entrepreneurs hate the idea of having lunch with clients, and you shouldn't be embarrassed if the idea intimidates you, too. Take heart: successful business lunching is a skill which can be developed just like other business skills. It just takes training and practice.

First, you must understand the purpose of the business lunch. Most novice lunchers believe its main purpose is to either conduct business or to eat lunch. Wrong! The primary reason is to *build a relationship.*

Thus, the business lunch is the time for you and your client to get to know each other better. One of Rhonda's Rules is "People do business with people they like." Often, it's not the products, prices, or company that make the sale—it's the person. Business lunches (and now, the increasingly popular power breakfast) are the perfect time for you and your prospect, client, supplier, or employee to get to know each other as people. This helps establish common interests and makes working together easier.

A business lunch is not a two-way street. You will be more interested in your client than she or he will be in you. Therefore the most important thing you can do at a business lunch is to listen. Ask questions about your guest as a person, not just about their business. Don't make it seem like an interview. Three of my favorite questions: "Where did you grow up?" "How did you like living in a small town/big city?" "Tell me about your family." You'll work together better if you can relate as human beings.

You don't need a particular reason or occasion to ask someone to lunch. Instead, try the straightforward approach: "We've been doing business together for almost a year. I'd like to take you to lunch and get to know you a little better" or the less direct "I'm often in your area. How about having lunch sometime?"

It's best to have your guest suggest a place for lunch. ("Is there a restaurant you've been wanting to try?") You don't have to go to the fanciest place in town, but avoid fast food joints. However, if you're thanking someone for a favor or business referral, take them to a special restaurant.

127

Don't be in a rush. Order "slow food" not "fast food." You want as much time with your guest as possible, so consider ordering soup or salad, an entree, and dessert. If you're dieting, have coffee or tea instead of dessert. Eat slowly. If your guest is doing most of the talking, they'll have less time than you to eat. If you finish first, they are likely to be uncomfortable and shut up. Then you'll never find out you went to the same summer camp.

And no messy food! Pass on the pasta and be careful piling chili on the burger. You don't want sauce on your tie or a two-fisted fight with a beanburger. You want food that requires as little attention as possible so you can focus on your guest.

Turn off your cell phone. If your guest is important enough to take to lunch, don't insult them with a ringing phone.

Pay for lunch, even if your guest says, "I can put this on my company's credit card." There are a couple of exceptions, however. Some men are uncomfortable when a woman picks up the tab, and some companies have rules against employees being treated for meals. Don't fight over the check.

Do's and Don'ts for Business Lunches

Do:

- **Listen**
- **Discuss common interests**
- **Order many courses**
- **Eat slowly**
- **Turn off your cell phone**
- **Pick up the tab**

Don't:

- **Dominate the conversation**
- **Discuss controversial topics**
- **Order messy food**
- **Drink alcohol**
- **Bring a lot of paperwork**

Don't bring any reports, presentations, or samples, unless specifically asked. If so, put them on the floor until you're asked about them or toward the end of the meal. It's certainly okay to make some notes when you get around to talking business, but don't try to do a lot of writing at the table.

I never drink alcohol at lunch because it makes me fuzzy all afternoon. I don't recommend drinking alcohol during business—you want to stay alert. Never order an alcoholic drink if your guest doesn't. If you do drink, stick to one drink, even if your guest drinks more.

A final suggestion—visit the restroom before lunch and watch your liquid intake. You don't want to have to get up from the table during lunch and you certainly don't want to be sitting there fidgeting. After all, you're nervous enough already. Good luck and bon appetit!

Powerful Presentations

"I'd rather have a root canal," my friend replied when I asked if she'd rather go to the dentist or give a speech. She's not alone. Most Americans fear giving presentations—whether to a room full of people or during a one-on-one sales call on a significant prospect.

Important presentations are intimidating. After all, you know you've got a lot riding on what you say and how you say it.

I vividly remember the most important meeting of my first year in business. I had sent out a mailing to a list of potential clients. A really big prospect responded, inviting me to come tell him about my business. I arrived early and sat in my car, reviewing notes I had on three-by-five cards, practicing what I'd say. I checked my hair and make-up. I looked at my watch. I reviewed my cards again, practiced again, checked my hair again, and on and on 'til it was time for our appointment. I was *so* nervous.

I'm happy to say I got the contract. It helped that I had prepared and practiced for that meeting. Since then, I've made hundreds of presentations, and I've learned a few critical skills that can greatly enhance any business presentation, regardless of setting or audience:

■ **Create rapport.** Usually the main thing your prospect or audience is sizing up is *you.* While you're focused on the substance of your presentation, they're figuring out whether you're a person they like and trust.

Relax a little and find ways to establish rapport with your listeners.

■ **Be prepared.** Preparation is critical, even for a small gathering. First, think about what you want to say—what are the most important points you want to leave your listeners with? Do you need to provide any statistics or supporting material? Research your audience as well; find out as much as you can about the people who will be hearing your presentation.

> The main thing your prospect or audience is sizing up is *you.*

■ **Get to your important points right away.** Even if you don't prepare a formal presentation, don't let the discussion wander. Be very clear about your key points and get to them quickly, when you know you have your audience's attention. You don't want to leave the meeting kicking yourself for having forgotten to mention the one thing you know could get you the job.

■ **Prepare a PowerPoint presentation.** If you have a lot of data to present, I recommend preparing a PowerPoint presentation. In critical meetings, a PowerPoint presentation keeps you focused, helping you to focus on your key points. Preparing a PowerPoint presentation is a good discipline for figuring out what you want to say even if you don't end up using the show itself.

■ **Practice.** Practice your presentation before you ever do one "live." If you're making sales presentations, schedule some of your least likely prospects first. Use those presentations as practice to sharpen your skills.

■ **Never assume your audience has read the material.** No matter what you've sent to people ahead of time, they probably won't have read it or let it sink in. I've sent potential clients copies of my books and some have still been surprised when I mention I'm an author!

■ **Have answers prepared.** Anticipate possible questions and have clear, concise answers ready so you won't be flustered. "I'm glad you asked that," you can reply, and then launch into your prepared response.

■ **Know what questions you won't answer.** Some things shouldn't be discussed in a first meeting or in a large group, and you should have an answer ready to deflect those questions. For instance, it may not yet be appropriate to discuss fees or terms. Have an appropriate response prepared. "It's a bit premature to discuss fees, since I don't have a complete grasp of the project yet."

■ **Close.** Don't end a presentation without a clear statement of what happens next. On a sales call, try to close the deal. If that's not possible, ask for the prospect to delineate the next steps and timeline. In a larger group, make certain the audience knows how to contact you. Give your presentation a sense of closure.

Getting Comfortable When All Eyes Are on You

Whether you're introducing yourself to 15 other entrepreneurs at a Chamber of Commerce meeting or describing your product to 300 potential customers at a trade conference, sooner or later you're going to have to get up in front of other people. Being comfortable when all eyes are on you is a competitive advantage. When you're at ease, listeners pay more attention to your message.

But how do you get over the jitters when standing in front of people?

■ **Stop looking in the mirror.** It's normal to check yourself before you meet with people, but there's a limit. If you've made certain your hair is neat, make-up fixed, and fly zipped, don't take "just one more look".

■ **Wear something that gives you confidence.** Whether it's a new outfit or your favorite tie, you'll feel more relaxed if you think your clothes are appropriate and make you look good. New clothes often give you a sense of pride in your appearance. But I know businesspeople who have one great suit or dress that they always wear for initial meetings or presentations. Make sure your clothes are clean and neat; you can hardly be relaxed if you think everyone's staring at the spot on your shirt.

■ **Wear or carry something that makes you feel terrific.** It can even be something no one else sees. There's terrific power in knowing you've got on sexy underwear or that you're wearing the watch your favorite uncle gave you. These tokens are more than superstition; they remind you that you're someone special.

■ **Concentrate on what you're good at.** Remind yourself of the special talents or knowledge you bring and let your confidence grow from those. Are you an expert in your subject? Do you excel at your work? Are you terrific at working with your customers? Whatever your skill or expertise, knowing you're capable makes you look and act more assured.

■ **Have something interesting to say.** When you keep people focused on what you're saying, they don't care what you look like. So work on making your presentation clear and compelling. After all, what you really want them to remember is what you said, not what you wore.

■ **Bring visuals.** If you're nervous when people look at you, bring lots of visual materials to distract them. While the audience is staring at your colorful charts, they won't be looking at your face. Completely petrified before you have to make a presentation in front of a group? Then prepare a PowerPoint presentation, and arrange to have it shown in a darkened room.

■ **Pay attention to others.** The best way to make yourself more appealing is to pay attention to your audience. Interact with them, ask questions, make eye contact, smile. Think complimentary thoughts even if you don't speak those thoughts out loud ("What a nice group," "She seems friendly.") When you think well of others, you give off a welcoming glow.

You may never get used to standing up in front of others, but it doesn't have to feel as bad as dental surgery. Just put on a great outfit, a special watch, and most of all a smile, and you'll be getting rave reviews.

Don't Get Barbecue Sauce on Your Business Card

An important client invites you to a barbecue. You realize there are likely to be other prospective business contacts there as well. Do you take business cards? How do you hand them out when you've got a hot dog in one hand and a beer in the other? Here's how to gracefully network at an informal social event.

■ **Be sociable.** Remember, it's a social event. People don't go to social events to conduct business. Mingle. Don't monopolize someone's time.

■ **Make small talk.** If you identify a potential business contact at a social event, engage them in conversation. Sports, new movies, even the weather are easy ice-breakers. Establish rapport by finding something you have in common to discuss.

■ **Arrange to follow up.** Once you've established rapport, it may be comfortable to discuss a modest amount of business. After all, they're going to ask you what you do, and you'll have your elevator pitch handy. But don't go overboard. This is *not* the time for a sales pitch. Instead, arrange a follow up with them another time.

■ **Take business cards, but don't hand them out too fast.** Always carry business cards in your wallet or purse. When you're at a purely business networking event, you can offer your business card when you first meet someone; at a social event, only give someone a card when asked for it or just before you leave the party.

■ **Behave yourself.** If a client invites you to a party, it's a business event for you. You can have a beer or glass of wine, but don't get drunk. Make sure those who are attending with you—spouse, partner, kids—understand that this is business and ask them to act appropriately.

Dress for Success in Your Business

What to wear? What to wear? That's not just a question about fashion; you've also got to figure out what to wear when you're running your business, whether from your home, an office, or when you're out meeting clients. For most of us who run small companies, deciding what to wear can be a dilemma.

If you're an employee in a downtown corporation, clothing choices are easy. You just follow the company policy. If everyone wears suits, you wear suits. If everyone wears casual clothes, you wear casual clothes.

In smaller businesses, apparel decisions are more vexing. You set the policy and often your co-workers or employees will take their cue from you. More importantly, you're likely to interact with a wide variety of people, whether customers, prospects, or vendors. Some of them will be dressed in suits and some in shorts. So you may conclude that what you wear doesn't matter.

But clothes are an important part of your business image—and your business attitude. If you're too casual, you may not seem professional to your customers, employees, or even yourself. On the other hand, if you're overdressed, you may be needlessly uncomfortable during your daily tasks or you may appear to be trying too hard when you meet with a more casually dressed prospect.

What you wear, of course, also depends on what you do and where you live. Certain industries, like high tech, have their own style of dressing. Tech workers are likely to be more casually dressed than those who operate in other, more conservative, industries, such as the legal or financial fields.

I've always found that I'm more productive when I'm dressed fairly decently—even when working at home or by myself in the office. Wearing sweats or sloppy casual clothes makes it easier for me to allow my business attitude to become as relaxed as my outfit.

> **Clothes are an important part of your business image—and your business attitude.**

Diane Parente, President of Image Development & Management of Ross, California, and author of *Mastering Your Professional Image,* says the key to business dressing is understanding the concept of *three levels* of dressing. "The basic rule is always dress at the same level or one above your customer. Don't be a level below, and don't be two levels above."

133

Parente described the three levels of business dressing as:

■ **Level Three, Business Formal.** When you have to look your most professional: while negotiating a big deal, giving a presentation, or calling on a downtown office. For men, this means a business suit. For women, this means a business suit or a dress with matching jacket.

■ **Level Two, "Spiffy" Business Casual.** "You can't wear a suit if your customer is in jeans," says Parente. That's going to make both of you uncomfortable. Instead, choose an outfit that looks great but less formal. This could be a good-quality sweater and nicely pressed cotton slacks for both men and women or a skirt or dress for women.

■ **Level One, Informal Business Casual.** For working with casually dressed customers, while traveling, or for meetings held in casual settings, such as resorts. Men and women can both choose casual trousers made of cotton, khaki, or corduroy. Combine this with a shirt (polo shirt or sleeved cotton for men; cotton or silk for women) or sweater. Women could also wear a long, casual skirt. Note that, according to Parente, even the most informal business casual doesn't mean shorts, jeans, or t-shirts. That's just casual, not business casual.

Working at home presents a different kind of dilemma. You can wear jeans, sweats, or shorts but try to look decent whenever you leave the house. You never know who you're going to run into!

If you're unsure how to dress, remember you're always wiser to dress better, rather than more casually, than your customer or prospect. And no matter what, *always* be clean and neat.

What Kind of Website Is Right for Your Business?

The other night, a friend told me he had just come from a company meeting. "We're redesigning our website," he said. They had hired a designer to make their website look better and to make it easier to use. This cost a bundle.

"Why are you doing this?" I asked.

"We want our website to be as good as our competitor's."

"But what do you want your website to achieve? What's the *purpose* of your site?" He didn't understand the question.

My friend is not alone. When it comes to websites, many business owners suffer from the "if you build it, they will come" syndrome. They imagine that if they put up a website, they'll automatically get thousands of new customers. While it's true there are a lot of potential customers out there in cyberspace, you still have to have a plan to make your website successful.

Most importantly, you need to be clear on what you are trying to achieve and make sure it's realistic. To help you understand what you can do with a site, I've divided websites into four main types:

1. **Transactional.** Most retailers hope to actually sell products over the Internet. Perhaps the best-known example is bookseller Amazon.com. The problem with trying to get customers to buy on your site is that running an online store is just like running a land-based store. It's typically a full-time job, and you have to spend time and money getting people to your location. You also have to learn how to merchandise your products just like in a real store.

> When it comes to websites, many business owners suffer from the "if you build it, they will come" syndrome.

2. **Promotional.** Perhaps you're dreaming of a website that will attract new customers from all over the world. They'll find you while surfing the net and then call you. This happens when customers have a very specific need or are willing to spend a long time searching. This approach is good for niche businesses offering a hard-to-find or relatively limited product or service. Promotional sites generally don't work for

businesses with thousands of similar online competitors unless you're willing to spend a lot of time and money making sure your site appears high in search results. If you're hoping to find new customers with a promotional site, ask yourself: "Will people really spend a long time to find a business like mine?"

3. Informational. One of the best uses of a website is to give detailed information about your company to potential customers and employees who hear about you offline. When I looked for a graphic designer, I asked friends for recommendations and then checked the websites of the designers whose names I was given. This gave me a chance to check their work and learn more about them before contacting them. An informational site serves as an in-depth company brochure, enabling you to easily update and change information.

4. Relational. Finally, a website can be a good way to build closer relationships with current customers. You can post specials, provide detailed information on topics relating to your services, and put up a FAQ (Frequently Asked Questions) list.

A last website tip: it's a good idea to get your own domain name. Ideally, your domain name should be the same as your company's name. If the name is clumsy or not available, choose something as simple as possible that is appropriate for your business. Most catchy names are already taken. To check whether a domain name is available, go to **www.networksolutions.com** and click on "Whois."

The Internet doesn't change business fundamentals. If you want your website to be a success, you're going to have to put time, money, and most especially, planning, into making it work.

Increasing Website Traffic

■ **Improve your search engine ranking.** Most people use search engines to find websites. Using software that crawls through millions of websites, search engines create lists based on key words and phrases. Two primary search engines are Google (**www.google.com**) and Yahoo (**www.yahoo.com**).

The important thing to remember is that search engines find you by looking through your site, so by doing a few simple things, you can improve your chances of being found:

1. Use phrases that searchers are most likely to type in. If you're a mortgage broker, make sure you use the phrase "mortgage broker" repeatedly on your website in addition to using sentences such as, "I'll help you find the best mortgage rate."

2. Refer to your geographic location. Many searchers will add a location to their search terms ("mortgage broker in Phoenix"), so be certain to mention your city, county, state, and country (if you do business internationally).

3. List your products or services individually. The more specific you are, the more likely it is that your website will show up in relevant searches. The mortgage broker's website might list "30-year fixed rate," "15-year fixed rate," "adjustable rate mortgages," and so on.

■ **Get listed in directories.** Directories list websites by topic area, and are compiled by humans, not software. You can submit your site for inclusion. At the best known directory, Yahoo (**www.yahoo.com**), go to the home page and scroll down to "Suggest a Site."

■ **Buy search engine placement.** Search engines sell premium listings for keywords, so that searchers see your ad when they type in those keywords. These listings can be very affordable, since you typically only pay for "click throughs" to your site. Prices are based on demand by advertisers for that term. In other words, "dining room furniture" is likely to be more expensive than "Windsor Chair." To learn more about Google's search term advertising program, Adwords, go to **www.adwords.google.com**.

■ **Get links from related sites and sources.** Make it easy for potential customers to click to you from other sites they're visiting. To help local residents and visitors find you, get listed on local directory websites, often run by local newspapers, Chambers of Commerce, or tourist bureaus. Ask the businesses you do business with to link to you. The mortgage broker might ask to be listed by real estate agents she works with and offer to list them on her website in return.

■ **Buy ads.** Just as in the real world, you can purchase ads to get your name known on the Internet. These work best when placed on sites that are closely related to your product or service, such as those listed above.

■ **Include your website address on everything.** Remember, most customers will find you in the real world first. So include your web address on every piece of printed material and packing material, as well as every advertisement and invoice. Be certain to add your website address to your business card and to your email signature as well.

Gold by Association

Dream of becoming a freelance cartoonist? Check out the National Cartoonists Society. How about starting a business cleaning windows? There's the International Window Cleaning Association. What if you want to earn a living cleaning out other people's closets? Contact the National Association of Professional Organizers.

No matter what business you're in—or want to start—there's an organization you can turn to for help. Whether you run the smallest home-based business or the largest multinational corporation, you'll find a group of colleagues in your specific field.

The number of industry associations and professional societies is staggering. In April 2002 the Internal Revenue Service reported 71,032 organizations designated under the tax code for trade associations. A more reliable number is around half that, since many groups have state and local chapters. But any way you look at it, there's a heck of a lot of trade groups.

I'm a big believer in joining trade or professional associations. Most people think of trade associations, if they think of them at all, as groups that lobby for legislation to protect their industry. They do that, especially on the national level. But associations are far more important to you and your business as a source of information, education, and marketing opportunities.

My belief in the value of industry associations goes back to my very first client. I was developing a business plan for a small apparel manufacturer in San Francisco. As part of that consulting project, I attended a meeting of a local designers organization. They shared information about design trends, future fashion colors, purchasing habits of department stores, and marketing opportunities. But perhaps the biggest benefit for my client was just having a group of colleagues with similar needs and greater experience to call upon.

> **No matter what business you're in, there's an organization you can turn to for help.**

A few months later, I had another experience with a trade association. This time my client was a florist; one of their specialties was providing large floral arrangements for office buildings. As a way of meeting—and impressing—a group of highly targeted potential customers, my client donated the flowers for the holiday party for the local chapter of the Building Owners and Managers Association.

Years later, another client had a trade association success story. He and his buddy had invented a new kind of skateboard. Before they even went into production, they exhibited at a sporting goods association trade show. Their board was a hit; they lined up their first big orders and found a manufacturer at the same time!

Industry and trade associations are a great source for:

■ **Education and training**
■ **Certification**
■ **Data, information, and publications**
■ **Networking with colleagues or customers**
■ **Trade shows for sales and marketing**
■ **Organized political activity and legislative representation**
■ **Information on suppliers**
■ **Support and advice from colleagues**

You can also get advanced certification in your field from industry or professional associations. Such certification can make you more competitive in your market and bring you new customers.

If you're looking for information to start a new business, or to expand your current business, the first place to check is with your industry association. I'm surprised at the wealth of information and data some associations have available. For instance, if you wanted to start a landscape business, you could find a guidebook to running a landscape business as well as data on operating costs and standard business forms from the American Nursery and Landscape Association.

To make it easier for you to find an association for your industry, I've compiled a list of hundreds of associations—with Internet links—on my website: go to **www.planningshop.com/associations**.

Now, get out there and meet your colleagues!

Customers and Sales

Who's Your Customer?

You've got to understand your customer to succeed in business. But if I asked you to tell me who your customers are, could you do it?

Let's say you've created a wonderful new breakfast cereal for children: "Yummy Tummy Oats." You've packed Yummy Tummy Oats with all kinds of good things: vitamins, minerals, great nutrition. You figure you're going to wipe out the competition because every parent wants a nutritious breakfast for their child.

There's only one problem: who's your customer?

When you decided to create a healthy breakfast cereal, you thought of your customer as mom or dad pushing the grocery cart down the cereal aisle, comparing the nutrition information on the side of the box. After all, it's parents who purchase children's breakfast cereal. They're the customer, right?

Not exactly.

How about the actual end user of your product—the kid—who couldn't care less about nutrition but wants cereal that tastes sweet and has cartoon characters on the package and toys inside? If you realize that the child is your customer, what do you do then?

"Okay," you reply smugly, "if both parents and children are my customers, I'll find a way to satisfy each of them." So you revise your formula and now make Yummy Tummy

Oats in three all-natural flavors: grape, strawberry, and chocolate. You invent a new character, Yummy Tummy Tillie, a cereal-chomping yellow dinosaur, and give away Yummy Tummy Tillie action figures inside every box. You're only one step away from making your fortune, right?

Not so fast. Let me ask you again, "Who's your customer?"

> **Many businesspeople think of their customers only as those people who buy or use the product. This is a mistake.**

What about the cereal buyer for the grocery store chain? The supermarket buyer couldn't care less about nutrition or yellow dinosaurs. He's seen kids' breakfast cereals come and go, and his concerns are more down-to-earth: how much money you're going to spend on advertising, how quickly you replenish inventory, whether you'll pay him a stocking fee to obtain shelf space. Parents and children aren't going to have a chance to buy or eat Yummy Tummy Oats if you don't meet the supermarket buyer's needs first.

On top of that, if you do not have your own sales and distribution force, you may first have to find a cereal distributor and convince them to carry your product.

The parent. The child. The store buyer. The distributor. That's a lot of customers you have to satisfy with each box of Yummy Tummy Oats.

The term "customer" can be confusing. Many businesspeople think of their customers only as those people who buy or use the product. They imagine that if they win over those customers, they'll beat the competition. In real life, however, there are usually a lot of people between you and the final consumer, and each of those people can control the fate of your business. We've all seen products disappear from the shelves only to be replaced by inferior substitutes. Often, it's because the company didn't meet the needs of its intermediaries.

You give yourself a competitive edge by thinking of each of those intermediaries as customers. Being responsive to the details that are important to distributors, retailers, and sales representatives helps you plan your marketing materials, operations, packaging, even the nature of the product itself. If yours is an industry where sales reps must purchase their samples, for instance, you can set yourself apart by supplying samples free. If retailers can fit more square packages on a shelf than round packages, you'll be more competitive by choosing a square package. When you realize you've got a whole chain of customers, you'll think about "customer service" in an entirely different light.

"Forget it," you say. "That's too many people to think about. I'll do away with intermediaries, and I'll market Yummy Tummy Oats directly to consumers on the Internet. No grocery store, no distributor, no intermediaries. So there!"

Good luck. Many business owners would like to think the Internet wipes out intermediaries, connecting producers directly to consumers. But more often than not, there are still many entities between you and your customer in cyberspace. In the case of Yummy Tummy Oats, your intermediary might be an online health food site, or children's site, or parent's site. You'll still have more than just parents and kids to please.

So, we're back to where we started, and I'll ask you again, "Who's your customer?" If you can't answer that, it won't matter how many Yummy Tummy Tillie toys you put in each box of cereal.

Getting to Know Your Customers

"What were they thinking?" How many times have you been frustrated with a product or service and wondered why it was designed so poorly? Why didn't the company that made it understand how real people act?

The sad fact is, in many cases, companies simply don't think about the customer. Sure, they think about how they can get customers to buy, but when it comes to actual product design, they focus on issues such as features, cost, and production rather than usability. What's often overlooked is how real customers really behave.

As small business owners, we're even more likely to fall into that trap. Although we think we know our customers well, the reality is we probably don't. Many of our products or services tend to reflect our own interests, needs, and abilities. Those aren't necessarily the interests or needs of our target customers. In our rush to get a product out the door or to get our company up and running, we don't have the time—or money – to do a lot of market research.

However, I've discovered the value of a process called "goal-directed design," conceived by Alan Cooper. Cooper, a pioneering software developer, came up with a method for companies to better understand how customers interact and use their products.

The key to Cooper's process is creating *personas* representing target customers. A persona is a single archetype that depicts, in great detail, what a typical target customer would be like. Then, as you develop your product or service, you keep that persona, or personas, in mind.

For instance, in my company, The Planning Shop, as a first step in designing a new line of books, we met in our conference room and spent a full day discussing the types of people who currently use our books. We then created about a half-dozen specific, fictional individuals who were likely customers. We gave each one a name, a personal description (age, gender, personality), business description (industry, business stage, revenues), and specific business need.

We use this process of creating personas for each of our books. It forces us to think carefully about who our customer is for each product—what they need and want and how they'll use it. Even for a book on business planning, for instance, *Sally Startup* has different needs than *Vic Venture*.

The first step of Cooper's process, ideally, is to get out of your office and meet with customers or potential customers. You don't need hundreds of meetings; just speak to a cross-section of the types of customers likely to use your product. To make these interviews most effective:

1. Go to them. See customers in the setting where they'll be using your product or service. It's preferable to conducting interviews over the phone or in a conference room.

2. Approach the process with a blank slate. You want to learn as much as you can, not just confirm your preconceived notions.

3. Ask open-ended questions. If you're designing a new product, ask questions about how your customers currently do whatever your product or service will address. Avoid leading questions, such as "Wouldn't you find it easier if you had a …."

4. Observe. Watch how your customers interact with your product (if it's already developed) or with whatever products they currently use. What do they do first? What seems clumsy? What else is going on around them at the same time? From observing, you'll almost certainly discover ways to enhance your product or service.

Once you interview customers, you'll have a lot of raw data. Now comes the important part: compiling that information into personas. Review your notes to find the characteristics common to major types of customers. Then, create a few fictional individuals—give them names, ages, personalities, descriptions—to represent customers with those characteristics. Create a handful of personas representing the major types of customers you serve.

Realistically, as an independent entrepreneur, you may not have the resources to go out and fully implement Cooper's data-gathering methods. But even using a highly simplified version of Cooper's process can be a huge help in better understanding your customers.

In fact, we don't have the time or money to do the research Cooper advises—at least not yet. But we've taken the first steps in creating our company's personas. We continually refer to these personas when making decisions about our books—content, layout, design. The use of personas has given us a quick and easy way to stay closer to the actual needs of our customers. And it's been fun, too!

Cooper's firm offers training in the persona process. You can find information about it at their website: **www.cooper.com.**

How to Get Your First Customer

So you've decided to go into business. Congratulations! You've got your product or service ready. You're prepared and eager to go. There's only one problem—you don't have any customers.

Sure, you need the money from customers. But you need more than that. You need the credibility that comes from having a client list. While the Starship Enterprise may "boldly go where no man has gone before," most customers only follow where others lead. Let's say I see two restaurants on the same street. One restaurant is bustling, with a line of customers waiting for tables. The other is completely empty, with just one lonely waiter standing there by himself. Which restaurant will I choose? Unless I'm starving, I'll almost certainly go to the restaurant that's full, even if I have to wait.

This follow-the-herd mentality is even more prevalent when it comes to serving businesses. Businesses like to know that others, especially other companies in their own industry, have used your product or service.

The fact is, you've got to have a track record for clients to feel comfortable with you. What a dilemma: you have to have customers to get customers. But don't despair; there are a number of tricks to snare that first one.

The simplest is to give your product or service away. This isn't as stupid as it sounds. Technology companies often give potential customers *beta* or trial versions of their software. They use this as a way both to improve their product and to expose future buyers to what they make.

Whether you're creating websites or wedding cakes, you, too, can treat your first customers as beta testers. Approach a potential customer but instead of trying to sell your product or service, offer it to them free if they will give you feedback on ways to improve. Be sure to treat these beta testers *exactly* the same way as if they were paying. Draw up a sales document, indicate what you're providing and what direct costs they'll pay (if any), and then specify that you are "waiving" your fee. Use this transaction to learn how you'll deal with paying clients.

> **It's a dilemma: you need to have customers to get customers. But don't despair; there are tricks to snare that first one.**

A bonus to this approach? My experience has been that most beta testers feel a strong sense of connection to the product or service they're evaluating. Not only are you likely to turn your beta testers into future

147

paying customers, I'm willing to bet they'll start referring others to you as well.

Another approach is to charge your early clients far less than they would pay elsewhere and less than you're likely to charge later. This is a type of introductory pricing approach. It's also fair, especially if you're in a new line of business. When I got my very first business plan client, I set an exceptionally small fee. It certainly wouldn't have been appropriate to charge my client a lot of money when I still had to learn what I was doing. I also worked my heart out for him; I wanted to learn as much as I could. He got a bargain; I got an education and a track record.

Another way to find your first customers is to ask your competitors for excess work they can't handle. Yes, I said competitors. One of the biggest mistakes I made when I started in business was that I avoided talking to others in my field. I figured they would view me as a threat. I was wrong. It turned out my competitors were a great source both of new business and of industry information. Competitors may also be interested in subcontracting or referring work to you.

If you can do so legally, or if you're on good terms with your former employer, see if there are customers you can take from your last job. Some of the most successful small businesses are those set up to serve the customers or offer the product lines that bigger businesses can no longer handle profitably.

A word of warning: if you're making a major career switch don't expect your friends, family, or former colleagues to be eager to be your first customers. These are folks who've thought of you in one context for a long time, and it's going to take a while before they'll see you in a new light. So get out there and market to strangers. And don't worry, it gets (somewhat) easier after you've done it for awhile.

Make More from Each Customer

Getting customers isn't cheap. It takes money and time to attract new ones. You advertise, attend trade shows, and maintain your website. This costs the same whether a customer spends $1 or $1,000. So it's far more profitable if you can make a bigger sale to each customer who comes your way.

I was thinking about this the other day when I went to a neighborhood beauty store. I needed a new eye shadow, and I went straight for what I wanted: one eye shadow for $8. I was ready to leave. But the very nice saleswoman came over and advised me of a much better deal. For $25, I could get three eye shadows, two lipsticks, one nail polish, and a cosmetic carrying case. An enticing offer, and by the time I left, I had a selection of beauty supplies and a $25 charge on my credit card.

What the beauty store did is called "up-selling." It's not only smart and perfectly legal, but if done right, the customer is appreciative of the opportunity to spend more. I walked away feeling that I got a good deal, not wondering whether the $8 eye shadow was intentionally overpriced. How could the retailer afford this kind of offer? Because their big expense is tied up in their overhead—rent, salaries, advertising—not in the cost of the eye shadow.

Many retailers try to up-sell their customers. If you've ever been to a giant warehouse discount store, you'll see that many items are packaged in multiples, whether twelve rolls of paper towels, or boxed sets of books, or four boxes of corn flakes. The result is that the customer makes a bigger total purchase on each visit, and it's much more profitable for the retailer.

> ## What could you offer your customers on a continuing or consumable basis?

Up-selling doesn't just occur in retail. If you need to get a will drawn up, don't be surprised if your lawyer offers you a complete estate planning package, which includes a few other documents you should properly prepare at the same time. The one-price package is a good value to you and a better sale for them.

A slightly different approach is "cross-selling"—selling related products or services. If you book an airline flight on a travel website, they'll offer you a discount if you also book your hotel at the same time.

One way to make more money from each customer is to find ways to produce continuing income rather than just making a one-time sale. Are there products or services your customers use up or use repeatedly—consumables? There's often more money in consumables than in the original product or service. Decades ago, Kodak figured out there was more profit in the film than the camera. Today, we see the same thing with cellular phones (the phones are inexpensive or free; you pay for the continuing service).

Service businesses, too, can look for ongoing revenue streams. Accountants frequently offer bookkeeping or bill-paying services. Instead of just preparing clients' tax returns once a year, they work for them all year long. What could you offer your customers on a continuing or consumable basis?

Of course, there's a risk that if you're overly aggressive when you up-sell, cross-sell, or offer consumables that a customer will view you as too pushy and leave.

But if you can honestly provide a more complete service or a better value by up-selling or cross-selling, your customer benefits. After all, it's more convenient to book all my travel needs at one time. I don't view the lawyer who suggests a full estate package as greedy, I think he's taking care of my interests. And I liked having those beauty products!

Turn One-Timers into Lifetimers

For the first decade of my consulting business, I depended on one-off clients: I'd do the work for them, and then they'd have no need for my services again. I'm not alone. Many businesses are built around one-time customers, but that's a dangerous business strategy.

I developed business plans. And once a person had a business plan, they didn't need me any more. Right?

Wrong. As I've learned in my own company, a successful enterprise needs to revise its business plan at least once a year. But I wasn't getting this potential recurring business. My income was completely dependent on finding new customers.

Of course, I was doing very well. Somehow the clients just kept coming. I'd like to believe it was solely due to the fact that I was a brilliant consultant (will you take my word on that?) but I was also lucky.

Selling every customer only one item—whether a business plan, a landscape design, or a kitchen remodel—is a precarious way to earn a living.

The truth is that whenever you run a business totally dependent on new clients, you're vulnerable. If economic conditions change, or a new competitor enters the market, you may suddenly see your flow of new customers disappear.

However, if you've managed to build up a stable of loyal, repeat clients—even if they reduce their purchases in a weak economy—you're better able to maintain at least a basic level of income and keep your business alive.

> **Your doctor, dentist, and auto mechanic all have you come in regularly; why not ask the same of your customers?**

Many of us know we need to become less dependent on one-off customers, but we don't know how. What if the very nature of our business means customers only need us one time? Regardless of divorce statistics, can a wedding planner really build up repeat business?

Well, that's a tough one. But even there, the answer is "Yes."

So what types of things can a one-off business offer their customers to create a renewable income stream?

■ **Tune-ups and check-ups.** Your doctor, dentist, and auto mechanic all have you come in regularly; why not ask the same of your customers? A landscape designer can provide semi-annual or quarterly garden updates. I could have offered annual planning sessions. And that wedding planner? How about offering—on a complimentary basis—to plan a small first anniversary dinner and then provide ongoing special anniversary and party (including children's birthdays) planning? This might not bring in a great deal of income directly, but it keeps your name in front of the client for referrals.

■ **Support services.** Many businesses dependent on one-off customers provide design or construction services. But most customers also need ongoing maintenance and support. For instance, a website designer's clients need site hosting and ongoing updates. Can you provide a one-stop shop, hiring a low-level staffer to do updates and subcontracting the hosting?

■ **Products.** Finally, are there products you can sell or create that customers need to replace on a regular basis? Consumables are a great source of continuing income. Just think about inkjet printers—the real money comes from selling replacement toner cartridges.

So what's holding those of us who continue to serve only one-off customers back?

■ **Fear of being bored.** Face it, working with new clients can be more interesting than working with the same customers over and over. Creating a new design is more fun than providing maintenance. But trust me, you'll appreciate the money from the humdrum stuff when new business dries up.

■ **Business structure.** Providing service to clients on a repeat basis means managing a more complex schedule, hiring subordinates, or dealing with subcontractors. That isn't the kind of business you want to run. But do you want to risk having no income at all?

■ **Ego.** I know what you're thinking. "My clients are hiring *me!* So I can't bring in anyone else to help with the ongoing stuff. And I've got all the work I can handle now." Well, your clients do want to work with you, but they'll understand that you have staff to perform some of the ongoing tasks.

Remember, you never want to lose a satisfied customer. Look for ways to keep—and serve—them on a repeat basis. Your bank account will thank you.

Sales Are the Heart of Business

We may not like to admit it, but sooner or later, all business comes down to just one thing: making sales. Maybe you started your business because you've got a terrific skill—designing homes, forecasting financials, catering great meals—but if you can't make sales, you'll have to work for someone who can.

People hate to talk about sales, even salespeople. It's as if making sales is shameful. But sales are the lifeblood of business. If you're the owner of a company—even if you have a staff of salespeople—you'll inevitably be involved in making some sales yourself.

I knew a shy man who started a business a few decades ago. He was a European gentleman, the kind of man who hesitated to even ask someone to pass the salt. As soon as he started his company, whenever he was on a business trip, if the person sitting next to him on the plane wasn't a potential customer, he'd change seats. I'm sure he was never pushy, he just looked for every opportunity to make a sale. He became a multimillionaire.

■ **Change your attitude.** It's natural to think of sales calls as an imposition on others, and if you're obnoxious, you are a nuisance. But if you select your target market carefully and offer the customer something of genuine value, then you have no reason to be hesitant or ashamed. In fact, you can feel good about making something useful available.

■ **Listen.** You can't make a sale if you're doing all the talking. Customers have to tell you what they want and need. You have no way of knowing whether your product or service will be of use to the customer unless you *listen*. One of the reasons we hate telemarketers so much is that they just rattle out a sales pitch.

> **Start with smaller customers, and don't forget them once you're successful. They can be the backbone of a company.**

■ **Know what you're selling.** In my first year of business, I lost a big client when he called and asked what I did. I fumbled my answer and by the time I figured out what to say, he had lost interest. You have to be able to present your product/service clearly and concisely and know what aspects meet your customers' needs.

■ **Make sales an ongoing process.** You can't immediately turn on a good sales program when income drops and forget about making sales when times are good. Sales are an integral part of your company, and regular communication with your customers helps them to remember you.

■ **Build relationships.** People buy from other people. Develop relationships with your customers. You can compete with big business by building strong customer relationships.

■ **Start small.** Many entrepreneurs would love to have Fortune 500 companies as customers. But big companies are the hardest to sell into. Start with smaller customers, and don't forget them once you're successful. They can be the backbone of a company.

■ **Make a plan.** Just like any other aspect of business, successful sales takes planning. Figure out which customers you'll go after, how you'll communicate with them, how many sales calls you'll make a day or a week, and how you'll follow up. Set specific goals.

■ **Keep your calendar out.** When you make a sales call, many customers legitimately won't have a need for your product or service at that time. So ask when you can call them again ("May I call you again in three months?"). Most people say yes. They'll be surprised when you call again, and they'll trust you more because you follow up.

■ **Be persistent rather than insistent.** Most people think you have to be pushy to be a successful salesperson; you don't. You just have to stick with it.

■ **Stop networking and start selling.** It's important to join trade groups and go to chamber mixers, but at some point you have to turn your contacts into sales calls. Get out those business cards you've picked up and make some appointments!

Responding to Prospects

Your phone rings. It's a prospective customer wanting information about your services and prices, requesting a bid or proposal. That's a good thing, right?

Well, yes and no. Obviously, it's great to have potential customers knocking on your door. But not all prospects are going to become paying customers—no matter how good your sales skills, how competitive your prices, or how outstanding the quality of your products or services. The sad truth is you can waste a lot of precious time and money answering inquiries and preparing bids or proposals for prospects who are not ready to buy or are just plain looky-loos.

Figuring out how much time and energy to spend on prospective customers is a delicate and difficult balancing act. You need to spend enough time to make a sale to a genuine prospect, but you don't want to waste too much time on those who won't ever buy.

Realistically, you have to be responsive to all potential customers. But there are ways to limit the time, money, and effort you spend on dead-end shoppers. Here's how:

1. Have general information prepared and available. Most prospects will try to figure out whether a company is a good fit for them before taking up too much of their— or your—time. Let's say you sell and install floor tiles. Do you specialize in commercial or residential? Do you only serve a specific geographic area? Do you install counter tops as well as floors? That kind of information enables prospects to weed themselves out before calling you. A great and relatively inexpensive way to provide this information is on your website.

2. Ask questions of the prospect. In professional salesperson terms, this is called qualifying the prospect. By asking a few simple, non-intrusive questions, you can get a much better sense of how serious the prospect is. Some questions to ask:

■ What's the scope of the project?

■ What's the time frame for the work to be started and completed?

■ How soon will you be making a decision on a vendor?

■ How many bids are you getting?

■ What other alternatives (not competitors) are you considering? (In the floor tile example, for instance, the question might be phrased as "What other types of floor coverings are you looking at?"

■ What are the most important considerations in your decision—price, quality, convenience?

Questions such as these give you a better sense of whether a prospect is ready to make a decision, whether they're likely to find you a good choice, and how much time to spend with them.

> **Figuring out how much time and energy to spend on prospective customers is a delicate and difficult balancing act.**

3. Don't get star-struck. It's easy to get excited if you're approached by a large or well-known company or customer. Don't lose your judgment. Such customers often take up more of your time, take longer to make decisions, and expect highly competitive bids. Sure, it would be nice to have the biggest company in town or the star of a major league baseball team on your customer list,

but is it worth it if you don't make a profit?

4. Give prospects a reason to make a decision sooner rather than later. It's human nature to put off making choices until the last minute, but that often leaves your business in a crunch. If you can, come up with truthful, positive ways to encourage customers to make a decision quickly—"I've got an opening in my calendar in two weeks but then I'm booked til May," or "I can get a discount on materials this month only."

5. Be cautious of prospects who want *too much information.* Some prospects use proposals as a way of getting free consulting services. This is true of both small customers and Fortune 500 companies.

6. Don't count your chickens before they hatch. It's easy to get excited about a prospect, especially if it's a big one. So keep a lot of balls in the air, and remember, a deal is not a deal until the check clears.

Writing Winning Proposals

"Can you send me a proposal?"

In many lines of business, submitting proposals is an essential part of business life. Yet, no matter how many proposals we've written, most of us freeze when faced with an empty computer screen and the knowledge that our words are going to decide whether we'll be making money—or not.

As a consultant for more than fifteen years, I submitted hundreds of proposals. Every time I wrote one, I worried about the same things: Am I accurately forecasting the amount of time and money this will take? Is this addressing the clients' real concerns? Did I tell the client enough or too much? What are the magic words that will make them decide to hire my firm?

The good news is that there are ways to make writing proposals easier and landing clients more likely.

The first trick is to create a template. Develop a standard format (or formats if you prepare more than one type of proposal frequently). That way, you don't start from scratch every time. I had a proposal template containing the information I included in every proposal. This meant the proposal was half written before I even started, and I never faced a blank computer screen.

Here's what I included in my proposal template:

■ **Background.** A brief statement of the problem. This basically restates how your potential client has described their situation. It lets them know you understand why they're undertaking the project.

■ **Scope.** This is a fairly detailed description of what you are going to do for the client so there can be no misunderstandings later. Be specific!

■ **Deliverables.** If you're creating tangible items for the client—such as a report or a brochure—list exactly what you'll be giving them.

> You need to put in enough information to show you've got the knowledge and creativity to do the job, but not so much that the client doesn't need you.

■ **Personnel.** Indicate who will be staffing the project and their qualifications. In many cases, this may be you alone, but in others you may have staff or subcontractors who should also be mentioned, especially if their qualifications add strength to the proposal.

■ **Timetable.** State when the project will start, when certain milestones will be reached, and when the project will be considered finished.

■ **Fees.** Clearly state how much you are charging for the project, which expenses are included, whether there is an allowance for possible overcharges, and all other fees.

■ **Equipment/Outside contractors/Other expenses.** If the project entails other major expenses—such as equipment rental, hiring outside contractors, or printing costs—describe who will be responsible for engaging/supervising these services and how they will be billed.

■ **Terms.** Detail when payments are due, how expenses that are not part of the project fees will be billed (e.g., at cost or cost plus 10%), what happens when payments are late (e.g., interest rate to be charged on amount due, cessation of work, etc.).

Many entrepreneurs find the hardest part of developing a proposal is figuring out what to charge. I preferred to work on a project basis rather than charging an hourly rate. That way I didn't have to keep an eye on the clock every time a client called, and the client wasn't surprised by a big bill at the end of a project.

But while I only gave the client an overall fee, to come up with an appropriate charge, I first made a detailed list of each step and estimated how much time it will take. From that list I could see what I needed to charge to make a fair profit.

It's also critically important to learn what *not* to put in a proposal. On many occasions, I had clients give me other consultants' proposals, some with excellent creative ideas they had given away in those documents. You need to put in enough information to show you've got the knowledge and creativity to do the job, but not so much that the client doesn't need you.

Finally, be brief and make your proposal look good. Most proposals for consulting work need only be one to three pages long. You can add supporting materials, such as brochures, client lists, testimonials. Make certain your proposal and supporting documents are as professional as you are.

Landing Big Accounts

Do you dream of landing a big corporate account? Fantasize about a national department store carrying your products? Lust for a Fortune 500 company to give you a contract for all their 692 offices? The world would be your oyster: money, prestige, flying first class. Get a grip. Huge companies can be a nightmare rather than a dream.

If you're trying to sell to a big company, you'll have a hard time finding the right person. Sure, your jogging pal may be a vice president, but she still may not be able to hook you up with the right decision maker (there could be 189 vice presidents). When you finally get the right name, and after you've left fifteen messages over three months, the guy tells you he no longer has that responsibility, "We transferred that to Western Division."

Once you finally meet with the decision maker, your work has just begun. People in big businesses often don't think the same way as those in small companies. You'll imagine he wants to save time and money, when he may only be interested in saving his job. He may just want to stay out of the boss's way or can't take time to think about changes.

Eureka! You manage to get him interested! Expect to be asked for detailed proposals, which take you weeks to prepare. Then more meetings, then revise your proposals. And then? If your contact isn't transferred, he needs the decision to be approved by the senior vice president, who's in Singapore for two months.

Expect hard negotiating over price and terms. Yes, it is true that many large companies are used to paying high prices, but they also know suppliers are eager for their business and are used to making demands.

> ## You'll have an edge if you've got someone to shepherd you through the process.

Even if you get the contract, your woes may not be over. One of my clients, an apparel manufacturer, was doing great until big department stores started buying from him: their orders were so large and their payments so slow, they tied up all his capital and eventually put him in debt.

Should you give up on corporate clients altogether? If you've been in business less than two or three years, I'd say yes. You'll waste too much time. Start with smaller companies, which are quicker and easier to secure.

If you've already to try to sell to a large client, keep some things in mind:

■ **Get an inside advocate.** Corporate decisions are often based on factors you can never know about (the CEO is emphasizing quality rather than cost this year or the boss hates the color green), so you've got an edge if you've got someone to shepherd you through the process.

■ **People change jobs frequently in big companies.** Meet a lot of people and stay in touch with them all, not just your advocate.

■ **Many different departments may buy your product or service.** Don't limit your activities to one area of a large company.

■ **Always ask for a time frame for a decision.** The company won't keep to that time frame, but having set dates gives you a reason to continually follow up.

■ **Figure out whether their business is truly profitable for you.** It may be great to have big orders, but do they make you enough money? It may be worth breaking even, or even losing money, if you know this will lead to other orders or other big clients. But be careful; give yourself limits.

■ **Carefully weigh how much debt to take on to serve a new client.** A small bakery got the contract to be the in-store bake shop for a grocery chain. They took out loans for new ovens, trucks, and staff. Within a year, they turned the bakeries into such a terrific profit center that the grocery chain decided to run it themselves. The bakery was stuck with massive debt and went bankrupt. Be careful.

Once you have your first big corporate account, you'll find it much easier to get subsequent accounts. Big companies like to follow other big companies and do what everyone else is doing—just like kids.

Sometimes the Best Word Is "No"

Years ago, there was a business book called *Getting to Yes*. Its goal was to help people negotiate deals and get positive responses. While everyone wants to get a "Yes," sometimes it's equally important to get a firm "No."

If there's a real hope that a customer will buy, you don't want to prematurely force an answer. But sometimes when a deal is really dead, nobody is willing to call the coroner. In these cases, a "No" is the best thing you can hear. Remember Rhonda's Rule: If you're going to get rejected eventually, it's better to get rejected soon.

Here's a typical scenario: A prospect calls. They're interested in your product or service. They ask for a meeting. You spend time preparing and then meet with them. They ask for a proposal. You spend days, maybe weeks, putting together a great proposal. After all, this could be *big*. You drive two hours or fly out to meet the district manager. They love you. You're excited. Now they have to run it by their superior. She wants just a few small changes. You put in more time. Now, the vice president has to approve it, and he's on assignment, and you've missed this year's budget cycle, and they're not sure when they're going to be able to get sign-off. Months go by. At this point, you've gone through a lot of your company's resources, yet you're no closer to a decision than when the prospect first called.

How can you avoid such frustration? Realistically, you have to be responsive to potential customers. And the bigger the prospect, the more obliging you're likely to be. But if you can find ways to limit the amount of time, money, and effort you spend on dead-end deals, you can free up your time for more profitable activities.

It takes a while to develop a sense of who's serious and who's just a looky-loo.

You can get a better sense of the timing by asking a prospect where they are in their decision-making cycle. "When do you need this?" Ask questions to determine how

> It takes a while to develop a sense of who's serious and who's just a looky-loo.

pressing their need is and when they'll make a firm decision. Keep your sales efforts proportionate; if the caller's going to remodel "one day," you might only want to send them a brochure; if they absolutely have to add a room before the baby arrives, get out your appointment book.

161

Give customers deadlines, incentives, or other reasons to hurry their decision making. These can be positive ("We've got a fall special that runs out this week") or they can be negative ("Prices go up after the first of the year").

Be wary of customers who want too much information. I've seen customers who use proposals as a way of getting free work. Bids and proposals are a tricky business: you have to show enough so the customer knows you are capable of doing the work, but you don't want to give away the store. Come up with some snazzy standard marketing information and limit the amount of material you develop on a custom basis for individual customers.

Keep a lot of balls in the air at once. One of the worst mistakes you can make is to put too much hope in any one prospect. You'll put in too much effort, and you'll be afraid to put on the pressure, which is often necessary to get a customer to say yes.

Learn to mentally shelve proposals that aren't progressing. You don't have to tell the prospect you're putting them aside, but don't fool yourself into believing something is happening. And perhaps most importantly, get over being afraid to hear the word "No." We all want to believe that if a prospect hasn't actually said no, the deal is still alive. So we all avoid asking the question, "Do you intend to make this deal?" But sometimes "No" is the most important word you can hear.

Making Cold Calls

There's a way to increase your business that you probably don't want to hear about: cold calling.

What exactly is a "cold call"? It's a sales call—on the phone or in person—when the person you're calling has not approached you or expressed interest in your products or services. (Conversely, "hot" leads are those who've already expressed interest in your products or services.)

I know you hate making cold calls, and we all certainly hate getting them. Who wants another call from a mortgage company, phone service, or credit card company? But here's the dirty little secret: cold calls work.

In our own businesses, we may neglect cold calling because we don't have time. Perhaps we think they wouldn't be effective in our type of business. More likely, we don't make cold calls because we hate the prospect of selling—especially to strangers. Who likes having all those people tell them "No"?

But cold calls can be effective, especially if you spend time to find appropriate potential leads. If your business is stagnant, or you're developing a new product or service line, cold calls can be a relatively inexpensive way to attract new customers.

You probably already do cold calling; you just don't think of it as a sales call. When you call a big company about forming a strategic partnership or exhibit at a trade show, you're out there looking to gain new business from prospects that aren't yet interested in your company. Viewed that way, cold calling doesn't seem as distasteful.

Most small businesses do not have the resources—nor would they find it effective—to just start calling prospects from a phone book. Moreover, national Do Not Call registries limit the numbers you're allowed to call. You'll be better off finding highly targeted lists, such as those from industry or membership associations.

> **Here's a dirty little secret: cold calls work.**

What's the secret of cold call success?

■ **Change your perspective.** Most of us think of a sales call as bothering the other person. But if you offer something you truly believe meets a real need and is a good value, then you're not a bother but a help. If you don't believe in what you're selling, don't sell it!

■ **Qualify your leads.** We really *hate* sales calls when they don't relate to us. Find ways to narrow down your target list. That saves you time and increases your success rate. What makes a qualified lead? Identify those characteristics that your customers share in common and concentrate on other prospects with those same characteristics. If you're targeting other businesses, research those companies on the Internet before you approach them.

■ **Listen.** Find out what your prospect wants and needs before you start your sales pitch. Make sure your product or service is a good fit with their needs. Otherwise, you're not only imposing on your prospect, you're wasting your own time.

■ **Develop a great pitch.** Be clear about what you're offering and the benefits to the customer. Write out your pitch and your most important points well before you make your first call, but don't just read it aloud! Think about the objections you're likely to hear and have responses ready.

■ **Take people literally.** If a prospect says, "I'm not interested right now," believe they mean right *now*. Perhaps they'll be interested another time. Ask if you can call on them at a later time.

■ **Don't be obnoxious.** Take "No" for an answer. If someone's not interested, why waste your time or theirs? Be polite. They may know someone else who's interested or their situation may change.

■ **Mind your manners.** If you walk in on someone and they're on the phone, wait until they're free. If you're phoning, and the person says, "Now's not a good time," ask when a good time would be to call back.

■ **Give yourself a quota.** Set a minimum—but realistic—number of calls you have to make before you can call it quits for the day. Stick to it.

■ **Stay in practice.** Cold calling is difficult, and it's easy to forget how to do it well. So make calls from time to time even when you aren't looking for a lot of new work.

■ **Don't get discouraged.** If you get turned down repeatedly, evaluate whether you've got the right list, pitch, or product. But don't let it completely defeat you. And don't take rejection personally.

Dealing with Difficult Customers

"I love my business; it's the customers I can't stand."

Customers! Can't live with them; can't live without them. They're aggravating, demanding, indecisive, inconsistent, and just a plain pain in the neck. Sometimes, you'd like them to just leave you alone so you can run your business.

Unfortunately, without customers or clients, you won't have a business to run. And when you consider the situation honestly, you realize you enjoy dealing with *most* customers. It's just that small—annoying—percentage that makes you want to pull your hair out.

Not all difficult customers are alike, however, so I've developed a field guide to help you recognize and deal with problem customers. This will help you distinguish the specific types of difficult customers when you run across them:

■ **Give them an inch.** Going the extra mile for a customer is good business, but sometimes it can come back to haunt you. When you give a customer something extra, most are grateful, but a few take advantage by continually pushing for more. Solution: Whenever you give a client something free, let them know the dollar value normally attached to that product or service, indicating that you are voluntarily waiving the charges—in writing. When they start asking for more, just smile and say politely, "I'd be delighted to do that for you. The cost is *x*. Shall I add that to the contract?"

■ **Just plain cheap.** Some customers always want the least expensive option, then complain if things aren't first-rate. They're constantly negotiating and renegotiating. Eventually, you cut corners so you can still make a profit, and your work—and reputation—suffers. Solution: Be less eager to land such clients. Don't low ball proposals just to get the job. Give them choices, in writing, making clear the downsides of the cheaper option—and make them sign off on their choices.

> **A small percentage of customers will drive you nuts. Don't let them affect the way you treat all customers—or you won't have many left.**

■ **Never satisfied.** As a manager, you know you have to positively reinforce your employees with praise and recognition. But some customers think the only way to get a job done well is to continually criticize. Even when you do superb work, they find something to complain about. Solution: Don't let it get to you. Praise your employees or co-workers in front of the client, so they know you value them. And, if you can, don't work for such customers again.

■ Micromanager. Nothing is as frustrating as a client who wants to stand over your shoulder, guiding—or second-guessing—your every move. But you know what you're doing or they wouldn't have hired you. Solution: Keep perspective. This kind of customer is either nervous or controlling; either way, it isn't a reflection on your capabilities. Communicate with them often and clearly. Let them ask questions. But do this in a formal way. Set aside a regular time when you will bring them up to date. Tell them you have to have some time and space so you can get the job done. Good luck!

■ Decide-o-phobic. Some potential customers will eventually turn into buyers, but they're incredibly hesitant. Others are looky-loos. How do you tell the two apart so you don't waste way too much time on prospects you'll never close? Solution: When trying to get a job, indicate time limits in your proposal ("This proposal not valid after…" or "Subject to additional charges after…"). Limit the number of times you'll meet with a prospect before getting an agreement; after that, inform them you have to charge a consulting fee. Once you've landed the project, give this type of customer a few clear choices for each decision they have to make, with deadlines!

■ Always busy. They hired you. They needed you. Now they have no time for you. You can't move forward because you need their input. You're not making money, you're not signing new customers. Solution: Give these clients deadlines. Let them know that you've got other commitments after a certain date. Start sending bills. If this happens a lot, structure your proposals so fees accrue if work is delayed due to customer inaction.

Remember, only a small percentage of customers will drive you nuts. Don't let those few affect the way you treat all customers—or you won't have many left.

Getting Rid of Your Best Customers

My friend Tony had a serious business problem. For more than a decade, he'd run a thriving consulting practice. He made a great deal of money and attracted world-class clients. In fact, that was the issue Tony needed help with; he had a very big client he wanted to "fire."

You might think Tony was nuts. Why would any businessperson want to get rid of customers who bring them a lot of money? The truth is that many companies need to jettison some customers for the good of the business or the personal well-being of the owner.

Typically, the most obvious reason to get rid of a customer is when their business is no longer profitable. They may bring you a lot of cash but with very little or no actual profit. That's not to say you want to dump every marginally profitable customer—you may need the cash flow to finance your overhead or growth. But there may come a time when you do have to end what seems like a significant relationship so your more profitable business activities can grow.

You may also want to get rid of a customer when they just become too much trouble. They constantly complain, pay slowly, take too long making decisions. They may not be draining your financial resources, but they may be depleting your emotional reserves. At some point, you just have to recognize that your life and your business are better off without them, even if your bank balance suffers in the short term.

Tony didn't have either of these problems. His client was great to work with and profitable. He was merely at a point where he wanted to develop new areas of expertise and change the nature of his projects. That one big client monopolized most of Tony's time, and while he liked the work, he'd been doing it for so long that it no longer presented much challenge or interest.

> **The truth is that many companies need to jettison some customers for the good of the business or the personal well-being of the owner.**

But getting rid of customers isn't easy. It's not only difficult to face someone and say, "I can no longer handle your account," it's also scary to turn down money coming in the door. To avoid dealing directly with these situations, many of us torpedo ourselves instead. We take on work and then do it poorly. We stop communicating. We overcharge and underperform. In the end, we may get rid of the customer, but we've also hurt our reputation and our self-confidence.

So what did I propose to Tony? First, that he assess his situation. Was this a temporary difficulty or truly a turning point in his career? We all experience frustration with our customers from time to time.

Next, could he really afford to lose this big customer? It takes a while to establish a new business or new business line. What was going to happen until he had lined up sufficient clientele to replace his current income?

Tony didn't want to leave consulting altogether; he just wanted different types of projects. I suggested to him that he start trying to secure those types of projects now, recognizing that he would have a transition period where he would be working many more hours and be pulled in two directions.

Perhaps Tony could have hired a new staff member to handle the client or most of their work. Why not grow his business instead of just changing it? Or perhaps he could have sold his current consulting practice—including the big client's contract—rather than just changing focus.

In the end, Tony felt he needed a clean break.

To fire his client, I suggested to Tony that he sit down and explain to the client that he had done everything he felt capable of doing for them, that he'd help them find another consultant and help orient the new person, but that he'd be ending the relationship. He did it. It wasn't easy. But soon after that, Tony landed a couple of new, smaller clients with projects in areas he wanted to pursue.

Encouraging Customer Complaints

No business owner likes to get a complaint from a customer. But there's something worse—when customers *don't* complain.

Of course, it's great if all your customers are completely satisfied. But if some of your customers walk away from you unhappy without lettting you know, you're in trouble.

Over the years, I've learned that one of the worst things that can happen to a company is for dissatisfied customers to leave quietly— while still dissatisfied. The damage these customers can inflict on a business is a lot worse than if they had complained directly to you.

Because, believe me, what they don't tell you, they're willing to tell other people—a lot of other people. Studies show a satisfied customer will tell four to five people about a good experience, but an unhappy customer will tell an average of seven to nine others.

If that's not bad enough, reports of a negative experience are twice as likely to affect another person's buying decision as a good report. An unhappy customer becomes a sort of Typhoid Mary, spreading a virus of negative comments about you.

Just as importantly, a customer who never tells you about a problem, never gives you a chance to correct it. Let's say a company's salesperson is very unpleasant to me. If I don't let the manager know, this bad apple can do more damage. If, on the other hand, I take the time and make the effort to complain, the manager can then train,

counsel, or if necessary, fire the salesperson and reduce the damage to the company's reputation.

So instead of cringing when a customer complains, welcome the opportunity. Complaints can be a good way to improve your company and keep customers for life. Take a good, hard look at how you react to complaints and incorporate the following into your customer feedback program:

> **Complaints can be a good way to improve your company and keep customers for life.**

1. Apologize. Saying "We're sorry" is an important first step to letting customers know you care when they have a problem.

2. Don't use the excuse "It's company policy." No phrase is more frustrating to customers than to be told they won't be listened to as an individual. The only policy your company should have is, "We do our very best to solve every problem. We want our customers to be completely satisfied."

3. Recognize a complaint for what it is: an opportunity and not a confrontation.

Only 20-50% of all customers with problems will tell you. Those who do are giving you a chance to improve your company and create an even stronger bond with them. If you handle a complaint well, you can turn a dissatisfied customer into a customer for life.

4. **Encourage feedback.** Make it easy for customers to let you know how they feel. Many companies give customers cards to rate the service and make comments.

5. **Don't mislead and don't overpromise.** Many companies get into trouble because they use misleading or confusing advertising or sales techniques to attract customers. This is bad business, often illegal, and a sure formula for complaints.

6. **Don't blame the customer.** "You ordered the wrong thing." "You didn't follow directions." Even if the customer is not always right, they always believe they are.

When you blame a customer, they see it as a personal attack. Why go back to a company for insults?

7. **Give front-line sales and service people authority.** My friend returned an $8 bath rug to a store and had to get three approvals for a refund. The store's bureaucratic policies lost a customer.

8. **Don't be cheap.** Correcting mistakes is a normal, and necessary, cost of doing business. Trying to save a few dollars but losing a customer is penny wise and pound foolish.

9. **Finally, but most importantly, admit your errors and solve the problem.** Every business makes mistakes; yours will, too. So don't take complaints as personal attacks. Just be determined to get to the root of the problem and make it better for the customer. If something is wrong, fix it.

Keys to Successful Sales

■ **Listen.** No sales skill is more important than the ability to listen. A great sales-person hears what the customer wants—their concerns and priorities. It's tempting to immediately launch in to a sales pitch. But by listening, you can better understand how your product or service meets the customer's needs and desires. If a woman shopping for a car says she likes to drive fast, focus on performance instead of cup holders or safety features. Don't just stick to your standard sales patter or tell the customer what you *think* they'll be interested in.

■ **Ask questions.** You can't listen to a customer unless you get them talking. Ask relevant questions to draw them out: "What do you like in your current car?" "What don't you like?" "What features are the most important?" Don't just ask questions to qualify them as a hot prospect such as, "Are you ready to buy a car today?"

■ **Tell them what they get, not what you do.** Customers don't want to know the ins and outs of your business; they want to know how you meet their needs. There's an old marketing axiom, "Sell benefits, not features."

■ **Be enthusiastic about the benefits of your product or service.** Genuine enthusiasm is contagious. If you truly believe you're offering the customer something worthwhile, you're likely to be an effective salesperson. On the other hand, if you don't believe in what you're selling, you shouldn't be selling it.

■ **Don't oversell.** Customers have some of their worst experiences when a sales-person makes promises that the company won't or can't keep. Yes, it's tempting to land a sale by telling the customer anything they want to hear (especially if you're a salesperson on commission), but that's almost certain to lead to customers being dissatisfied or disappointed.

■ **Be honest.** Lying is not only unethical and possibly illegal, it's a sure-fire way to lose customers and potential customers. You may even find yourself facing a lawsuit.

■ **Compare yourself to (but don't criticize) your competition.** Yes, I know, your product or service is so much better than your competitor's, and they're really not very nice people, either. But disparaging your competition makes you appear malicious. Instead, factually—and positively—compare your benefits and value with those of your competitor.

■ **Don't argue.** You'll never win an argument with a customer. They'll just take their business elsewhere. As soon as you find yourself arguing, stop.

■ **Don't overload your customer.** A few customers will want to know everything about your product or service, but most people just don't have the time or attention span. Concentrate on those aspects of your product or service that are most relevant to your prospect and on your significant competitive advantages.

■ **Build relationships.** One of Rhonda's Rules is: People do business with other people. We all prefer to do business with people we like and trust. Consider the lifetime value of a customer, not just the one-time sale. Often, you might want to make a little less profit to begin an ongoing customer relationship. Get to know your customers; find out about their businesses or families. One way small businesses can compete with the big guys is by building strong customer relationships.

■ **Don't be judgmental.** The guy in the torn jeans may be a millionaire. The petite woman may be the CEO of the biggest company in town. Be careful not to judge people by how they look. Don't judge prospects by how they behave, either. You may think the man who asks detailed questions about a car's features is a more serious shopper than the woman who just wants to know the price, but the woman may be the customer who's ready to whip out the checkbook.

Leading Your Team

Who Do I Want to Work With?

Nothing affects your day-to-day work life more than the people you work with. If you're going to run your own business, try to work with people you like.

You may not be eager to work with anyone. When I started my first business, I remember saying, "I don't want to work for or with anyone." Over time, however, that changed.

Even if you work by yourself out of your home, you'll work with other people: customers, vendors, advisors. Perhaps you work with them over the phone or through email rather than in person, but they can still make or break your day. You may even find yourself "working" with people you never consider co-workers, like the after-school babysitter who watches your kids while you work in your home office. Yikes! Suddenly you're spending your time with a tongue-pierced sixteen-year-old, discussing what to wear to the prom. How did this happen?

As you structure and grow your business, carefully consider who you want to work with and why. Examine whether their goals, work styles, and values fit with yours.

Consider a few of the types of people you can have as part of your total team:

■ **Partners.** Want someone to share every up and down, every gain and loss? Get a partner. However, remember that partners own the business, too. Your future is tied together, even if they are only a minority partner. Make sure you spend a lot of time with a potential partner. Do they share your business goals? Are they willing and able to work as hard as you? Get a written agreement and review it with a lawyer. Have clear-cut definitions of responsibilities and authority. A messy "divorce" from a business partner is as difficult as any other kind of divorce.

> Suddenly you're spending your time with a tongue-pierced sixteen-year-old, discussing what to wear to the prom. How did this happen?

■ **Investors.** You are married to your investors for the life of your business, so proceed carefully. You may feel lucky to get anyone's money, but if you have a fearful, intrusive, or controlling investor, you may soon regret taking their money. Have they invested in other companies before? If so, speak to the entrepreneurs who've worked with them. What are their financial and business motivations? Are those goals a good fit with yours? How actively do they engage with the companies they invest in?

175

■ **Employees.** On a day-to-day basis, the people you'll work with most are your employees. Even if you start your company as a sole proprietorship, as you grow, you'll need employees. You'll gain the most—in satisfaction as well as in revenue—if you hire well, manage thoughtfully, help your employees continually develop, and reward them appropriately.

■ **Customers.** You may not feel like you have very much choice about who your customer is, but you have more control than you imagine. Target the types of clientele you'll enjoy working with as well as those who are most financially rewarding.

■ **A "Business Buddy."** The best source of advice for an entrepreneur is another entrepreneur. For years, my friend Jennifer (another management consultant) and I would call each other often to discuss pricing, client problems, proposals. If you have a number of friends in business, you can get together regularly to discuss your current projects and marketing approaches and to solve problems that you're facing.

■ **Entrepreneurs' organizations.** Business groups are a great source of support, referrals, information, and sometimes even new clients. In addition to entrepreneurs' groups, seek out trade associations. Members of these can help you cope with your industry-specific issues.

■ **Family members.** Many people choose to work with members of their family or rely on their family for advice and support. Some entrepreneurs are fortunate to have this work well. But working with family members puts a strain on both your personal relationships and your business. No matter how supportive, spouses and children can lose patience hearing nitty-gritty details about your work. And do you really want to tell them when things aren't going well, since you know they'll be worried?

Going from Doing to Leading

My business is growing, and I'm having a tough time. Not for all the usual reasons such as increased expenses, hiring new employees, or developing additional sales channels. I'm dealing with all of that, but those issues are a piece of cake compared to the real challenge: having other people do things I'm used to doing myself. It's tough to go from do-er to lead-er, from first violinist to conductor.

Entrepreneurs all face this issue as their businesses expand. In order to grow your business, you need to hand over responsibilities to others: whether routine administrative tasks, key sales calls, or critical product development. You don't have time to do these things and guide the development of a growing company.

It's really tough to let go. After all, we started and grew our businesses ourselves. We're good at what we do. We have pride in what we've created. Our livelihood is at stake. And, let's face it, we're people who are used to being in control. People who have pride in their work—and do it well—are naturally fearful that others won't do it as well.

Deborah used to be my office manager. A few years ago, I promoted her to Academic Marketing Director, and we hired someone else to take over most of Deborah's tasks. She experienced the same discomfort about letting go of her responsibilities that I'm experiencing now. "I felt an emotional ownership of the systems I created; I was anxious about anyone doing it differently."

How did Deborah learn to go from office manager to crackerjack marketing pro? How did she navigate the transition? What could she teach me about my changing role in an expanding company?

> **If I want good people to take over some of my work, I'm going to have to allow them to use their brains, not just their hands.**

"Recognize you're going to have a certain amount of frustration," Deborah advised me. "But as long as the work gets done and gets done well, you have to keep focused on why you're making the change. Remind yourself why you're not doing those tasks any longer. Stay focused on the stuff that needs you now. And remember, if you can't let go, you're going to lose good employees."

That's an important thing to keep in mind: good employees chafe under constant

177

supervision and second-guessing. If I want—and need—good people to take over some of my work, I'm going to have to allow them to use their brains, not just their hands. If I give them a job, I'm going to have to allow them to do it.

This means I have to learn to be comfortable—more comfortable than I am already—with employees doing things differently than I would. I don't mean allowing them to do things worse than I would, just differently. After all, not everything has to be done my way to be the right way.

Of course, this doesn't mean that I, or you, can just hand off tasks to employees. You have to train employees in specific tasks. They have to know the standards you want maintained, the methods you need utilized, and each task's purpose and importance. Of course, they have to be told all relevant details such as budgets and deadlines.

It's okay to set limits: schedule time for review and feedback, especially when employees are just learning. And let them know which decisions still need your approval.

Then you have to let them do their jobs. Most importantly, let them know they're being given responsibility because you know they can handle it, not just because they're a warm body. Most people try to live up to the trust they're shown.

Be gentle on yourself, too. Remember, you're also learning a new task: how to be the leader of a growing organization. You're going through a transition—from do-er to lead-er—and all transitions take time.

Finally, recognize that while your role is changing, you're still the boss. You're the one who sets the overall vision, direction, and standards of your company. You're still in charge.

A Field Guide to Advisors

It seems the minute you start a business, everyone gives you advice. Suddenly, your unemployed brother-in-law Sheldon, a failure at everything, is now a business expert. "You know what you should do," Sheldon says, cornering you at a family gathering, "sell everything half-price. That'll pack the customers in." Right, Sheldon. The customers will come but the profits will go.

Unsolicited advice doesn't stop when your business grows. In fact, it may only get worse. Ask the head of any Fortune 500 company, and they'll tell you they get a stream of suggestions from stockholders, market analysts, and people sitting next to them on airplanes.

It's a jungle out there. What you need is Rhonda's Field Guide to Advice Givers, a handy tool for helping determine what advice to listen to and what to ignore:

■ **Experienced industry businesspeople.** Listen to these folks! Novice entrepreneurs often believe they know better than those who've been around a long time. After all, the old fogies have been too dumb to figure out changes in the market, technology, or some other aspect you're about to seize on, right? Well, yes and no. The realities of an industry don't go away overnight. So listen closely even if you don't follow their advice to the letter.

■ **Potential investors.** A few years ago, I was raising money for a business and went through a series of meetings with various venture capitalists. Each one immediately knew the key to making the business successful, and each one's key was different, of course. With potential investors, listen carefully to glean whatever insights are of value, nod while they speak, and when you leave the room, weigh their advice against your own knowledge. Just because these people are rich doesn't mean they know better than you.

> **Customers can give you ideas for new or improved products or services. Ask for their feedback.**

■ **Investors.** Your investors are, in essence, your partners, so their advice has to be given serious consideration. In some cases, they call the shots. But with investors, the advice-giving and advice-taking process should become a two-way street. It's part of your job to help your investors know enough about your business so that when

179

they give suggestions, they can be informed and well-reasoned.

■ **Customers.** You'd better be listening to your customers because they're the ones who determine whether you stay in business. It's tempting to dismiss the advice of customers because it often comes in the form of complaints. Instead, look for ways to gather just as many insights and suggestions from customers in positive situations. Customers can give you ideas for new or improved products or services. Ask for their feedback.

■ **Employees.** Your employees can provide a rich vein of insight and advice for your company. Ask for their advice and ideas; listen to them carefully. When you can, act on their suggestions. Obviously, not every idea can be implemented. The key is to create an environment where employees know their advice is welcome, valued, and given a careful hearing. Employees often know the ins and outs of some aspects of a business better than the owner.

■ **Board and advisory committee members.** Board members of corporations have legal authority over that company, so decisions of board members must be followed. That means it's critical for you to listen to the advice and concerns of all board members. Advisory committees are set up specifically to get the advice of people you respect. You've asked these people to give you their time and lend their name to your enterprise. So give their advice the attention it deserves.

■ **Friends and family.** The people who are closest to you have their own motivations and their own fears when they give you advice. When your spouse suggests you'd be more productive if you didn't work in the living room, they may just want to get your stuff out of their way. When your mother suggests it's time you close your business and look for a job, it may be that she's uncomfortable seeing you struggle. Be careful—and be gentle—in how you respond to the advice of friends and family. You may find it's best to seek advice only on certain clearly defined issues ("Should I wear this suit to the meeting?") rather than asking open-ended questions ("Do you think I'm doing the right thing?").

I Get By with a Little Help from My Friends

When I consider what I'm thankful for, I start with my family, my friends, and my good health. But somewhere high on my list are the people who have given me guidance in my business and career. Most of these have been informal relationships, but for two of my companies, I've set up "advisory committees."

A group of advisors is one of the most valuable assets an entrepreneur can have. They bring experience, skills, contacts. An added benefit is that most members of my advisory committees have become my close friends as well.

Most people, of course, like the idea of an advisory committee, but don't know how to form one—who to ask, what to ask of them, how to reward them.

First, recognize the difference between an advisory committee and a board of directors. A board of directors is a legal entity, with legal responsibilities and liabilities. You have to be very careful about who you choose as board members because they control your company. If you have investors, especially venture capitalists, they'll expect to be on the board.

An advisory committee, on the other hand, is informal. Advisors have no legal authority and assume no liability. Because the committee is informal, there are no set rules, such as how often they have to meet, how many people must be on it, and so on. You can structure the advisory committee to meet your needs and their schedules.

> **A group of advisors is one of the most valuable assets an entrepreneur can have. They bring experience, skills, contacts.**

In fact, your advisory committee can be so informal, you don't even have to call it a "committee." You can just have a few people who've agreed to let you turn to them for advice. But I've found that forming an official entity creates a closer bond between you and your advisors. If you've asked the right people, they'll consider your request carefully before accepting, and when they do, they'll take their role seriously and be even more committed to your success.

Who should you ask? First of all, people you respect. The point of advisors is to give advice. So look for people with good judgment, experience, wisdom. Ideally, of course, you'll find wise folks who are also seasoned entrepreneurs or from your industry. Be careful when choosing potential investors. They can be terrific sources of advice and possibly money, but if they later choose not to invest, for whatever reason, it can send a negative message to other potential investors. I'd be very wary of asking potential customers, employees, or, naturally, competitors.

You don't need many advisors; in fact I've never had more than five or six. And you don't have to ask everybody at once. You can add advisors as you progress.

How often should you meet? Perhaps never. With one company, I never held even one meeting of my advisory committee. I just called on individual members when I had specific concerns. One member helped me build my financial statements, another helped shape our marketing efforts, others introduced me to contacts or suggested conferences to attend. All read my business plan, provided me with real-life insights, and would return my phone calls when I needed help on a particular problem.

I was careful not to call too often. Advisors aren't signing up for a job. I'd keep them informed about what the company was up to, sending them emails, announcements, and inviting them to company events. I'd have lunch with each of them about once a quarter. But I respected their time.

The advisory committee for my new company has met once. But I've met with individual members many times and call some fairly frequently.

What do you pay them? Not cash. Most people you want as advisors aren't motivated by money; they're motivated to help you succeed. For a fast-growing incorporated business, granting stock to advisory committee members is the most appropriate form of compensation. That way, they'll share in your eventual success. Of course, make sure your advisors get any company trinkets such as t-shirts, coffee mugs, pens.

Building a company can be lonely work. You'll find advisory committee members can be a great source of help and comfort. They can give you guidance, contacts, friendship. I know I'm thankful for each and every one of my advisors, past and present.

Partnership Tips

Before you enter into a partnership, be sure you've taken care of the following:

■ **Draw up a legal partnership agreement.** Be clear about the ownership division, who owns what percentage of the company, how decisions will be made, how disputes will be settled. If your company is organized as an LLC, make clear how profits and losses will be distributed.

■ **Write up a buy/sell agreement.** With the help of an attorney, figure out how ownership will be transferred if one of you wants to leave or buy the other out, or if something happens to one of you. This is **critically** important. Decide now how you will handle things if your personal relationship falls apart.

■ **Together clarify your company and personal goals.** While these may change over time, it's important to sit down and decide how big you want the company to become, what kinds of products or services you're going to offer, how much money you'll take out of the company, and how much you'll leave in for growth. Make certain you both share the same vision and goals for the company.

■ **Develop an internal business plan.** Together, write up a business plan for your internal use, projecting out for at least 3–5 years. This helps to make certain you have a shared concept of the company and understanding of the company's strategy, activities, and priorities.

■ **Assign responsibilities.** While the partners may want to work on everything together for the first few months of a business, over time each partner will have their own areas of prime responsibility. Clarify who has responsibility and authority over which aspects of the company.

■ **Establish regular partnership meetings.** Once the business is up and running, it will be difficult to find the time to communicate with each other regularly, but it's critical for success. Set regularly scheduled meetings to discuss business issues and make certain you are communicating.

■ **Be polite.** Say "please" and "thank you" and "I appreciated that." A partner is an easy person to take for granted. A little bit of courtesy can make daily life a lot more pleasant.

Working with Friends

Working with friends can be an enjoyable, highly successful experience. After all, you know, trust, and respect each other. But working with friends is always tricky. You may each see the relationship differently. While you may think your friend appreciates the work you've sent their way, they may feel like they're doing you a favor. If their work is unsatisfactory, it may be hard to complain.

So take steps to be extra cautious when working with a friend:

■ **Be professional in your dealings and establish a client/consultant relationship right from the start.** Make it clear that work time is for work; social time is for socializing. Try not to mix the two in the same phone call or meeting.

■ **Clearly establish fees, timetables, and expectations.** Sign your normal contractor agreement or letter. Who pays for expenses? The more direct you are, the less room for misunderstandings that can seriously strain your relationship.

■ **If a friend is doing work for you for free, first determine if they will do this on a "time available" basis or if they will do it to meet your deadline.** Don't ask—or allow—a friend to work for free if you have a strict timetable. Force them to accept some payment, however low, because you'll be making demands on their time, and make your deadline clear.

■ **Communicate with each other throughout the project.** Establish when and where you can call about work—day or evening, home or office. Even if you're used to talking to your friend at 11 p.m., they may not want to discuss business at that hour.

■ **If you can afford it, pay your friend's regular rates.** If you can't and you've hired your friend because of special rates they've offered you, express gratitude and also realize they might not treat you the same as full-fare clients.

■ **Pay your friend promptly.** If you owe a friend money, it could add a great deal of tension to your personal relationship.

All in the Family?

"My cousin's looking for a job."

Terrifying words? Not to me. While most employers dread the idea of hiring someone's relative, I've had (mostly) good experiences with nepotism.

Don't get me wrong, hiring relatives is tricky. Family spats can carry over to the workplace. Other employees may feel that a relative gets special treatment, and a host of problems can crop up. As a result, most companies adopt policies against hiring more than one member of a family.

But there's another side: great employees often have great relatives. Sticking to a strict rule that you'll never hire someone's relative may keep you from getting the best employee out there. After all, if you have an employee with outstanding work habits and intelligence, why wouldn't you want to hire a brother with the same qualities?

Of course, just as with any hiring decision, you have to use good judgment when hiring relatives. In fact, I tend to apply higher standards when dealing with family members, especially my own. Here are a few other things to keep in mind:

■ **Don't hire someone's relative just because they "need" a job.** You're running a business, not a social service agency. More importantly, there's a good chance your brother-in-law Sheldon "needs" a job because he's not very good at holding one down. Better to stare your sister in the face now and say, "Sheldon doesn't have the qualifications we need," than to have a big family blowup when you later have to fire him.

> **Great employees often have great relatives.**

■ **Ask specific, detailed questions about the relative's qualifications before you agree to interview them.** People rarely see their own relatives clearly, especially their children. They're likely to say, "He's a wonderful guy" or "She's so smart." That doesn't tell you if they've had relevant work experience or training. Always leave yourself an out: "I'm not sure Chris has the computer skills we need."

■ **Don't have relatives report to one another or work too closely together.** It's one thing to have siblings work for the same company in different areas, but if they work together on the same project, you're likely to see old family patterns emerge. If something goes wrong, don't be surprised if you hear, "He started it." "No, she started it."

■ **Watch out when hiring spouses! Years ago, I hired Arthur, the husband of one of my best employees.** That turned out very well; Arthur's still with me more than five years later. But spouses or domestic partners working together can present a number of difficulties. There are logistical issues, as vacations or family emergencies may leave you doubly short-handed, and there are behavioral issues: a terrific worker may suddenly change dramatically with a spouse around. In a new or small company, having both breadwinners work for the same company puts a lot of stress on a family and their budget, meaning more stress on you.

■ **Be careful about working with your own spouse.** I know of a few businesses where husband and wife successfully work side by side all day. But I've had a number of clients where either the business or the relationship (or both) ended up on the rocks. Tread carefully!

■ **Be toughest on your own close relatives.** I'm old fashioned enough to think it's good for the boss's kid (or niece, nephew) to have to work their way up, and it's good for other employees to know that the boss's brother doesn't get a free ride. Before you hire a relative, make it clear that they're going to have to prove themselves and will be held to the highest standards. And never supervise one of your relatives directly.

No matter what, never, ever play favorites. Make sure the rules apply to all—employees must do their jobs well. Otherwise, they're fired. Even your mother.

Getting Ready to Hire Others

Entrepreneurs like to be in charge. You don't start your own company to have someone else call the shots; I certainly didn't. But if you want to grow your business, you're going to have to hire others. If you want employees who are productive and motivated, then you're going to have to allow them a certain measure of control. You won't be able to call all the shots all the time.

While it's hard enough to get used to the idea of having others make decisions in your company, the problem is exacerbated because many entrepreneurs have never had positive role models of how to be a good manager. Having a string of bad bosses gives little preparation for being a good one.

Many of us have to spend time learning to be a good boss. We may excel at what we do, but being a boss isn't a natural skill.

The old-fashioned concept of being a boss meant issuing orders and having others follow. If we're honest, this idea probably still appeals to a lot of us. Many entrepreneurs hire their first employees with the idea that they'll do a lot of the dirty work the entrepreneur no longer has time for. They'll be an extra set of hands, not extra brains.

If we want our companies to grow, we need extra brains, no matter how smart we are. So we have to allow our employees to think, not just to carry out tasks. This requires leadership, not just management. So how do we become leaders, not mere managers?

First, while this may seem self-evident, hire well. Just as it's easier to be a good parent if you have good kids, it's much easier to be a good boss if you have good employees. You can't choose your kids, but you can choose your employees. In the press of business, we're often tempted to hire anyone we can get, but you'll be much more confident sharing authority with someone you consider capable and trustworthy.

> **Many of us have to learn how to be a good boss. We may excel at what we do, but being a boss isn't a natural skill.**

Next, never give someone responsibility without also giving them authority. If you're going to give someone a job, allow them to do it; don't make them come back to you for every decision. This means you have to learn to be comfortable with people making some decisions that are different from those you'd make. Learn to recognize that some decisions are just different, not wrong. Not everything has to be done your way to be the right way.

Sometimes, however, employees will indeed make what turns out to be a wrong decision. How do good bosses handle that? They spend time with the employee learning why a decision was wrong and how to avoid it the next time rather than rehashing the history and looking for blame. And they lighten up. Hey, we've all made a lot of wrong decisions.

Many bosses dole out information as infrequently as bonuses. As a result, employees often don't have enough data to do their jobs well. You can't just hand off tasks to others; you've got to sit down and spend enough time so they know all the relevant details: the project's purpose, customer pressures, deadlines, budgets. Let them know their limits: can they deal with the customer directly? How much can they spend without coming back to you? Be clear on the importance and priority of each task.

Most importantly, let people know they're being given responsibility because you know they can handle it, not just because they're a warm body. Most people try to live up to the trust they're shown.

Finally, recognize that while you want to be a good boss, you're still the boss. You're the one who sets the overall vision, direction, and standards of your company. Organizations need leaders, and employees will respect leaders who respect them.

Building a Virtual Staff

Do you work alone? If so, you juggle a variety of tasks at the same time. One minute you're the marketing director, the next you're the computer specialist, then you're in charge of accounting. How are you ever going to do the stuff you actually went into business for—the core functions that make money?

Take heart. Just because you have a small business, even a one-person business, doesn't mean you can't have a "staff" at your beck and call. Consider outsourcing. I worked alone for fourteen years and during that time, I found ways of building an infrastructure of outsourced consultants and professionals to assist me.

Don't go it all alone. Find capable professionals, consultants, and assistants and treat them as your virtual staff. *Voila!* You're now the CEO of a great team.

Here's how to build your virtual team:

1. **Identify the key functions you need to have addressed.** At the top of this list is accounting and bookkeeping. Next, you probably need help with technology, and you may be smart to find someone to help you with marketing. Of course, it's always advisable to have a good lawyer. If you're very busy, you may need someone to run errands or help with mailings.

2. **Evaluate whether some "positions" can be filled by companies instead of individuals.** For instance, I recommend purchasing the upgraded tech support for your most important software, especially for the first few months or year. That way, the company's tech support becomes your in-house tech specialist.

3. **Recruit service providers.** Interview a number of potential providers just as you would interview applicants for any job opening—discuss their fees, their services, and your business. Network with other business owners to get recommendations for appropriate and excellent service providers.

4. **Keep your virtual staff on call.** Line up your providers before you need them. If possible, give them a small assignment before you have a big project or big problem.

5. **Recognize this is going to cost money.** Sure, you're going to have to pay these providers for work you're now doing yourself. But sit down and consider whether your time is better spent finding more clients or doing your own bookkeeping or website building.

Are Two Better Than One?

Small companies used to be called "Mom and Pop" businesses. While that term may conjure up a picture of a couple happily working by each other's sides, the reality is that running a company with your spouse or partner can strain both the business and the relationship. Take steps to improve your chance of success.

Think through the ramifications:

■ **Financial security.** Your family income will be entirely dependent on one business. As a family, you may have greater financial stability when each spouse brings in an income from a different source.

■ **Time off.** It may be difficult for both of you to take vacations or other time away together. In a family emergency, who will take care of the business?

■ **Impact on other staff.** Few staff members will tell you when it's your spouse who messed up the accounts or alienated a customer. Both you and your staff will want to protect your relationship, sometimes at the expense of the business.

■ **Inability to escape problems.** What will you talk about over dinner? Or on your rare days off? Most of us want our home lives to provide a certain respite from our work and our work to give us some change from our home life.

Develop a written partnership agreement that includes provisions for:

■ **Ownership.** Be clear about who owns what percent of the company. Understand the legal and tax ramifications as well as the emotional aspects of legally sharing the business.

■ **Decision making.** Discuss and delineate each person's area of responsibility and decision-making authority. Who gets final say?

■ **Contingencies.** What happens if the relationship fails? Which partner, if necessary, leaves the company? How will the value be decided and distributed? If you're married (or even co-habitating), understand how divorce laws can impact the future of your business. In community property states, you may have to sell or close the business to divide the assets.

■ **Employee status.** Delineate the "employment" terms for each spouse, such as pay, time off, ability to quit. This is particularly important if one spouse is just "helping out." Will they be able to take time off whenever they choose or be expected to show up to work every day?

Hiring Your First Employee

During many of my years in business, I worked alone. But one of the best decisions I ever made was to hire my first employee.

Hiring your first employee is financially, logistically, and psychologically challenging. But a question I often ask people who've been self-employed for a number of years is, "Are you creating a business or are you creating an income?"

Now, there's nothing wrong with building a business that provides personal income; the overwhelming majority of entrepreneurs do just that. But at some point, you may decide you want to build a company that multiplies the value of your knowledge and skills, creating something of ongoing worth. That means getting help.

How do you know when it's time to hire your first employee?

Most business owners wait until they just can't handle all the work they have. This means you're going to be frazzled long before you get assistance. Even worse, during the time you're overworked, you're probably going to turn away—or turn off—customers. And you're almost certainly going to have stopped prospecting for new clients.

Instead, ask yourself: "How much time can I free up if I get some assistance? How much more money can I make?"

Getting help doesn't mean immediately going out and getting a full-time employee.

You can start with a part-time worker or even outsource some tasks. One of the biggest time-gobblers, for instance, is handling financial matters—generating invoices, paying bills, entering data. Can you find a reliable, trustworthy outside bookkeeper to do most of this for you? Just think how much easier it will be when it's time to prepare your taxes!

My first "employee" was a part-time administrative assistant. Wow! Suddenly, instead of waiting in line at the post office or packing up boxes to send clients, I could actually be doing my work.

> Recognize that you have to relinquish some control if you want your employee to be effective and satisfied.

But it also meant I had someone working out of my home, someone I had to tell where I was when I was out of the office. That was a difficult adjustment. But, to be honest, it kept me more focused for more hours of the day. And that meant I made more money, even though I was paying some one else as well.

I was fortunate that my first assistant, Ann, was a joy to have around. Together we started figuring out what the job really entailed and how I could use her to maximum advantage.

One lesson I learned from Ann was the importance of hiring someone you really click with, especially for your first employee. That doesn't mean looking for a friend, but finding someone with whom you can communicate easily. You want to feel comfortable having this person in your home, small office, or store.

Before you look for your first employee, write down all the things you might want them to do. This list is likely to be way too long, unrealistic, or contain the wrong job duties. The two biggest mistakes:

1. **Handing over *too much* authority**

2. **Not giving over *any* authority**

Recognize that you have to relinquish some control if you want your employee to be effective and satisfied. No one is going to be a miracle worker, solving all your problems.

Prioritize what you'd like done. Be realistic. You're not going to find someone who loves data entry and who also excels at sales calls. Those are two different personality types. When choosing employees, here's an important rule: hire for attitude; train for skills.

To find applicants, start by networking with other business owners and through professional and entrepreneurial organizations. And don't forget the classifieds, in newspapers or online. I found Ann by running an ad in my local newspaper.

Hiring an employee is an investment in your business. Like all investments, it means giving up something now for greater rewards later. Yes, you'll have to take some money out of your own income. Yes, you'll have to set aside some time for training. Yes, you'll have to give up some privacy. But in the long run, you can build a bigger, more profitable business with the help of others than by trying to go it all alone.

Learning to Be a Boss

Years ago, I inherited a difficult secretary who always left work early. I was only twenty-eight, and she was a sassy New Yorker who could make mincemeat out of me. One day I finally got up the nerve to confront her. She replied defiantly, "I'll stay until 5 now, but once daylight savings time ends, I'm leaving before dark." At 5 p.m., it was perfectly safe in downtown San Francisco, even in the dark.

I lost sleep that night deciding whether I could bear to confront her again. But the next day, I took her aside and said firmly, "The office hours are 9 a.m. to 5 p.m. If you don't like it, quit. If you don't work 'til 5, you'll be fired." She quit two weeks later, and I was glad to see her go.

I'd like to say that after this, my confidence as a boss blossomed, but it wouldn't be true. It took time, lots of time.

Being a boss is tough. It's incredibly demanding, but it's often given little thought. Being a boss is like being a parent: you must inspire, lead, motivate, discipline, and reward. Just as we wrongly expect people to know how to be a parent once a baby is placed in their arms, we also expect people to know how to be a boss once their first employee is hired.

What makes it harder is many people who start their own businesses have never had a good boss as a role model.

Bad bosses seem to fall into one of two extremes: they are either too lenient or too tough. But those aren't the real problems. You get into trouble as a boss, just as you do as a parent, when you fail at five basic requirements: setting standards, fairness, listening, respecting, and rewarding.

> **Being a boss is like being a parent: you must inspire, lead, motivate, discipline, and reward.**

■ **Set standards.** The best way to set standards is by being an example to others. Employees resent being held to higher standards than the boss. Clearly state your expectations, and try to be consistent. Develop and distribute clear policies. Even a small company should have a basic manual outlining benefits, holidays, sick leave, and such. Let employees know on what basis they will be judged and stick to those.

■ **Be fair.** Make certain your standards are reasonable and fair, and that the goals you set are actually reachable. Don't change the rules constantly; we've all had bosses who one day want things one way and the next another. Be careful not to play favorites, and never use benefits to manipulate employees. A company I worked for gave longer maternity leaves to female employees that management liked and "punished" women it didn't like with shorter leaves. This is a sure way to gain both an unhappy workforce and a lawsuit.

■ **Listen.** Learn to talk *with* and not just *to* your employees. Many employers fail to use one of their most important resources—their employees' minds. Enlist their suggestions and set goals together. Have problem-solving sessions where employees help devise solutions to company problems. Make it clear, however, that decisions usually lie with you. Before reprimanding an employee, seek their explanation of why they failed to perform. Share information with your employees so they understand some of the constraints on the company.

■ **Respect.** Recognize the unique skills and talents of each person who works with you. Demonstrate to them that you believe they are capable of doing their job, even if it takes some time for them to learn. People generally live up to the trust—or mistrust—that others show them. As employees gain in experience, allow them to make independent judgments and decisions.

■ **Reward.** Everyone wants acknowledgment for a job well done. Give credit to all employees who do their jobs well and reward those who perform exceptionally. Rewards don't have to be only money; find fun or creative ways to congratulate people publicly. Recognize and reward teamwork, not just individual performance. Never criticize or discipline employees in front of others.

Being a boss is a skill that you have to learn—and relearn. Just like any other business skill, perfecting it takes practice, thought, and input from others. Don't be embarrassed to take classes or read books to improve your "boss" skills. After all, the bestselling book for decades was Dr. Spock's *Baby and Child Care,* a book that helped people learn something that's supposed to come naturally.

Attracting, Hiring, and Retaining Great Employees

It's a jungle out there. The future of your company depends on the quality of your employees. Yet, it's a challenge to find and retain outstanding workers. This situation isn't going to change anytime soon.

In the U.S., we're in the midst of a demographic baby bust. There weren't a lot of babies born twenty-odd years ago, leading to a smaller overall labor pool today. That means there's lots of competition for the best employees.

To stay competitive, you have to continually sharpen your skills in attracting, hiring, and retaining employees.

Attracting Great Employees

■ **Give yourself time.** You won't always know in advance that you have an opening, but when possible, start the candidate-hunting process as early as possible. The more time you have, the less you'll feel pressured to hire an unqualified candidate just to fill the position. It's better to leave a job open than to hire the wrong person.

■ **Create an ongoing recruitment campaign.** Just as you need an ongoing marketing campaign to attract customers, you need an ongoing campaign to attract employees, especially if you have a lot of employees and natural turnover. In a small business, that doesn't mean constantly running ads; it means developing a network of referral sources, reminding everyone in your company to be on the lookout for great employees, and being visible in the community.

■ **Be creative in your ads.** When you place a help-wanted ad, create as much attention and interest as possible. Use unusual and creative phrases, but be honest. I always stress that we are a dog-friendly office, which increases the number of applicants.

■ **Be in the game on salary and benefits.** As a small company, you may not be able to pay more than big companies or give as many benefits, but you'd better be fairly competitive. You can't be so far apart that any applicant would feel like a fool for accepting your job. Offer creative benefits. We give employees their birthday as a paid holiday.

■ **Be flexible.** Many applicants want flexible work schedules to avoid rush hour or to be home by 4 p.m. with the kids. You'll have a larger applicant pool if you challenge yourself to think of ways to offer applicants more flexibility.

■ **Get a reputation as a great place to work.** Good employees know they're in demand; they're going to be very picky.

195

Sure, all applicants look at tangible rewards such as salary and benefits. But in the long run, what attracts the best employees (and encourages current employees to recruit others) is building a company that's a great place to work.

Hiring Great Employees

■ **Hire for attitude, train for skills.** Don't get hung up looking for specific skills, such as knowledge of a particular computer program. If you find a smart and willing person, you can send them to a class. Obviously, if you need someone to fly a plane, you need an experienced pilot, but most tasks can be taught.

■ **Hire the un-usual.** Increase your applicant pool by expanding your vision of a typical employee. Do you usually hire young people? Try recruiting retirees. Have you considered more actively seeking people with disabilities? Sometimes the best employees don't look like the ones you already have.

■ **Develop your interviewing skills.** When you're interviewing applicants, don't do all the talking! Many employers are as nervous as prospective employees when they're in a job interview and talk too much. Most of the time the candidate should be talking, not you. Have a few questions prepared in advance; it's not fair to just say, "So, tell me about yourself." Ask what about the job appealed to them, what skills they're particularly good at, what about their last job they didn't like. Ask some questions that give you a sense of the applicant as a person, but be careful not to ask questions that are illegal.

It's perfectly legal to ask about hobbies, interests, and what a candidate's long-term goals are.

■ **Check references.** I'm always surprised by employers who never bother to check references. Even if you have no reason to doubt the honesty of an applicant, you can learn a lot by checking references. Don't look at the reference check merely as a way to confirm employment but also as a way to learn how to work more effectively with your new employee. Some of the questions I asked included, "What kind of training, either for skills or for attitude, would you suggest to make the applicant an even better employee?" "What job duties required you giving more direction than others?" "What duties did the candidate particularly enjoy or do well?"

■ **Act fast.** Good applicants don't stick around long. If you see someone you really like, be prepared to decide and make an offer. But don't ever hire just because you have a job to fill. It's better to keep a position open than to be stuck with the wrong person.

Retaining Great Employees

■ **Recognize achievement.** Everyone wants to be appreciated. When an employee does a good job, let them know you noticed. Say "Thank you" a lot. Find ways to recognize employees who do their jobs well on a day-to-day basis as well as those who accomplish something unusual or significant.

■ **Reward.** As important as it is for employees to get verbal recognition for their contributions, it's also great for them to get tangible rewards. This doesn't always have to be a major salary increase or bonus; sometimes just an unexpected treat can go a long way. For instance, when a public relations firm in Houston signed a major new client, the owner rewarded the staff for all their hard work by taking them to a fancy lunch at a nearby mall and then gave them each $100 to spend.

■ **Give salary increases.** Your employees know what other people in similar jobs earn. They know the salaries you're giving to new employees and what their co-workers make. Don't wait for an employee to become dissatisfied with their pay and ask you for a raise; they may just leave.

■ **Be realistic in your expectations.** It's human nature to focus on what an employee is missing rather than what an employee offers. For example, I once knew an attorney who had a terrific secretary; she easily handled complex legal matters and anticipated his every need. But she arrived late for work, and he hounded her until she quit. Let's face it: no one's perfect (not even you!).

■ **Create a "blame-free atmosphere."** Your very best employees want to be able to use their judgment and their brains. They'll thrive in an environment where they know they can make decisions and take chances without getting berated if something goes wrong.

■ **Share.** Employees feel a stronger sense of ownership when they know the company's overall goals and strategy. Share information. Also, look for ways for employees to benefit financially from the company's long-term financial success, whether in the form of profit sharing or with some equity interest in the business.

> **To stay competitive, you have to continually sharpen your skills in attracting, hiring, and retaining employees.**

■ **Enable employees to grow.** After a while, the best employees get bored doing the same job. If the only way they can grow is by leaving, then they will. Instead, invest in your employees. Help them take classes, learn new skills, take on new responsibilities.

■ **Install a "revolving door."** No matter what you do, some employees will want to move on. Be supportive of employees' personal goals. Make them feel welcome to return. Stay in touch with them; invite them to holiday parties. They'll be more likely to return or send other potential employees your way.

Who Do You Want on Your Team?

It takes many types of players to make a winning team—in baseball or in business. What kinds of players do you want on your team?

- **Babe Ruth.** Aims for the fences. People admire and follow him; he's larger than life. He wins big, but also loses big. Remember, the Babe had 714 homers, but 1330 strike-outs. One Ruth is a star; a team filled with Ruths is a disaster.

- **Cal Ripken.** Shows up and gets the job done. Ripken played in the most consecutive games ever. He doesn't hold any hitting records, but he batted in over 1600 runs. Remember what Woody Allen said, "Eighty percent of success is showing up."

- **Jackie Robinson.** Blazes new trails. His skills are great enough to enable him to change the rules, and he's willing to make the many personal sacrifices that go along with being first. He makes the future possible for others. He's a hero.

- **Sandy Koufax.** Seeks perfection. Koufax, my favorite player of all time, is arguably the best pitcher in the history of baseball. But perfection comes at a price, and perfectionists often flame out. Koufax's career was cut short by injuries.

- **Don Larsen.** Shines for a moment. Larsen is the only person who ever pitched a perfect game in the World Series, but overall he had a mediocre career. But for one brief period—or assignment—he can be a superstar.

- **Rickey Henderson.** Makes the most of what he has. As the all-time leader in stolen bases, Henderson didn't need to hit homers to make a contribution. In the history of baseball, only Ty Cobb scored more runs than Henderson.

- **The Alou Brothers.** They stick with family. Matty, Felipe, and Jesus Alou all played in the same outfield together. Together, they were stronger than any one Alou alone.

- **The Mascot.** He's the cheerleader, helping everyone refocus their attention when things go bad. This is, after all, supposed to be fun.

Making the Most of Employees

When you run a small company, you can't afford to waste resources. Yet many business owners often waste one of their most valuable assets: their employees.

I'm always surprised when I encounter an employer who views having employees as a necessary evil to be endured rather than a resource to be developed. If you waste the intelligence, energy, or skills of employees, it's just like throwing money out the window.

The surest way to get the most from employees is by treating each with respect. Your attitude toward the people you hire goes a long way in determining their attitude about the job. Remember, they aren't just "human resources," they're people.

Employees want their minds and judgment to be valued. No matter what kind of work a person does, they like to have a sense that their opinion and input counts. When you allow your employees to think about how to solve problems, not just carry out specific tasks, you can unleash an amazing amount of creativity and energy. To do so, however, they'll need information, patience, and a sense that they won't be "punished" if they make an honest mistake.

To make your employees more productive, remember:

■ **Hire well.** If an employee is smart and capable they'll help your business grow. Hire for attitude and adaptability, rather than merely for skills. Look for the ability to learn quickly, common sense, good work habits, and a willingness to take on any task.

■ **Train.** It's hard to take time away from your own work to train someone else, but you'll save far more time in the long run. If you have to, train after regular work hours when you can give the new employee your undivided attention. In a small business, employees should be able to pitch in on just about any job, so don't just train for specific tasks. Instead teach them about the whole business and emphasize problem solving.

> **Your attitude toward the people you hire goes a long way in determining their attitude about the job.**

■ **Communicate.** Perhaps the biggest mistake companies make is failing to share information. Have short, frequent meetings, maybe only ten minutes at the beginning of the day, and share both bad and good news. Employees feel included and empowered when they know what's going on.

■ **Motivate.** Three men are working in a rock quarry. A passerby asks each of them what they're doing. The first one stops and grunts, "Digging up stones." The second one stops and says, "Feeding my family." The third one continues working and replies, "Building a cathedral." People who share a common vision work harder. Share your vision and enthusiasm.

■ **Empower.** Give your employees the ability to make certain decisions. Nothing is worse for morale, or for the bottom line, than an employee who is only allowed to follow narrow rules. Most employees will learn how to do their job better than you can teach them. Let them use their brains, not just their backs.

■ **Evaluate.** You can't expect employees to improve if you don't give them regular, constructive feedback. Employees are better able to meet your needs if you let them know when they do well and how they could have done better. Give specific suggestions, don't just complain.

■ **Acknowledge.** The least productive thing an employer can say is, "I don't need to thank employees; they get paid." We all need to be thanked and recognized. Find opportunities to get the staff together to acknowledge jobs well done. Give small acknowledgments—plaques, certificates, t-shirts—to recognize even small achievements.

■ **Reward.** Pay people decently, reward them when you're successful, and give them as much sense of security as you can. Employees don't work well when they're worried about how they'll pay the rent or whether they'll have a job next month. Job security, good pay, and decent benefits help make a much more productive staff.

In a small company, it's hard to match the financial benefits of a big corporation, so it's even more important to make every employee feel valued, included, and respected. If you help your employees grow, they'll help your business grow.

Getting Employees to Use Initiative

One of my favorite management sayings is "Hire people you trust, and trust them." It's not easy. As a business owner, you need to make sure your business is safe, that money isn't being stolen, and that customers are being properly served. But all too often, while trying to prevent failure, you may also be preventing success.

Without realizing it, many managers undermine their own best intentions. For example, a few years ago, a client complained to me about his employees: "When they see something wrong, why don't they just fix it? Why do they turn to me for every little thing?"

But as we spoke, I watched my client. He hovered over his employees, frequently popped up from our table to check or criticize their work, and intervened when a worker was talking to a customer.

Many business owners exhibit the same inconsistency. While saying they want their workers to take more responsibility, they second-guess decisions or require employees to get permission for everything. They're always looking over other peoples' shoulders.

The result? Workers become unmotivated and dispirited. You lose the creativity and ingenuity of your best people.

So instead of organizing to avoid failure, what does it take to create an environment that enables and encourages success? How can you structure your business so employees will use their brains and take initiative?

■ **Allow mistakes.** An employee who is not allowed to make mistakes, who is criticized or punished for making the wrong choices, soon stops making any choices. Stop thinking of mistakes as "failures." Instead, use these opportunities as a chance to teach employees how to make better choices. One way a business owner can help develop a blame-free atmosphere is by acknowledging their own mistakes. The former head of 3M frequently told employees how he personally "killed" Post-its twice because he didn't think they would be a success. Clearly, the boss is not always right.

> How can you structure your business so employees will use their brains and take initiative?

■ **Share your vision.** Employees are far more willing to work hard and take responsibility if they understand the larger goals and context of their work. What is the passion that drives you to own and run this company? What important need does your company fill? People want more than just a paycheck from their work; they want meaning and purpose.

■ **Share information.** Many managers hoard information the way a miser hoards cash—doling it out as meagerly as possible. This means employees often don't understand the implications of their actions. One of my first summer jobs was typing twelve-page pre-printed contracts at a banquet hall. My boss told me how each department used the information and how someone's wedding depended on me typing everything right. He helped me realize why it was important for me to slow down and check my work.

■ **Lose the "My way or the highway" attitude.** Most of us start our own businesses because we like being in control. But if we want to be truly successful, we have to permit others to do some things their way. As long as the overall goals of the company are being met, give employees room to implement strategies in their own ways. They might even surprise you and come up with better ideas than your own.

■ **Give employees authority and don't interfere when they are making independent decisions.** If you require every decision to be approved by you, your employees will turn to you for every little thing. Show them you trust them, and even let them overrule you to meet the needs of a customer.

■ **Don't blame the messenger.** At one company I worked for, if you pointed out a problem, you owned that problem. The already overburdened workers quickly learned it was smarter to just shut up.

■ **Treat each and every person with respect.** You never know where the next great idea is going to come from. At one airline, a woman in accounts payable noticed the huge cost of storage bins. On her own initiative, she contacted a local manufacturer who could make the bins for just a few dollars. She saved the company tens of thousands of dollars a year. Who knows? Your company's next great idea could come from the janitor.

Avoiding BADD Boss Syndrome

Morning thoughts of an entrepreneur…

- **While jogging.** Envisions new product line that will revolutionize industry and triple sales;

- **During shower.** Thinks up new ways to inexpensively manufacture product for export and double sales;

- **While getting kids dressed.** Plans new marketing campaign that will bring in youth market and double sales;

- **Over breakfast.** Thinks up ways to totally reposition current products and double sales;

- **During drive to work.** Remembers idea thought up on weekend for a new gardening tool, considers selling current business, starting gardening company instead;

- **On last few steps from car to office.** Suddenly remembers crisis with major client, but draws a blank on how to deal with it.

Sound familiar? This entrepreneur is suffering from what I call Boss Attention Deficit Disorder.

Like children who can't sit still, people who have BADD Boss Syndrome are easily distracted by their own creativity. They're smart; often, they're brilliant. But their creativity and intelligence means they're always thinking up new concepts and strategies. Inevitably, their company loses focus, they don't excel at any one thing, and their employees are driven to distraction.

Take "Kyle," for instance. Kyle designed video games as a hobby and had invented a line of games he thought could sell. He wanted to both design and manufacture the games. He also intended to open a store to sell the games. Part of the store would be a video arcade for customers to play the games. Since customers would be coming in to purchase video games, they might also want to rent and buy other videos, so he'd have a video rental area in his store too. People renting videos often don't have time to cook, so he'd have a take-out pizza counter. Since parents might come and watch the kids, he'd give them something to do and add a laundromat.

> **People who have BADD Boss Syndrome are easily distracted by their own creativity.**

Can you count how many businesses Kyle wanted to start at once?

Under the weight of all his other ideas (some of which might even have been workable) Kyle's core product (his video games) got buried. Kyle could have invented the best video game ever, but instead of spending his time perfecting his game and finding distributors, he'd be fixing the washing machines.

Kyle was a novice, but even owners (and managers) of big companies suffer from BADD Boss Syndrome. Years ago I was a consultant to a very large company whose CEO had a bad case of BADD Boss Syndrome. In less than two years, the company launched six new divisions. He continually moved key personnel to manage these new endeavors, while existing projects languished. Not surprising, the company soon got into serious trouble. Their resources were overextended and they ended up neglecting current clients, all because the boss couldn't stay focused.

How can you avoid becoming a victim of Boss Attention Deficit Disorder? How can you reduce the effects of BADD Boss Syndrome if you're already a sufferer?

I've come up with a list of ten suggestions. Perhaps on the way home from work, you can think up ten more, we could publish them, maybe start a magazine for BADD Boss Syndrome victims, add a support group program, sell them vitamin supplements, launch a website…

Ten Tips to Avoid Boss Attention Deficit Disorder Syndrome:

1. Define your "bread-and-butter" business so you know what pays the bills.

2. Spend at least the first half of the day attending to that core business.

3. Keep a visible list of current projects.

4. Put all new ideas on a separate list.

5. Separate ideas into those that solve problems and those that are "creative."

6. Have a partner, key employee, or consultant tell you "why it won't work" and remember their job is to be negative.

7. Set aside a specific time to evaluate and prioritize new projects.

8. Establish a limit on the number of new projects undertaken at any given time.

9. Respect current demands on employees and avoid distracting them from core work.

10. Stop being in such a hurry; great ideas don't vanish.

Inexpensive Ways to Reward Employees

■ **Well days.** Once or twice when I was a young employee, if I really needed a day off, I'd call in sick. But the guilt from lying to my boss always made me actually feel ill. I decided that when I became a boss, I wouldn't make my employees lie to me about wanting a day off. Instead, my employees get "well days." In other words, if something is going right in their lives—they've just fallen in love, their child is receiving an award, their best friend is in town visiting—they can call in "well." Sure, this isn't really different from having a floating personal leave day, but it recognizes that employees' lives outside of work are important.

■ **Birthdays.** I've always considered birthdays special, so in my company, employees get their birthdays as paid holidays. Be careful about this benefit, however. Some people would rather work on their birthday than be alone.

■ **Awards.** We have a very small office, but a few years ago, I light-heartedly named one of my employees "Employee of the Week." All he got was an email and a round of applause, but it was enlightening to see how much he enjoyed the recognition. The idea caught on, and every once in a while, we'll name an Employee of the Week. Sometimes they even get a candy bar!

■ **Food.** It's amazing how much people like food. You don't have to provide free food regularly, but when anything special has happened, an easy, inexpensive way to celebrate is to bring in food or take the staff to lunch.

■ **Flexibility.** Few things are as greatly appreciated by employees as having the ability to adapt certain things to their own needs. Typically, the most important area in which flexibility is valued is in their schedule, whether it's starting work a half hour later to get a child to school or leaving work a little early occasionally for other needs. Giving employees a reasonable amount of flexibility will often engender a great deal of loyalty.

■ **Say thank you.** The least expensive thing you can do is to thank your employees. All of us appreciate being appreciated.

Money and Financing

Money Lingo

■ **Red ink or in the red.** On accounting ledgers, negative numbers used to be written in red ink. So the expressions "red ink" or "in the red" refer to showing a loss.

■ **In the black.** Positive numbers, on the other hand, were written in black ink. So if your accounts finish "in the black," you've come out with a profit.

■ **The bottom line.** At the top of your financial statements, you list your income. You then deduct your expenses. The number you're left with on the last line is how much money you've made—or lost. That's your company's "bottom line."

■ **Overhead, fixed expenses, or your nut.** These terms refer to each month's expenses, even if you don't make a sale. Fixed expenses include rent, utilities, insurance, and administrative salaries. Your "nut" is the total of these fixed expenses.

■ **Variable expenses.** Costs that change over time. In other words, if you run a sporting goods store, your rent is fixed every month, but your marketing expenses vary depending on how many advertisements you decide to run.

■ **Cost of goods sold (COGS).** This refers to what it costs you to purchase the inventory you sell or to purchase the raw materials to manufacture your products.

■ **General and administrative expenses (G&A), or Operating expenses.** Costs to operate your business other than COGS or direct sales costs (such as sales commissions). This includes all overhead expenses whether fixed or variable.

■ **Revenue.** Total amount of money received from sales.

■ **Income.** The amount of money received from any source. You can, for example, have money coming in to your business from loans or investments.

■ **Profit.** Money you have left after deducting expenses.

■ **Gross profit.** The amount of money you receive after deducting the cost of goods sold and sales commissions but before deducting general and administrative expenses.

■ **Net profit.** The amount of money you receive after deducting the cost of goods sold, sales costs, and general and administrative expenses.

■ **Net loss.** The amount of money you're in the red if, after deducting expenses from revenue, you've lost money instead of having made money.

The Bottom Line of Business

There are many reasons to be in business, but the bottom line of business is the bottom line.

We're often uncomfortable talking about money, even in a business context. Promoters of 'get rich quick' schemes have no trouble mentioning money: "Make $10,000 a week in your spare time working from home!" But the rest of us usually approach the subject more delicately.

We each bring our own personal issues to the topic of money. Sometimes we're conflicted about wanting to make money. We may associate the idea of being interested in money with the kind of people who are interested in nothing but money, and we don't want to be like that. Some may feel unworthy of having money or afraid they won't know how to handle money once they have it.

Almost all of us are uncomfortable talking about money. Money, after all, is one of the few things left in modern life that we don't discuss openly with even our closest friends or family members. You may know all the intimate details of your buddy's romantic life, but he probably would never tell you how much money he makes.

In a business context, this discomfort with money often becomes a reluctance to deal with budgets, bookkeeping, and accounting. Most of us are intimidated by numbers. More often, we just find it unpleasant to think about cash flow and profit margins and, especially, debt.

Well, it's time to get over that.

Money and numbers are essential components of business. If you're going to be in business, you have to learn to deal with money and numbers in a matter-of-fact, business-like fashion. You have to be able to look at your financial reports without thinking they're a report card on your character, discuss a raise with an employee without feeling you're under attack, and tell a client the price of your services without being embarrassed.

That doesn't mean you should start boasting about every dollar you make or obsess about every line of your budget; it's more about developing a healthy understanding and respect for the role money and numbers play in your business.

So recognize this: it's okay to talk about money. If a customer's bill is overdue, it's polite to tell them. If you're meeting with a prospective client, it's appropriate to say how much you charge. If you're hiring a consultant, it's reasonable to ask not only their hourly fee, but how much the whole project will cost and to set limits. You have no reason to be uncomfortable discussing such matters—these are all normal business topics.

So stay cool when the topic of money comes up; it's part of doing business. And I hope your bottom line is always "in the black."

Money Management Tips

■ **Send out your bills.** I'm amazed by the number of businesspeople who wait months before billing clients or customers. Get in the habit of billing immediately when you've delivered a product or service. Make certain you do your billing at least once a month. Remember, the longer you take to send out your invoices, the greater the chance you won't get paid at all.

■ **Review your books regularly.** You can't manage your money without knowing the facts. At least once a month, but preferably once a week, look at your accounts payable, accounts receivable, income statement, checkbook balance, and cash flow.

■ **Look ahead.** When looking at your books, don't just look at the present. Look at the past and then look toward the future, creating income and cash flow projections. Be conservative!

■ **Watch where you put your money.** Those of us in smaller companies usually leave all our money in one checking account. Sit down with your banker or investment advisor to discuss accounts that can generate income on money you don't need immediately. Sweep accounts automatically switch excess cash into interest-earning accounts.

■ **Line up a backup source of capital.** To prepare for those inevitable cash flow crunches, line up credit sources in advance. A good source is a credit line from a bank. Another, more expensive, alternative is to have credit cards with high credit limits you can use for cash advances when you need them. (When you don't, let them sit, unused, in a drawer.)

■ **Manage your growth.** Growth costs money. Typically, you have an increase in expenses long before you have an increase in income. Plan your growth carefully so you have the financial ability to fund it yourself or comfortably pay the debt you'll incur.

■ **Get a retirement account.** An excellent tax shelter for those who are self-employed or sole proprietors is the self-employed retirement account. You'll save money now and have a more secure financial future later.

■ **Save.** Every business has income fluctuations. The best way to have cash when you need it is to put some away when you've got it.

Where Do Numbers Come From?

While no child has ever asked, "Mommy, where do numbers come from?" it's a question adults ask me often. For new entrepreneurs filling out financial forms, especially if they've never done projections before, numbers seem daunting.

Once you have an established company, you have a fairly good sense of how much things cost, how large a staff you'll need, and the sales you're likely to make. But when you're just starting out, facing line after line in your financial statements, numbers appear a complete mystery.

They're not—at least not entirely. Just remember Rhonda's Rule: Numbers are the reflection of decisions you make.

Every decision you make when planning your business has a number attached: If you choose to exhibit at a trade show, there's a cost associated with that; if you choose to locate your business in one town versus another, there's a cost to that.

The key is to create your financial projections after, or at the same time as, you plan your business. Problems arise when you complete your financials before you've made critical business decisions, or when you do projections from the "top down" rather than the "bottom up."

Top down numbers are enticing to work with because they always come out looking good. Here's how they work: You look at the big picture—the total market size,

growth rate, average sales price, average profit margins, and so on. These numbers are typically found through demographic, industry, and research data.

You make what seem to be reasonable assumptions. Perhaps you assume you'll capture 4% of the existing market or improve upon competitors' existing profit margins by 2%. Then you fill in each line of your financial statements to make the totals come out to the big numbers projected.

> ## Remember Rhonda's Rule: Numbers are the reflection of decisions you make.

For instance, let's say you've invented a new, improved golf club. Here's an example of top down numbers (recognize that I'm making these figures up—I don't have statistics on the size of the golf club market):

"Total annual sales of golf clubs are $2 billion. We'll achieve at least 1% market penetration for our superior club within 3 years: amounting to $20 million in annual sales. With a profit margin of 15%, we will have a net profit of $3 million."

Sounds good, doesn't it? Top down projections result in some very positive numbers—the kind that excite you and any potential investors. They just don't happen to have much relation to reality. When investors start asking tough questions, these numbers are hard to defend.

The best financials are developed from the bottom up. You start by planning your business—doing the real business-building legwork, examining different distribution channels, identifying suppliers, developing a staffing chart.

So let's say you're that same golf club manufacturer and you're building your financials from the bottom up. Here's how it would work:

You first compare different distribution channels: direct online sales, sales through general sporting goods shops, and sales through specialty golf retailers. Choosing

one, let's say selling through specialty golf retailers, will have associated costs and impact on income. You'll also need a sales force to sell to those shops, you'll exhibit at four sporting goods trade shows a year, and you'll advertise in *Golf Retailer* magazine. All this will cost something, too. You'll receive 40-45% of the final sale price of the golf club, since the retailer will take half and the salesperson will receive a commission.

Now, you're starting to get real numbers to plug into each of the lines of your financial forms. You've got numbers for advertising, numbers for staffing, numbers for income.

Yes, this takes work, but there's help. The best place to start is by speaking with others in your industry, attending trade shows, contacting your industry association.

By the time you're done, numbers won't seem so mysterious. They'll be real and they'll be yours. You'll learn not only how to do financial projections but a whole lot more about your business as well.

Finding Money for Your Business

I give presentations to entrepreneurs all over the country, and I'm always asked the same question: "Where do I get the money to start or grow my business?"

Before you start looking for money, figure out how much money you actually need. Most people underestimate how much it truly costs to start a business. Even if you're starting a business requiring little funding, such as consulting, you'll still need cash to pay your living expenses and personal bills.

A good place to start is by knowing the difference between the two basic types of financing: debt and equity.

■ **Debt.** You borrow money and must pay it back, usually whether the business does well or not.

■ **Equity.** An investor puts money into your business in return for a share of ownership and future profits. If the company fails, you most likely will not have to pay them back.

There are two other primary funding sources that don't get as much attention: personal assets and income.

■ **Personal assets.** You use existing personal funds, such as savings, or convert other personal assets (such home equity) into money you can use for your business.

■ **Income.** The absolute best way to finance a business is by going out and making sales.

Financing from income gives you the most control over your business and the most peace of mind. You don't have investors, and you don't have loans. But raising money through income is typically a very slow process. And it's not an option if you need funds before you can make even your first sale.

> **You need to know the difference between the two basic types of financing: debt and equity.**

Those are the major categories; specific funding sources include:

■ **Investors.** People will tell you it's always better to finance a business using other people's money. But other people's money comes with a nasty attachment—other people. They'll own a piece of your business and may even control whether you'll be able to continue to operate the business.

■ **Savings.** It's best to start a business with your own money. You don't get into debt, and you don't give up equity. Of course, you're also risking your long-term financial security. This is a more comfortable choice

213

for those who are younger. If your savings are owned jointly with a spouse or partner, be certain that they accept your plans; it will save a lot of grief later on.

■ **Home equity.** You may have built up significant equity in your home, some of which can be turned into cash by a home equity line of credit or refinancing your mortgage. Be careful, especially if this is your first business. You want to make sure you'll always have a roof over your head.

■ **Credit cards.** Accountants will tell you credit cards are a terrible way to finance a new business; you'll face high interest charges and put your own credit-worthiness at risk. But most entrepreneurs use credit cards for many start-up expenses.

■ **Friends and family.** Getting family or friends involved in your business is dangerous, but there are exceptions. If the person truly understands the risk involved, grasps the nature of your business, and is someone with whom you can communicate, the situation may work. Just be sure to draw up the necessary legal paperwork.

■ **Line of credit.** Typically, the first type of outside funding a business will get is a business line of credit. The bank sets a maximum amount of money you can borrow; you use as much or as little of this total amount as you need, giving you a way to help manage cash flow.

■ **Term loan.** For larger expenses, such as equipment, vehicles, or property, you'll need a fixed loan that you pay back over a set period of time. You may also be able to get a term loan for business expansion, especially if you have an existing, profitable company.

■ **Vendor financing.** Suppliers have a vested interest in seeing you grow; the more you grow, the more you'll buy from them. Many equipment vendors offer financing. Discuss your growth plans with other suppliers and see if you can negotiate favorable payment terms.

Just remember, finding money takes longer than most people think. So plan accordingly—don't wait until you're in dire straits to find the cash to keep your business afloat.

Start-up Money from Banks?

When asked why he robbed banks, notorious thief Willie Sutton replied, "Because that's where the money is." When looking for financing, many novice entrepreneurs also think of going to a bank, assuming that's where the money is. But they might find they're just about as welcome as Willie.

Banks can indeed be an important, even critical, part of financing a business. In fact, as your company develops, you'll want to find a good bank and develop a strong working partnership. But you'll find banks generally aren't an appropriate place for start-up capital.

Banks' lack of responsiveness to new business loans can be frustrating. It's important to understand the role of banks in comparison to other kinds of financing sources. A key concept is appreciating the "risk/reward ratio." In other words, there's a direct relationship between the amount of risk you ask someone to take and the reward they receive. The greater the risk, the greater the rewards.

Let's look at two financing sources: an angel investor and a bank.

An angel investor looks at your business plan, experience, and team, and decides whether you have a good chance of success. In return for giving you money, they get a piece of the ownership in your company. If you fail, you don't pay them back. But if you become a smashing success, they get a portion of every dollar you make. High risk. High potential reward.

Now, look what happens if you go to a bank. In return for lending you money, they charge you interest. They get the same amount of money whether your business barely makes it or becomes a Fortune 500 company. Limited reward. So they have to limit their risk. Instead of looking at how big your company might eventually become, they're concerned about your ability to repay the loan.

> **As your company develops, you'll want to find a good bank and develop a strong working partnership.**

Typically, banks look for what are referred to as the "Three C's of Credit." If you approach a bank for a loan, expect to have the following examined:

■ **Character (or Credit).** The most important thing a bank will consider is how you've handled credit before. There's a Catch 22, however. If you've never borrowed money in the past, you may have a hard time borrowing money now. In the early years of a business, most banks will look at the owner's personal credit history rather than at the business itself. Most of us have established some credit history through credit cards, mortgages, or car payments. Banks will examine your credit report to see whether you paid your bills on time and repaid loans in full. A way for a business to establish its own credit history is by setting up accounts with suppliers (printers, office supply stores, shipping services) or landlords, so the business itself will have start to have good credit "character."

■ **Capacity.** There's an old belief that banks only lend money to people who don't need it. To some extent, that's true. Banks only lend money to those with the likely ability—or "capacity"—to pay back the loan. In other words, do you make enough money to be able to handle all your debts and responsibilities? Unfortunately for most business owners, the main criterion banks typically use is the historical ratio of your profits to your debts. This means that in new and growing businesses, some business owners with other substantial assets and a good credit history may still look as if they don't have the capacity to handle a loan.

■ **Collateral.** To reduce risk, especially on very large loans, banks may require you to pledge other valuable assets as security for the debt. Often, as in the case of real estate or equipment loans, the collateral is the physical asset you're about to purchase. But it could be anything of value. Keep in mind, though, that banks are in the business of lending money, not repossessing machinery or stores, so they're still going to be looking at your ability to repay the loan itself.

As frustrating as it may seem, banks prefer to lend money to companies that have been in business for at least one or two years. But don't be discouraged: as your business grows, you'll find your bank to be an important, even eager, partner.

Prepare to Get Your Loan

Be prepared! That's not just the Boy Scouts' motto. It's good advice before you approach a bank for a business loan.

According to the U.S. Small Business Administration (SBA), credit cards are the primary way entrepreneurs finance their businesses. But as businesses grow, a majority—55%—get their financing from a bank, credit union, or other traditional lending source.

If you've ever gone to a bank for a loan, you know it's not easy. Most banks require the same basic information about your business, so it pays to be prepared to answer these fundamental questions before you approach one:

How long have you been in business?

Before a bank officer spends much time with you, they want to make certain yours is the kind of business they'll lend to. Most banks only lend to companies that have been in business at least two years. If yours is newer, you can seek an SBA loan or personal line of credit (see below).

What kind of loan are you looking for?

Banks offer three main types of loans:

1. Term loan. This is a loan for a set amount of money, over a set period of time, typically with a fixed interest rate. In other words, you might borrow $100,000 for five years at 8% interest. Then, you pay back a portion of the loan and interest monthly over the life of the loan, typically in equal installments. You'll need a term loan when you're making a major purchase, such as real estate, vehicles, or large equipment. A bank will want to see that your current income is sufficient to cover the monthly payments and that your growth plans are realistic. They may also want a business plan.

> Most banks require the same basic information, so be prepared to answer these fundamental questions before you approach one.

2. Line of credit. An LOC is much like a credit card, only without the plastic, and typically with a lower interest rate. The bank assigns you a certain credit limit, and you can borrow any amount up to that limit as needed. You can pay back the funds on your own schedule (with minimum monthly payments), but you'll likely have to pay off the entire amount at least once a year. Interest rates can fluctuate, and you'll be charged an annual fee regardless of whether you use the LOC or not.

217

A line of credit is a good way to finance cash flow fluctuations; ask for a credit line when you must pay for inventory, raw materials, or other expenses long before your customer pays you. The bank will typically decide whether to grant you a line of credit based on the amount and quality of your accounts receivable. They may also give a newer business a credit line based on the owner's personal credit.

3. SBA loan. The Small Business Administration does not give loans; instead, it guarantees loans by banks to small businesses that involve more risk than a bank is usually willing to take. Banks that make a lot of SBA loans often have separate staff handling them. SBA loans are best for those who are starting a business (banks don't usually lend to start-ups) or purchasing the business's real estate, or for strong businesses that have some problems qualifying for regular bank loans.

How much money do you want?

Have an idea of how much you want to borrow before you call on the bank's lending officer. Banks will often limit a line of credit to the amount of your accounts receivable. Requests for loans of more than $100,000 are probably going to be sent to a central office for processing and to receive more scrutiny.

Are you profitable?

This seems like a trick question. After all, you wouldn't need money if you were rolling in dough. Banks understand that. They just want to see that you're not losing money, that you can pay your bills, and that you're likely to stay in business. They will ask you for your tax returns for the past two or three years and may ask for projections for future years.

Do you have good credit?

The bank will run a personal credit check on you and any other owners of the company. Unless you have a fairly large company, your personal credit score and history will be critical to the bank's decision on whether to lend your company money. The bank will also check with Dun & Bradstreet and your company's creditors to review your company's credit history. Be prepared to offer excellent business credit references. You can check your personal credit score at www. myfico.com and get your company's Dun & Bradstreet report at www.dnb.com.

Are you willing to personally guarantee the loan?

Until your business gets very large, expect to sign a personal guarantee for your company's loans. The bank wants the security of knowing that you will be responsible for the loan even if your company goes out of business. All owners, and part owners, of the company will have to give personal guarantees.

Show Me the Money?

You've probably heard that it's best to build a business using OPM, or Other People's Money. Isn't it an inviting thought to risk somebody else's savings instead of your own?

Hold on! Don't just rush out that door looking for a venture capitalist or angel investor. Taking on an investor is a huge decision.

The first thing to realize is you're likely tied to your investors for the life of your business. If things go wrong, there may be no easy way out of a relationship with an investor other than closing the business. In fact, if you come to a parting of the ways, your investors may have more power to get rid of you than you to get rid of them. So proceed carefully!

Don't forget, investors legally own a piece of your business. While laws vary from state to state, investors have certain rights even if they own less than 51% of the company. Moreover, most investors will negotiate their rights before they agree to give you funding. Their involvement can range from receiving a percent of profits, to control of the Board of Directors, to putting in their own people to manage the business. So don't think you're just going to take their money and never hear another peep from them.

Having investors makes dealing with taxes and legal issues more complicated and expensive. For tax purposes, investors are entitled not only to a share of your profits but to your losses as well. And believe me, many a rich investor would like to have losses to offset other income. Indeed, if things are going badly in your business, some investors may be motivated to force you to close up shop just so they can take a tax loss.

> **Looking for investors? The first thing to realize is you're likely tied to them for the life of your business.**

Three types of investors fund growing companies:

1. Venture Capitalists. Serious venture capitalists (VCs) are professional investors who raise money from institutional sources (banks, securities firms, and the like) and wealthy individuals to invest in companies with exceptional promise. Generally, they only invest substantial sums of money (millions of dollars) and only in companies with the potential to grow very big very fast. VCs have high expectations of return on their investment and take an active role in managing the companies they invest in. They can be more interested in a quick financial return than in the long-term health of your company.

2. Angel Investors. Angels are individuals who invest their own money in growing companies. Because it's their own money (rather than institutional dollars or other investors' funds), angels can make more diverse choices about the types and sizes of companies they invest in than VCs can. They may also have a longer timeline in terms of financial returns. Angel investors vary widely in the quality and nature of assistance they provide for you. Over the last few years, a number of angel capital groups have formed to help individual investors link up with worthy new ventures. You can find a list of a number of such angel capital groups at www.AngelCapitalAssociation.org.

3. Friends and Family. Getting family or friends involved in your business can be tricky, but there are exceptions. If the person truly understands the risk involved, grasps the nature of your business, and is someone with whom you can communicate easily, the arrangement may work. Just be sure to draw up the same legal paperwork as you would with a stranger.

Spend time getting to know potential investors before you take their money; you're tied to each other for a long time. Find out if they've invested in other companies before. If so, speak to other entrepreneurs who've worked with them. What are their financial and business motivations for investing? Are those goals a good fit with your own? How much control do they want in the business? What time frame do they require for getting a return on their investment?

Of course, when you need money for your business, you may feel lucky to get the money from anyone. But over time, if you have a fearful, intrusive, or controlling investor, you may regret having "married" an investor when it's so hard to get "divorced."

Using Credit Cards to Finance Your Business

■ **Plan ahead.** If you're thinking of starting a business, but are still employed, it might be a good idea to get a few new credit cards or increase your credit limits while you still have a regular paycheck. Some credit card companies won't extend credit to the self-employed until they've been in business for two years or more. Just be careful not to apply for too many cards at once—it can increase your interest rates or cause lenders to turn you down.

■ **Get cards with low rates even if they have higher annual fees.** You may be used to paying off the total amount due every month with a regular salary, but that may not be possible when you're self-employed, especially in the early months or years. Lower interest rates may be more important to you now.

■ **Get your spouse involved.** If you're using a personal card for business expenses, let your spouse know your plan to pay back the debt. Discuss credit card expenses with one another so you're not both racking up debt at the same time. Make sure you have your spouse's understanding and approval; after all, their credit may also be affected.

■ **Consider all your financial needs.** Come up with a total financing plan for your business and personal expenses. If you're financing your business from savings but meanwhile charging all your personal expenses on credit cards, the effect on your credit rating will be the same. If your business and personal budgets absolutely depend on racking up a lot of credit card debt, rethink your business plan.

■ **Use credit cards for short-term cash flow needs.** Credit cards are effective when you've got an order or contract and need to purchase supplies. Then you are using the card merely to manage cash flow, and you know where the money is coming from. Make certain your customer is a good credit risk, however.

■ **Use "checks" when a business doesn't accept credit cards.** You may need to charge an expense from a business that doesn't take credit cards (such as a consultant or graphic designer). If you don't have the cash, and are managing your finances carefully, you can pay with a check that is written against your credit card account. Use these only when you've got a good chance of income coming soon to cover the expense.

■ **Don't get carried away.** It's tempting to believe that if you have high credit limits, you can spend a lot of money. Or that if you're able to pay the minimum monthly fees, you're handling your debt well. Don't be misled—debt is still debt, and it continually piles up. Put a limit on how much total debt you'll incur before you cut off your own credit and start paying down the entire amount due.

Tax Tips

■ **Get the right professional help.** Do you still get your taxes done by a tax preparation service in the mall? Perhaps this worked when you were an employee or your business was tiny, but you may have outgrown that solution. It's probably time you found an accountant who specializes in business taxes or is familiar with your industry. A good accountant can help you understand and assess the tax implications of your business decisions.

■ **Select the right corporate structure.** Are you operating as a sole proprietorship or partnership rather than as a Limited Liability Company or corporation? If so, you may be losing out on some tax advantages and possibly putting your personal assets at risk. Moreover, you are probably increasing the likelihood of being audited, especially if you mingle personal and business expenses.

■ **Set up a good bookkeeping program and record-keeping system.** To the IRS, bad account records mean you have something to hide, even though you know they just mean you're disorganized. Moreover, most small companies lose legitimate deductions because they don't keep adequate records. Track your expenses in a good accounting program and keep the receipts neatly filed.

■ **Set up a retirement plan.** One of the best tax shelters available for the self-employed and small businesses is retirement programs. If you have no employees, you can shelter a significant portion of your bottom-line profit from taxes.

■ **Apply for a Federal Tax ID Number instead of using your Social Security Number.** This doesn't save you any money in taxes, but the IRS likes it better, and it's just a better business practice. Once you have a Federal Tax ID number, you won't have to give your Social Security Number to everyone you do business with. A Federal Tax ID Number is easy to get.

■ **Avoid trouble.** If you have employees, you'll have to pay penalties on any goofs you make with payroll tax. Save money; get a payroll service.

■ **Self-employment tax.** One surprise you encounter when you first set up your own business is the high cost of self-employment tax. It can take a huge chunk out of your earnings. Discuss ways to legally minimize this tax with your accountant.

■ **Timing.** A little advance planning can save a great deal of money. Knowing the best time to send invoices, order inventory, buy new equipment, and so on, can have an impact on your taxes. Discuss with your accountant when your fiscal year should begin, as well.

Buy or Lease?

When you're starting or expanding a business, you've got lots of things to spend money on. With each purchase, you face the same question: should you buy or should you lease?

All kinds of things can be leased: furniture, equipment, vehicles, technology, telephone systems. Leasing is tempting: you'll spend less money now. For a rapidly growing or new business, minimizing cash outlay is a serious concern. But leasing costs more in the long run, sometimes a lot more.

When considering whether to buy or lease, what are the trade-offs?

Advantages of Leasing

1. You hold onto your money. Cash is one of the most precious assets a company has. Money gives you time—time to stay in business, time to grow. Buying means tying up cash, giving you more pressure to succeed faster.

2. Flexibility. When you buy something, you're stuck with it, even if your needs change or technology improves. If you can negotiate the right terms, leasing may allow you to update or expand your equipment or furniture, or perhaps even get out of the commitment altogether.

3. Lower start-up costs. Leasing enables you to get a lot more now for a lot less. Buying twenty desks will cost many thousands of dollars. But leasing those same desks may only be a few hundred dollars a month.

4. Maintenance and support. When you lease or "outsource" technology or advanced equipment, the biggest benefit may be technical assistance. If you need to set up an internal email network, it may be cheaper (in the long run) to buy your own routers, firewall, and such. But do you have the staff to configure and troubleshoot such a system? It may be smarter to find a lease that includes technical setup and maintenance.

> For a growing business, minimizing cash outlay is a serious concern. But leasing costs more in the long run, sometimes a lot more.

5. Tax advantages. The IRS doesn't allow you to write off the total cost of certain purchases in one year. Instead, those costs may have to be spread out over many years. When you buy, you spend the money all at once but only receive a fraction of the tax advantage at one time. Most lease payments, on the other hand, are fully deductible the year they're paid.

Advantages of Buying

1. Lower total cost. The lifetime cost of many things is considerably cheaper if you buy rather than lease. A desk chair may cost $200, and you may keep it for many years. That same chair may cost $20 a month to lease, making its one-year cost $240.

2. Less overhead. When you've bought something, you won't have continuing monthly payments. You won't feel as stressed about money when you have a bad month.

3. Flexibility. Most leases are for a set time period. You can't easily get out of them. If you move, go out of business, or change the way you produce your goods, you'll still have payments on whatever you've leased. If you own your own equipment, furniture, or vehicles, you can take them with you, or sell or donate them.

4. You've got an asset instead of a liability. Once you've bought something, it's on your books as an asset of the business, increasing your company's value. A lease payment, however, shows up as a liability, decreasing your company's overall value.

5. Tax advantages. The IRS allows you to write off, or "expense," up to a certain dollar value of purchases (including furniture and certain equipment) every year. If you're having a good year, buying provides a better deduction than leasing.

There are pros and cons to both buying and leasing. Which do I recommend? Rhonda's First Rule: Buy less expensive items; lease more costly ones. It generally doesn't make much sense to lease a fax machine or printer—they're only a few hundred dollars. But if you need a major piece of equipment, don't tie up your cash. Rhonda's Second Rule: The more unsure you are of your plans, the more you should lease, especially if you can get short-term leases. Third Rule: Check the tax situation. Some deductions can make leasing actually cost less than buying. And Rhonda's most important Rule: Don't get more than you need. Cash in the bank beats a nice desk chair any day.

Say Charge It!

Credit cards: We like using them and so do our customers. But many smaller companies, especially those that deal primarily with other businesses, don't accept credit cards. However, many customers, even business clients, prefer to charge expenses. Using a credit card makes it easier for them to manage cash flow and track expenses, and the cards often earn them miles they can use for travel.

Accepting credit cards benefits you as well as your customers:

- **It increases the number of customers who will do business with you.**

- **You receive payment right away.** If you bill your customers yourself, they may take thirty days or more to pay.

- **The credit card company—not you—assumes the risk of non-paying customers.**

- **You have less paperwork, since you don't have to send invoices or statements.**

These benefits come at a price, however. Some fees:

- **Discount fee.** The credit card issuer (typically a bank) takes a small percentage (2-4%) of every charge. This covers the cost of administering the credit and assuming the risk, as well as the cost of marketing.

- **Transaction charge.** This is a small set fee (25 to 50 cents) for each transaction regardless of amount.

- **Monthly minimum.** This is the minimum amount you'll be charged per month regardless of how many charges you do.

- **Setup fees.** These are the costs for originating your account.

- **Equipment purchase or leasing.** In many cases, you'll have to pay for credit card processing equipment. If you are doing only Internet charges, you might not have equipment charges.

- **Chargebacks.** This is the amount the issuer will charge any time a customer refuses payment on a charge of yours stating dissatisfaction with the product.

Here's how these fees add up: Let's say a customer is buying something for $100.00. If the bank's discount was 2%, the transaction fee $.30, and monthly minimum $20.00, that $100.00 transaction would cost you $2.30. If you processed ten $100 transactions in a month, your total charges would be $23.00. If you only made five transactions, the credit card issuer would only have made $11.50 ($2.30 times five), and you'd be charged another $8.50 to meet your monthly minimum of $20.00.

The manner in which you accept credit cards affects your costs. If a customer presents the card to you in person, and you can physically see and swipe the card, there's a lower cost than if you're accepting phone, fax, mail, or Internet orders. The reasoning behind this is that there is less fraud committed when a customer presents a card in person.

> **Accepting credit cards increases the number of customers who will do business with you.**

Deciding which provider to use depends on how you'll deal with credit cards. If you'll be making very few credit card transactions, look for a low monthly minimum, even if the discount or transaction fee is somewhat higher. If you expect to be charging large amounts, shop for a low discount rate even if the monthly minimum is higher. Look to the future, too. Once your customers know you accept credit cards, will more of them take advantage of that option?

If you're not ever going to see or swipe cards, you theoretically shouldn't have to pay for the credit card equipment. However, that's in theory. Many companies make you lease the equipment anyway, but don't accept those fees without asking.

Once you decide to accept credit cards, be careful to follow the issuer's rules. A travel agent once wanted to charge me a few percentage points above the posted cost of a vacation package for using a credit card. Credit card companies typically have strict rules prohibiting merchants from applying such extra charges.

As more and more customers, even business customers, use credit cards, you, too, may find yourself asking, "Would you like to charge that?"

Do I Need to Collect Sales Tax?

When I purchase something from a local business, I pay sales tax. I may not like the extra cost, but it's a pretty seamless transaction—the seller tacks on the appropriate percentage, and I pay the total amount. But what happens when I'm the seller? How do business-people know whether to collect sales tax?

Here's the short answer: you must collect sales tax on most goods and some services that are delivered to a customer in any U.S. state in which you have any physical presence.

The long answer is much more complicated. Sales tax rates and rules vary from state to state, city to city. According to the National Retail Federation, 45 states and 7,500 cities, counties, and jurisdictions impose sales taxes.

What's a small business to do? Here are a few of the most-asked questions about sales taxes:

Who pays and collects sales taxes?

States give these taxes various names: sales tax, franchise tax, transaction privilege tax, use tax, and more. Some are the responsibility of the seller, others the buyer's responsibility. But governments figured out that it was more reliable to make the seller collect the tax. So, businesses are typically responsible for collecting sales tax and sending it to the state.

What kind of paperwork must I deal with?

Generally, if you're going to collect sales tax, you must get a license from your state. On each taxable transaction, you calculate the applicable sales tax, collect it from the buyer, keep tax records, and then file a tax return and pay the taxes to your state. You'll pay monthly, quarterly, or annually, depending on your level of sales.

> **According to the National Retail Federation, 45 states and 7,500 cities, counties, and jurisdictions impose sales taxes.**

What kind of products are subject to sales tax? Which are not?

Each state makes its own rules, so you must check your own state law. Typically, most products sold to end users are taxable. Major exemptions:

■ Prescription drugs

■ Food, especially groceries and non-prepared food

■ Animal feed, seed, and many agricultural products

■ Products that your customer is going to resell, such as raw materials and inventory

Do I have to charge sales tax if I'm selling a service?

Once again, rules vary by state. Many states exempt services. And within a state, the rules can be inconsistent.

If I do business in more than one state do I have to collect taxes?

The U.S. Supreme Court has twice ruled that states cannot require businesses to collect sales tax unless the business has a physical presence—or "nexus"—in the state. But physical presence is pretty loosely defined. If you have any location, facility, employee, call center, address, or even one independent salesperson in a state, then you have to collect taxes in that state.

Sales Tax Information Resource

An excellent resource for information on state tax rates and rules is The Sales Tax Clearinghouse: **www.thestc.com**. Click on the link to "Table of state tax rates and DoR webpages" to find a link to your state's sales tax authority. You can also click on "Lookup Rates" to find the sales tax—state, county, or local—for any address in the U.S.

Do I have to charge sales tax if I'm making a sale on the Internet or a catalog sale?

The rules are the same for Internet sales and catalog sales: You have to charge and collect sales tax when you deliver the product to a state in which you have a physical presence.

One thing's for certain, if you're going to be making sales in any state with a sales tax, talk to an accountant! It's not easy to figure out all the details on your own.

Spring into Savings

Spring cleaning means clearing out cupboards. But I've got another suggestion for sprucing up: tidying up your bills.

Few of us who run small companies like combing through the fine print on our monthly invoices. But by spending a half day once or twice a year to re-evaluate our monthly expenses, we can substantially lower our overhead.

Here's the plan for your Spring Savings Session:

■ **First, collect advertisements and promotions for the types of services you use.** This will give you ammunition when negotiating with your current provider.

■ **Set aside a few hours, preferably in the morning, to make phone calls.**

■ **Collect the most recent statements of all accounts you pay regularly, not just monthly, but quarterly, semi-annually, and annually.**

Now get ready to make calls. For each account, you'll call your sales rep, agent, or customer service and do the following:

■ **Ask.** This may seem tough, but it's surprisingly uncomplicated. Just say, "Hi, I'm calling about my account. I see I'm paying a rate of (insert your rate here). Is there any way I can lower that?"

■ **Probe.** Don't take a simple "No" or "That's our standard rate" for an answer.

Ask if they have rates for new accounts or larger customers. Ask to have those rates applied to you.

■ **Negotiate.** Since few customers take the time to call for better rates, most companies will offer you something. Take that as a starting point, not a final offer. Mention the other deals you've seen or been offered.

> **We can substantially lower our overhead by spending a half day re-evaluating our monthly expenses.**

■ **Be courteous.** Make vendors want to keep you as a customer. If you're belligerent, they'll be happy to see you go.

Be certain to re-evaluate these costs:

■ **Local and long-distance phone service.** There's a world of competition for telephone service. In addition to per-minute rates, you can buy flat-rate service with unlimited calls. Some providers offer frequent flyer miles. Call every provider in your area and compare. Don't hesitate to switch. The first time we renegotiated our phone rates, we cut costs by two-thirds!

■ **Wireless/Cellular service.** Talk about confusing! I defy anyone to figure out even the best wireless service contract. But look at your past bills to see if you're paying for too many or too few minutes (resulting in high per-minute charges). Ask for special concessions, such as a new phone or a "good customer" credit on your bill before signing another contract.

■ **Credit cards.** By calling every provider, we were able to lower the interest rate on every credit card used in my company. Most credit card companies are willing to negotiate rates, especially if you have good credit scores. If they're not, take one of their competitors' offers (but be certain to pay on time). You may have to call every year, since these rates are continually adjusted.

■ **Rent.** If your town has a glut of commercial space, it may be a good time to renegotiate your lease. Of course, there has to be an incentive for a landlord to lower your rent—perhaps you're willing to take a longer lease? If your lease is up, negotiate hard or move.

■ **Vehicles.** If you've got a car or van that needs frequent repairs or guzzles gas, consider getting a new one, especially if you can get a good deal or very low interest rates.

■ **Insurance.** Ask your agent to review all your policies. Don't just look at lowering premiums—make certain you've got the appropriate coverage for your current needs.

■ **Shipping.** From time to time compare rates from different shipping companies. Even if you want to stick with your current shipping company, try to negotiate more favorable terms or discounts.

Sure, any one of these savings might not be very significant, but to paraphrase an old quote, "A few dollars here and a few dollars there, and pretty soon, you're talking about real money."

Details, Details, Details

Nine Ways to Ensure Your Company's Survival

1. Provide a great product or service. This means continually improving and updating your offerings. It means ongoing training or professional development. In the long run, you're going to be judged by the quality and consistency of your products or services.

2. Be competitively priced. You may not be the cheapest provider around, but you have to be competitively priced. Even loyal customers will leave if they feel they're not getting their money's worth.

3. Give them something extra. Surprise your customers by providing a little additional touch. My car mechanic washes my car before returning it; a hairdresser could provide a short neck massage.

4. Stay in touch. People are busy; it's easy for them to forget about you. Contact your customers at least once a quarter.

5. Set an annual growth goal of 20%. Twenty percent doesn't seem like much; you'd like to double your sales. But it's easier to implement a marketing plan with a realistic target than one that aims for explosive growth.

6. Increase your product/service offerings. One way to increase income is to offer additional product or service lines. You'll get additional revenue from current customers and attract new customers. Just make sure you don't lose focus from your core offerings.

7. Develop a marketing plan. I'm always surprised at the number of entrepreneurs who just expect their business to grow without any action or planning on their part. Face it, if you want to survive—let alone grow—you have to get out there and market.

8. Manage your cash flow. More businesses fail from a lack of cash than a lack of profits. On paper, a business can be making money, but they may not have the money in the bank to pay their bills. Be cautious with your fixed expenses and get a line of credit from the bank to even out cash flow.

9. Lower your costs. Just increasing income doesn't ensure long-term survivability—you have to keep a handle on your expenses, as well. Make it a habit to periodically compare prices from new suppliers, especially on big ticket items such as insurance, rent, and telecommunications.

Tips and Tricks for Business Life

Here's a quick reminder of some of the large and small techniques to get ahead in your business:

■ **Develop—and practice—your Elevator Pitch.** This is a brief sentence that describes what you do. You can use it whenever you introduce yourself to others, even in a social setting. You're more likely to get word-of-mouth referral business if others understand what you do. And you sound more confident if you don't have to search for words.

■ **Think of the long-term value of the customer, not just the one-time transaction.** Since it costs a lot to attract a customer, it's typically smarter to retain an existing customer than to make a fuss over a minor dispute.

■ **Get a mileage-earning credit card for business purchases you now pay for by check.** Then immediately pay off the credit card bill. Ask your vendors if they accept credit cards. Our printer allows us to pay by credit card for the printing of our books. The miles add up fast this way!

■ **Use your cell phone in hotel rooms for long-distance calls.** It's usually much cheaper than using a calling card (and many hotels charge for local calls).

■ **If more than 50% of your business comes from one customer or distribution channel, diversify.** Don't become overly dependent on one source for your long-term economic well-being.

■ **Don't nickel-and-dime clients with charges for phone calls, overnight delivery services, copies, and such.** Figure those costs into your hourly or project fees. You'd be surprised at how many clients who never blink at being billed $100 an hour get peeved by being charged $12 for a FedEx delivery.

> If you work from a home office, set office hours. Make time for personal and family life.

■ **If you're giving a customer or client a discount, let them know it! When you send the bill, be certain to indicate the regular price and then the voluntary discount you're giving them.** That reminds them they're getting a special deal.

■ **If you use the Internet a lot while traveling, check motels targeted to long-term business travelers.** Many offer free high-speed Internet connections.

■ **Keep your notes from phone calls or meetings in a spiral-bound notebook on your desk.** Get rid of all those little pieces of paper with important phone numbers or To Do lists.

■ **Build a database of your current and former customers or clients.** Stay in contact at least once a year, but preferably quarterly. The only way to get word-of-mouth referrals from current and past customers is to remind them you exist.

■ **Join your trade association.** Participate in the local chapter if one exists. Attend a national industry convention at least every two or three years. Subscribe to, and read, an industry magazine or email newsletter.

■ **Keep a list of your best referral sources and best customers where you can see it frequently.** Contact these people at least every one to three months.

■ **It's okay to "fire" clients.** A few reasons to end a client relationship: they don't pay their bills, are unethical, want you to take on work you're uncomfortable performing, soak up all your time and energy, make you hate your business.

■ **View customer complaints as an opportunity to learn how to improve your** product or service rather than merely criticism.

■ **Hold a planning session every year.** Review your long-term goals, set annual sales targets, evaluate your target market, industry, and competition. A day set aside for planning can help you be more successful all year long.

■ **Never compete on price alone.** Make sure you have other competitive advantages that make your customers want to purchase from you even if a competitor undercuts your price.

■ **If you work from a home office, set office hours.** Set time aside for personal and family life.

■ **Do everything with integrity.** Treat everyone fairly and honestly, including employees, customers, and vendors. Don't rationalize bad behavior by saying "It's only business." Be someone worthy of respect.

Overwhelmed by Too Many Choices

Here's something no one tells you about running your own business: You have to make lots of decisions. So many decisions, in fact, that it's easy to become what I call "decide-o-phobic."

Sure, you know you have to decide which product or service to sell and how much to charge, but there are all those other nagging choices: what to pay employees, which computers to buy, insurance to get, loans to apply for, advertising to use, and phone, Internet, and wireless services to choose.

It's exhausting!

These daily choices can be so overwhelming that you can easily start avoiding making any decisions. Once, at the end of a tough work day, I met a friend at a Chinese restaurant. Faced with a multi-page menu, I felt totally defeated. I told my companion to order me anything, I didn't care, just so long as I didn't have to make even one more choice.

Now, I'm hardly a shrinking violet; I'm not the type who's overwhelmed by having to choose between an egg roll and a won ton. But it's the little decisions, made over and over and over each day, that grind you down.

Entrepreneurs can't afford to be decide-o-phobics. In fact, learning how to make decisions is a critical business skill. By being able to make decisions quickly and well you are able to get on with the real work of running and growing your company.

There are two keys to becoming a better decision maker: developing a positive mindset and adopting some practical procedures.

Decision-Making Mindset

1. Recognize that any decision is almost always better than no decision. In our business lives, if we neglect to make decisions, there are usually consequences. Can't choose which health insurance to get? Your best employee might quit out of frustration. Can't decide whether to exhibit at a trade show? The deadline might pass before you make up your mind.

> **Entrepreneurs can't afford to be decide-o-phobics. In fact, learning how to make decisions is a critical business skill.**

2. There's no perfect choice. We often procrastinate thinking that the perfect option will come along if we wait long enough. It won't.

3. You're going to make mistakes. Sure, you'll regret some of your choices, even some big ones. Allow yourself—and others—to make mistakes; that's part of doing business.

235

4. "It's only lunch." Years ago, a friend said that people in his office would agonize over where to go for their mid-day meal. Many choices just aren't worth driving yourself crazy over. Keep perspective; will your business really be affected if you choose one wireless phone service over another?

Practical Decision-Making Tips

1. Empower your employees. Your employees have brains; let them make some choices. Do you really need to be the one to decide which shipping service to use if you've got an employee perfectly capable of doing research and making the choice? Don't just throw decisions at employees: tell them your priorities (do you want the lowest priced shipping service or the most reliable?), let them come to you for input, and then never second-guess or criticize them.

2. Set a deadline. To avoid procrastination, give yourself a "drop dead" date for making a choice. Allow yourself enough time to do the necessary fact finding. But make a decision by your deadline, regardless of how much homework you've done.

3. Establish decision-making meetings. A successful entrepreneur drastically reduced the time it took to make choices at his company by declaring that some meetings were for discussion and others for decisions. At decision-making meetings, choices must be made. In my company, we know we will make big decisions and set direction at our annual planning meeting.

4. Give yourself fewer options. Narrow your choices down to two or three at the most. People get overwhelmed by too many alternatives. Here's a trick I use when trying to decide something with another person: One of us lists three options—only three—and the other can either choose one or veto one.

5. Get good advisors. It's easier to make decisions if you find people you trust, whether it's your accountant, attorney, insurance agent, employees, or sister-in-law.

6. Don't second-guess! You can evaluate your decision at an appropriate time, but once you've made a decision, carry it out.

How to Get More Hours in a Day

The one gift most business owners and managers dream of is more hours in the day, but we're all stuck with just the same old twenty-four. What we can do, however, is make those hours more productive:

1. Create an "Operations Manual." As you deal with a task, jot down the steps you've taken to complete it. That means you won't have to reinvent each process every time. This also makes it much easier to train employees if you have any.

2. Create templates. Instead of recreating forms or letters you use repeatedly, create blank templates of documents such as invoices, statements, proposals, product/service descriptions, basic letters of agreement, and so on. You may find some generic templates as part of your software programs or gather more industry-specific forms from your trade association.

3. Prepare standard answers to email or phone inquiries. It's likely that potential or current customers will ask many of the same questions over and over again. Don't answer with a new email each time, just cut and paste. But try not to sound bored when you give the same answer to one customer after another.

4. Maintain a calendar and keep it visible. You can use a paper desk or wall calendar, but you may find features of calendar software programs (such as pop-up reminders) helpful. Be careful, however, that you don't forget appointments when the computer is off.

5. Make a To Do list. Keep it somewhere where you can see it all the time, either on paper or on your computer. Look at it frequently and revise it daily. Check off tasks as you complete them—that gives you a sense of accomplishment.

6. Prioritize. Often the things that are most important to your business don't have deadlines. Make sure those vital tasks are on the top of your To Do list.

7. Set time aside. Make appointments with yourself to do important tasks and don't allow interruptions. Make certain you schedule time for marketing so you can build your business. Schedule time to send out invoices. You can't get money in if you don't send invoices out.

8. Reduce shopping. Keep a list of all the things you need so you reduce the number of trips you make. Stock up on supplies so you don't have to make a frantic trip when you run out of printer ink.

9. Eliminate errands. Keep a list of errands and do a number of them at one time. Schedule your errands for the end of the business day, rather than during prime work time. Investigate delivery or pick-up options for frequently used services (such as shipping).

10. **Keep frequently used files handy.** Get a desk with at least one file drawer so you can access the files you need easily. Use files of different colors for different types of information—client work, bills, suppliers—so you can quickly find information you need. Mark your files by year, so you can easily archive older files.

11. **Become a power user of email.** Take time to learn a few key steps in your email program, particularly how to set up files and filters. That makes it much faster to find past email correspondence.

12. **Handle mail once.** Ideally, deal with mail as soon as you read it. If you don't need to keep it, throw it out. Otherwise, file it immediately. If you have to take action, do so. Eliminate that pile of mail getting ever higher on your desk.

13. **Do the most important things early in the day.** You're inevitably going to fall behind. Take care of those "must do" items at the start of your workday.

14. **Turn off the phone.** Wean yourself from the need to answer every phone call. Let an assistant or voice mail pick up. You'll have a better chance of finishing your work if you don't let the phone become an interruption and distraction.

15. **Deal with things as they arise.** If a customer has a problem, get it solved. If a supplier has overfilled, straighten it out. This doesn't mean you have to do everything immediately—you can set aside time each day to return calls or answer correspondence—but deal with these issues today.

16. **Get help.** You're probably overworked because you're overworked. You've got more work than one person can do, so get others to do some of the work instead. Can you afford an assistant or another salesperson? If you can't afford full-time help, get part-time assistance, hire contract workers, or use outside companies for bookkeeping or secretarial service.

17. **Take care of yourself.** If you're sick, weak, or burned out, you're not going to be productive. Pay attention to your overall well-being. Eat properly and healthfully. Get enough sleep. Exercise, if only to go out for a brisk walk at lunch. And at some point every week, relax. Remember, the word "recreation" means to re-create, so use some recreation time to renew and re-create yourself.

Would It Kill You to See a Lawyer?

Question: What do you have when you've got three lawyers buried up to their necks in cement? Answer: Not enough cement.

Nobody likes lawyers. Even lawyers make lawyer jokes. Yet lawyers are a necessary, even valuable, part of business life.

Taking care of your company's legal health is like taking care of your personal health: an ounce of prevention is a lot more pleasant than a pound of cure. Time after time, I see entrepreneurs end up in legal battles costing thousands of dollars that could have been avoided with a $200 trip to an attorney.

Your first visit to a lawyer should happen at the beginning of your business life. When I started my consulting practice, I spent two hours with a lawyer. We not only wrote a basic letter of agreement for me to use with clients, we also discussed how to price my services and collect overdue fees, and tax issues.

A number of other legal issues arise when starting a company. First is determining what corporate structure you will take. Most of us begin as sole proprietors. There's no formal structure for a sole proprietorship. Just make certain that you're the only one who has any ownership interest in your company.

But if you're going to form a partnership, a corporation, or a limited liability company, consult a lawyer. Be aware that if you're working with another person, you may be in a legal partnership even if you don't draw up any contracts, so it's definitely advisable to consult a lawyer. Draw up a contract spelling out who owns what and what happens if you eventually divide or sell the company.

If you're new to business, you will also want to discuss such issues as protecting the name of your company, necessary business licenses, taxes, and dealing with vendors and land-lords. If your business has employees, consult a lawyer about issues of hiring and firing employees and what kinds of records to keep. If anyone is investing or lending you money, get a lawyer to draw up a clear contract with all the details of the financial arrangement.

Consultants, and companies that hire out-sourced workers, need at least a basic understanding of how the law treats independent contractors. If you're not incorporated, and if you aren't careful, you can easily get in hot water with the Internal Revenue Service.

The best way to find a lawyer is by asking for referrals, especially from others in your industry. It's always better, and cheaper in the long run, to get an attorney who has experience with your type of business.

Most lawyers charge by the hour, but some have set fees for specific tasks, such as incorporation. Interview your prospective lawyer and ask about costs before engaging their services. You have the right to choose someone you're comfortable with and can afford.

All Those Little Government Things

■ What's a FEDERAL TAX IDENTIFICATION NUMBER and where do I get one?

A Federal Tax Identification Number is the same thing as a Federal Employer Identification Number (FEIN or FIN) or Employer Identification Number (EIN). Your EIN identifies your business in the same way that your Social Security Number identifies you. If your business has employees, or is a corporation, LLC, or partnership, you'll need an EIN. Even if you're a sole proprietor, you may want an EIN because many companies you do business with will ask you for a tax ID number, and using an EIN is more secure than giving a personal Social Security Number.

It's easy to get an EIN. Go to www.irs.gov and get Form SS-4 or call 1-800-TAX-Form to get the form by mail. Be prepared to answer the questions on that form, then call 1-866-816-2065 (toll-free), and the IRS can assign you an EIN over the phone.

■ Do I need a STATE IDENTIFICATION NUMBER?

States may assign you identification or account numbers for various purposes. Here's an easy way to find your state's requirements and resources on the Internet: type www.(your state's abbreviation).gov in your search window. Arizona would be www.az.gov. Look for links to help businesses get started in that state.

■ Do I need a BUSINESS LICENSE?

Typically, you will need a business license. Most cities or counties require every company doing business in that jurisdiction to have a license. However, you probably won't need a license for a home-based business. Check with your local governments.

■ What's a RESALE LICENSE?

A resale license enables a company to purchase goods or materials for manufacture or sale without paying sales tax, because the tax will be charged to the ultimate consumer. In other words, if I own a sporting goods store, I can buy golf clubs from the manufacturer without paying sales tax, since I'm going to sell those golf clubs to a customer, and I'll charge the consumer the sales tax.

■ What's a "DBA," or FICTITIOUS BUSINESS STATEMENT?

If you use any name other than your own personal name for doing business, you'll need to file a "doing business as," or fictitious business, statement, usually with your county government. In almost every case, you'll also have to publish this information in a local newspaper.

Remember the Independent Contractor Deadline

Someone once quipped, "Being a consultant means never having to say you're unemployed." As the number of unemployed has ballooned, the number of self-employed consultants and other independent contractors has also increased. After all, if you can't find a job, you might as well try going into business for yourself.

If you're one of those newly minted independent contractors—or if you run a business that hires any independent contractor—there's a critical date for you to remember.

The date is January 31. That's the deadline for businesses which have used independent contractors to send Internal Revenue Form 1099-MISC to those independent contractors they've paid more than $600 in the last year and to file those forms with the IRS. It's also the date that independent contractors should start contacting any company that hasn't sent them a 1099 for work done in the past year.

Few areas of employment law are murkier than those that determine who qualifies as an independent contractor for tax purposes and who doesn't. And few areas of tax law can get a business—or an independent worker—in more trouble with the IRS.

Here's why:

As a business owner, you naturally want to reduce your costs as much as possible.

When you use a worker, you can pay them in one of two ways:

■ As an employee, which requires you to pay additional payroll, Social Security, and unemployment taxes, or

■ As an independent contractor, which requires you to pay no additional taxes.

The IRS aggressively pursues companies that inappropriately pay workers as independent contractors instead of employees.

As a worker, you can work:

■ As an employee, receiving less money in your pocket now due to withholding taxes but also enjoying more worker protection

241

■ As an independent contractor, receiving more money in pocket (since there are no withholding taxes on your income), enjoying no worker protection, and being required to pay your own taxes at the end of the year.

Obviously, many businesses would prefer to treat "employees" as independent contractors and avoid all those pesky taxes and worker protections. Equally obviously, the federal government, states, and cities, want to make certain that anyone who's really doing the work of an employee gets treated— and protected—as one.

So watch out! The IRS is particularly aggressive in pursuing companies that intentionally, or unintentionally, inappropriately pay workers as independent contractors instead of employees. The IRS has gone after huge corporations as well as small businesses, and once they find a violation, they're likely to go through your back years' taxes as well.

Making the task more difficult is the fact that IRS guidelines aren't crystal clear. They used to have a laundry list of rules governing independent contractor status, but the IRS, responding to legitimate needs of businesses for greater flexibility in hiring independent contractors, made the rules broader. But that means there's more room for misunderstanding.

The main issue the IRS tries to determine is who "controls" the worker. They look at three areas.

■ **Behavioral.** Does the worker control how they do the work? In other words, the IRS looks at issues such as who controls:

• When and where the worker works
• What order or sequence of work the worker follows
• What tools or equipment a worker uses
• Who determines where workers purchase supplies

■ **Financial.** Does the worker have a significant investment (for instance, do they own their own tools), can they make a profit or loss, do they make their services available to others, work for other businesses?

■ **Type of relationship.** How permanent is the relationship, is there a written contract, is the worker responsible for their own benefits, is the work performed a critical and regular part of the business?

Because the rules are somewhat fuzzy, the IRS does provide some protection for businesses that make mistakes in qualifying employees as independent contractors, as long as those mistakes were made in good faith. They'll look to see whether a business relied on advice of an attorney or accountant, followed industry practice, treated workers consistently. But—and this is important—there's absolutely no protection for any company that doesn't file an IRS Form 1099 for an independent contractor. So don't let January 31 slip by without getting those 1099's in the mail!

Home Office Issues

For fourteen years I ran a business from my home. I enjoyed working from home, and I'm not alone. The growth in home-based businesses has been so explosive that some home builders design houses especially for home-based entrepreneurs, with extra work space, storage, and separate entrances.

Working from home presents unique challenges. Here are four of the most common:

1. Where should I meet with customers?

When you work from home, you'll often arrange to meet clients at their offices. That avoids the problem of clients in your home.

If you'll often meet customers at your home, it's best if you set up a work space separate from your family surroundings. If possible, have a separate entrance or path to your office that doesn't go through the kids' playroom.

If you need to meet customers somewhere other than their offices, look for neutral locations, such as restaurants or coffee houses. However, if you have many such meetings, find office space you can use on an occasional basis. Executive suite services often offer hourly office rentals. Or make an arrangement with another company (such as a law firm) to use or rent a conference room or extra office from them.

2. What about phones and the Internet?

After your toddler answers a call from your most important client, you'll see why it's necessary to install a separate phone line for incoming business calls. If you want to be listed in the Yellow Pages or business section of the phone book, some local phone companies may require you to have a business phone line. An extra phone line for business enables you to have a business voice mail message on that line and a family message on your other line.

> After your toddler answers a call from your most important client, you'll see why it's necessary to install a separate phone line for incoming business calls.

Get a fast Internet connection if you're working from home full time. Once you get used to fast service and being constantly connected to the Internet, you'll discover it makes email communication and finding information much easier.

243

3. What tax deductions can I take?

When you work from home, one murky area you'll encounter is the matter of which expenses are deductible as business expenses and which are not.

Expenses you would incur whether or not you were working from home—postage, office supplies, advertising—are treated the same way as they would be in any other business. You claim those expenses as part of your regular deductions for the cost of doing business.

However, you have an additional tax savings option for your home office if you qualify. The home office deduction enables you to deduct a portion of the cost of the part of your house or apartment used exclusively for business. Be careful! There are many things to consider before taking a home office deduction, including the fact that this deduction is rigorously examined by taxation authorities, as well as the fact that taking this deduction will have tax implications when you sell your home. Discuss this—and all other home office deductions and business expenses—with your accountant or tax advisor.

4. Should I get a business mailbox?

When I first started working from home, I wasn't comfortable giving my home address to strangers or putting it on a marketing brochure.

One alternative is to get a Post Office box from the U.S. Postal Service. However, then your only address is a P.O. Box and that may not give a professional impression. Moreover, the Post Office usually doesn't accept mail from private delivery services such as Federal Express or UPS.

A better alternative is to rent a mailbox from one of the many private mailbox providers. This gives you the advantages of keeping your home address private, having a secure place to receive mail, and knowing there will be someone who can sign for and receive packages for you.

Working from a Distance

A long, long time ago, let's say twenty-five years ago, people who owned businesses actually worked in the same building as their employees. Their customers came to their stores or offices. There wasn't an Internet—no email or instant messaging. No faxes. Long distance phone calls were expensive.

Today we've got outsourcing, telecommuting, virtual companies, independent contractors. These new business twists make it possible for people to work together without ever being under the same roof.

Technology has made working with others across the country, even across the world, possible and affordable, with many advantages:

■ **More options.** Whether you're hiring an employee or a consultant, you can find someone with more experience in your industry or exactly the job skills you require when you can draw from a wider geographic area.

■ **Expanded market.** Just as you can choose your employees or service providers from a greater geographic area, you now also have a bigger pool of potential customers. It's easier to specialize in a niche product or service and still find a large enough market.

■ **Lower cost.** You can save money when an employee, partner, or contractor works from their own space. Any added telecommunications costs are more than made up for by the money you save on rent and overhead.

■ **Lifestyle options.** Do you want to live in a small rural town but have Fortune 500 companies as clients? Does your valued employee's spouse have a job offer in another city? Does your independent contractor want to be home with the kids? Lifestyle choices are driving the rapid growth in remote-location working relationships.

> Perhaps the most valuable things lost when you don't work face-to-face are all the good ideas that never get thought up.

But for all these advantages, there are also pitfalls:

■ **Lack of communication.** You share a lot of information informally when you work right next to someone. Once you're working with people from a distance, those informal information-sharing opportunities disappear, and it's much harder to give feedback, share company developments, solve problems.

■ **Loss of team spirit.** It's much more difficult to pull together when you're not actually together. Working in a group, there's a sense of being part of a team pulling toward a common goal. When employees are remotely located (especially in a very small company) you can lose the critical mass necessary for that sense of shared mission.

■ **Increased isolation.** One of the biggest challenges facing a person working independently is the sense of isolation. It's easy to feel alone when you're working alone.

■ **Loss of synergy.** Perhaps the most valuable things lost when you don't work face-to-face are all the good ideas that never get thought up. Sometimes you've got to literally put your heads together to come up with new strategies and solutions.

To counterbalance these negative effects, you can enhance your long distance working relationships by following a few steps:

1. Set clear goals and standards. At the beginning of any project, or phase of a project, get together (preferably in person) and review expectations and timelines. Remember, it's much harder to clear up misunderstandings when you're not working side by side, so get things as clear as possible from the start.

2. Establish and maintain a regular reporting routine. Don't just say you're going to keep in touch. Get out your appointment books and establish set times to report in. Set up a weekly staff meeting by phone.

3. Use email. Email is a quick and cheap way to share information. And, unlike phone calls, it produces a written record. Send a weekly update of what's going on to all employees.

4. Use instant messaging. If you're not familiar with instant messaging, ask a teenager. They use this instantaneous (faster and even more informal than email) Internet technology to chat back and forth in real time. When you have remotely located employees, I.M. can become your virtual water cooler.

5. Use the phone. It's easy for something in writing to be misunderstood. There's less chance of confusion when you're having an actual conversation. The phone is a more personal form of interaction and creates a stronger personal bond.

6. Meet in person. Nothing beats "face time" for building and maintaining relationships. Get in the car or on a plane and spend some quality time together.

Preparing for the Unexpected

Floods. Fires. Tornados. Earthquakes. Natural disasters can hit any small business anywhere. I've had my business interrupted twice by natural disasters—a flood and a major earthquake. I've been lucky; all I've ever lost was power and a few days' work. Others will not be so fortunate: they'll lose inventory, customer records, equipment, and income. Hopefully they'll never lose a life.

Every business, no matter how small, needs an emergency preparedness plan. It doesn't have to be complicated, and you don't have to practice fire drills. A few simple steps can save you money and heartache.

The preparations you make depend on the dangers your location is likely to face. Bolting down bookshelves may be more important in Santa Barbara than Salt Lake City, but many steps can be critical for businesses anywhere, of any size.

■ **Emergency plan.** Before disaster strikes, determine the critical components of your business. Here's how: for a one-month period, keep notes on what you do and what you need to accomplish those tasks (employees, data, power, phones, Internet, physical access). What would happen if an emergency struck? How would you get phone messages? Can you get your email from a remote location? How would you contact your employees? Where could you work? Make contingency plans for every aspect of your business.

■ **Insurance.** As awful as a disaster can be, its effects will be less devastating if insurance covers the financial losses. Granted, disaster insurance can be expensive, but this type of insurance should be evaluated in the same way as any other business expense. Consider business interruption insurance, which covers you even if your business doesn't suffer physical damage but you lose income due to the effects of a disaster, such as closed roads or loss of power.

> **Before disaster strikes, determine the critical components of your business.**

If yours is a home-based business, examine your policies and talk to your insurance agent. Most homeowner policies don't cover things such as computers, tools, and samples. So adjust policies accordingly.

■ **Data.** Our businesses rely on our records, so it's critically important to regularly back up your computer data and store copies of both digital and paper data off-site. On-line data backup companies offer relatively inexpensive options for storing data over the Internet. At the very least, in small companies, the boss can take a backup copy of records home once a week; just make sure they are stored at least a mile from the office or store. Get a fireproof safe for vital documents; make copies and store those off-site or with your attorney.

■ **Power.** Purchase auxiliary generators for vital business equipment. You can also obtain inexpensive backup power supplies to give you about a half-an-hour's extra power for computers, giving you time to back up records.

■ **Safety.** In case of disaster, the most important thing is safety: for yourself, your employees, and customers. Keep flashlights (with fresh batteries) on hand so you can leave the building safely in the dark. Develop evacuation plans; know how to exit your building in the dark or in a fire. And (okay, I lied) conduct fire drills.

■ **Employee backup.** Emergencies also come in the form of personal disasters, such as illnesses and accidents, so make backup plans in case you or key employees become unavailable. Make certain that someone knows where your records are and has the power to deposit checks, and pay bills, and can contact customers. This could be a key employee, an attorney, even a family member. Just make sure you trust them!

■ **Contingency vendors.** Remember, a disaster elsewhere can prove to be a disaster for you if your business depends on distant key suppliers. Develop a list of alternatives in case your regular supplier becomes unavailable.

Finally, keep in mind that disasters have psychological as well as physical and financial effects. You and your employees will need time to readjust, so expect distractions and extra time spent around the water cooler recounting just where they were when the dam broke, the tornado struck, or the earth shook. Stay safe!

Go Outside and Play

The weather's heating up and business has you down. You need a vacation! When you're in business for yourself, you can't just pick up and go. What you need is "Rhonda's Handy-Dandy Vacation Escape Guide for the Self-Employed."

The three key ingredients in Rhonda's Guide are:

- **Attitude**
- **Ability**
- **Action**

Master these three and you'll vastly increase the chances of getting your own suntan this summer.

■ **Attitude.** Repeat after me, "I have the right to take a vacation." Typically, the most difficult part of arranging a vacation is making the commitment to go. Of course, you must first decide if you can afford both the cost of the trip itself and any lost income. But that's not the big hurdle for many business owners. They often feel that the entire business will fall apart if they leave, they haven't "earned" a vacation, or they have to wait until "the timing is better."

Face it: the timing is never good. Working year round without any breaks is bad for both your health and the health of your business. You can't get perspective on your business while you're caught up in day-to-day pressures. I always get new insights and renewed enthusiasm for my business from a vacation. Vacations help prevent "burnout,

which can be a bigger long-term threat to your company's viability than a week at the beach. Even more importantly, vacations are good for you and your family and loved ones. If you're self-employed, business monopolizes a disproportionate amount of your time and attention. Every year make your family the center of your life for at least a week or two.

> **Repeat after me:
> "I have the right to take
> a vacation."**

■ **Ability.** Now that you've decided to go, you need a plan to make your absence work. The plan itself depends on the nature of your business, how long you'll be gone, and whether you want to be out of touch altogether.

Two kinds of vacation plans work best: those made well in advance and last-minute getaways. Schedule long vacations well in advance to give you time to complete major projects and find other people to cover your work. If you work alone, you may want to ask someone in the same industry to handle

249

client emergencies or inquiries from new customers. If you do, decide with them how to deal with issues such as who bills the client, how much will be charged, how income will be split, and who gets to keep new customers.

Last-minute getaways can be great. Seize the opportunity when you see a break in your schedule and can get out of town! Just don't make this your only vacation plan, especially if other traveling companions depend on your schedule. Somehow, work always seems to fill any available time, and you may find you never get a break at all.

■ **Action.** It's no longer possible to put up a sign saying "Gone fishing" when you're away. You've got to have a better way to communicate with customers in your absence.

First, cover your phones. Voice mail is the easiest solution. Record a message indicating which day you'll return. (You might add an extra day to give yourself time to catch up on your first day back.) Even if you plan on checking messages while you're away, don't mention this or people will expect you to return their calls. If you have a number they can call in an emergency, leave that.

Vacation Planning Tips

■ **Find someone to mind the store.** Customers and clients expect to reach someone instantaneously. Line up an employee or colleague who's prepared to step in for you.

■ **Cover routine tasks.** Arrange for routine tasks to be handled in your absence. If you're going for more than a week, consider giving someone you trust completely a Power of Attorney.

■ **Set a vacation date in the future and stick with it.**

■ **Make it hard to back out.** Get your reservations reserved and deposits deposited. Plan to go with others who won't let you off the hook easily.

I've seen ads that show a mom doing business on her cell phone at the beach, but I'm not convinced that trying to take calls on your vacation is such a good idea. If you do, it becomes a working vacation instead of a family vacation. Ask yourself "Will the world, or my business, really come to an end if I tell customers I'm away for a week?" (And isn't it about time for the assistant manager to learn how to handle problems without constant guidance from you?)

The same is true with email. There is nothing more frustrating for a traveling companion than to see only the back of your head while you pour over email messages. Most email programs have an auto-responder that can send a reply telling correspondents you're on vacation, so it doesn't seem like you've just ignored their message.

Take at least one vacation a year without calls, email, or checking with the office. Go ahead, live without business for a brief while. You'll find that both you and your business survive. You'll return to work not only with a better tan but with a better, more energized outlook toward your business.

Business Lessons from Baseball

One of the reasons I'm a big baseball fan is that the sport has so many parallels to real life. Here's what baseball teaches us about running a business:

It's a long season. Like baseball, business takes patience. Forget "get rich quick" schemes. It takes a while for your concept, marketing, planning, and operations to gel.

■ **Stick with it.** Every baseball player and team goes through losing streaks. In business, you're also going to have setbacks; you can't let those throw you. Sooner or later, especially if you learn from your mistakes, things are likely to turn your way (unless, of course, you're a Cubs fan).

■ **You need management.** Baseball is a game of strategy; you can't just go out there, throw a few balls, and expect to win. In business, this means having a plan, evaluating your decisions, keeping an eye on the big picture.

■ **Don't depend on one star for success.** Just as no team can depend on one star to win every game for them, you can't depend on one star customer (or one distributor or channel) for your success. If you're overly dependent on one or two customers, you need to strengthen your lineup.

■ **To win, you need both offense and defense.** No team can win a game on offense or defense alone. The same is true in business. You need offense: making sales, creating new products, beating your competition. But you also need defense: taking care of your internal operations, watching cash flow, managing employees.

■ **Swing for the fences.** Occasionally, you've got to go for that home run, that big customer, new product, or expensive advertising campaign.

■ **Depend on "small ball."** Home runs get all the glory, but baseball games are typically won one base at a time. The same is true in business; you build a business one customer, one sale, at a time.

■ **Have faith.** As the song from the musical *Damn Yankees* says, "You've gotta have heart." As an entrepreneur, you have to believe in yourself—over and over again.

■ **Have fun.** Ask any Cubs or Red Sox fan, and they'll tell you winning isn't everything. Sure, you've got to make a profit, but you also want to enjoy going to work.

■ **If you bat .400, you're in the Hall of Fame.** In baseball, even the biggest stars fail in seven out of ten attempts to get on base. You want to do better than that, but you certainly don't have to be perfect to be a success.

A Dog's View of Business

Allow me to introduce myself: I'm Cosmo, Rhonda's dog. I know you're looking for Rhonda's advice on business, but I put my paw down and insisted she take a break.

So instead of Rhonda, I'm offering you my advice. Think a dog can't know much about business? Well, from my bed under Rhonda's desk, I've had a unique vantage point. I've heard her on the phone; I've sat in on meetings. I've learned a lot. So allow me to share my dog's-eye perspective on what it takes to build a successful company.

■ **Loyalty.** Nobody knows more about loyalty than dogs. We canines virtually invented it, which would make us great in business. First, we'd start by being loyal to our employees. We'd recognize they're the ones who make our lives possible. A dog would never turn on someone just because they're having a bad day.

■ **Next, we'd be loyal to customers.** Dogs don't leave their humans just because a different human offers tastier treats. Sometimes people start looking at customers solely as dollar signs, not as people. Relationships are what makes business work.

■ **Patience.** If dogs were as impatient as humans, we'd have given up on our owners a long time ago. People make mistakes or disappoint you. If you're going to live with humans, be willing to put up with a lot. They take time to learn, to change, to get things right. But they really are worth sticking around for.

■ **Perseverance.** I love to play fetch. I can retrieve a ball for hours and hours and hours. Rhonda doesn't like this game. But I get her to play it anyway. How? I keep at it. Now, I'm not saying you should use my methods—barking, pulling at her skirt, whimpering miserably—but it takes persistence to get ahead. Some humans want to "get rich quick." That's not the way it works. It's like Rhonda says, "The best way to be an overnight success is to work at it for years."

■ **Gratitude.** How do dogs get humans to do what we want? Not just by making "puppy dog eyes." We also wag our tails or lick your faces. We let you know when you've made us happy. Canines know humans are suckers for appreciation. Try it. When someone does something that pleases you, try wagging your tail (or a more appropriate human equivalent).

■ **Playtime.** This is where I truly excel. Fetch. Tug-of-war. Chew up the shoes. What's life without play? But you'd be amazed at how many humans forget to play. Play is called "recreation." Think about that word: re-create—create again. That's what you're supposed to do, re-create yourself by taking time out, being playful, enjoying your life. Otherwise, it's just a dog's life. Woof!

Doing Well by Doing Good

Every entrepreneur hopes to do well. We'd all like to make a lot of money and have a big, profitable customer base. But over the years, I've realized that most entrepreneurs want to do more. They'd not only like to do well; they'd like to do good. They'd like their business to contribute to their community, respect the environment, and play a positive role in the lives of their employees and customers.

I'm not naïve or simplistic. I strongly believe that building an honest, responsible business with a healthy bottom line in and of itself makes a valuable contribution to our economy and society. Such businesses buy supplies and materials, often employ others, and obviously meet a customer need.

Over the years, however, I've learned that companies with a sense of integrity and purpose actually have a competitive edge over companies that are solely focused on the bottom line.

Being socially responsible helps you:

■ **Attract and retain employees.** A corporate culture committed to good corporate citizenship enables employees to feel that they are part of something important. Company programs allowing employees to use job time to be involved in community causes are viewed as a benefit. Prospective employees look at a company's values and social commitment when comparing job offers.

■ **Attract and retain customers.** People like to do business with companies they respect. Some customers are attracted by specific company policies; they prefer to buy products that aren't tested on animals or that are recycled. But all customers are attracted to companies that consistently deal with them honestly and fairly.

> **Companies with a sense of integrity and purpose have a competitive edge over companies that focus solely on the bottom line.**

■ **Reduce employee misbehavior.** Businesses that act with integrity and honesty toward their employees, customers, and suppliers are more likely to have employees who also act with integrity and honesty toward the company and their fellow workers. An atmosphere of honesty helps keep everyone honest.

■ **Stay out of trouble.** Being a good corporate citizen—in your advertising, employee treatment, or environmental policies—makes it less likely that your company will face trouble with regulatory agencies, or taxing authorities, or face lawsuits or fines.

Being a good corporate citizen may involve participating in programs outside your own company, doing such things as contributing funds to community programs, enabling employees to volunteer for such programs, or adopting or identifying your company with specific issues or programs.

First, however, good corporate citizenship begins with a company's own internal practices and policies, including:

■ Obeying the law, acting ethically, and being honest and responsible in all your dealings

■ Treating employees fairly and with respect, compensating employees fairly, and considering the well-being of employees when making decisions

■ Being honest and fair to your customers and suppliers, and in your advertising

■ Being aware of the impact your actions have on the environment

A critical aspect of being a good corporate citizen is making certain that what you sell is of the quality you promise. Some steps can be followed to ensure that it is.

■ Design your products or services to achieve the results desired and advertised

■ Ensure high and consistent quality of manufacture and production so that the design specifications can be met

■ Use trustworthy suppliers and subcontractors so that the standards you hold, such as manufacture quality and environmental standards and treatment of employees, are continually maintained.

Your responsibility to your customer begins even before they buy from you—with what you tell them about your products, and services, or your company itself. Many companies get in trouble because they use misleading, confusing, or even false advertising or sales techniques to attract customers. They may not be intentionally dishonest, just eager to make a sale resulting in overstating what a product can deliver.

Before you begin an advertising program, familiarize yourself with what constitutes deceptive or dishonest marketing. The Better Business Bureau has worked with the advertising industry as well as leading corporations to develop an Advertising Code, which you can find at www.bbb.org/app.

When your company does good, you'll find you also do well.

Great Faith. Great Doubt. Great Effort.

On my desk I have a small book of Zen quotations I open from time to time for inspiration. One quote that has stuck with me over the years—and that I find myself repeating as I run and grow my business—is "Great Faith. Great Doubt. Great Effort."

Great Faith. Great Doubt. Great Effort. Three things that are necessary to bring anything meaningful to fruition.

■ **Great Faith.** To build a business you must believe in yourself and your ideas. At first this is exhilarating. After all, you can envision something others cannot. You're the one who can create a new business, process, design, or technology. You're the one who can imagine something that has never existed before. You're the one who believes it's possible to make your vision a reality.

It is not only the quality of your ideas but the strength of your faith in those ideas that enables you to attract others to work with you, invest in you, support you.

But great faith is also exhausting. It's impossible to stay on an emotional high, even if things continually go well. And they will not always go well. When your business encounters pitfalls, detours, and slowdowns, others will look to you for reassurance. You will then have to call on the reserves of your faith in your project to bring back the momentum, to reassure others. This will happen when your own faith is most challenged.

That is why you have to have great faith, because your vision and dedication have to be strong enough to withstand the doubts of others and your own doubts, as well. When others believe you are drowning, you have to be the one who can still reach the shore.

■ **Great Doubt.** If you do not bring a healthy and respectful appreciation of the challenges you'll face when building a new business, you'll be unable to withstand the difficult times. I have met many would-be entrepreneurs who have "fool-proof" ideas for businesses or inventions they think cannot fail. They're unlikely to succeed, because nothing is fool-proof, and they lack a sufficient level of doubt.

Even the best-laid plans and the best-planned businesses can fail. You must be able to see and anticipate potential problems. If you have no doubts, then you won't be prepared to deal with setbacks. Instead, you have to recognize that there will be great difficulties, and you need to be able to adapt, regroup, re-energize. It is doubt that prepares you for this.

Moreover, you must challenge yourself. You must be willing to take a clear-headed look at your plans, your abilities, and your competition so you can respond accordingly. Great doubt is part of success, not necessarily an indication of failure. I remind myself of that every time I find myself sleepless at 3 a.m., daunted by all the things I have to do to make my business a success.

■ **Great Effort.** Nothing succeeds without hard work. No great business is built on ideas alone; great businesses take perseverance and hard work. I've seen hundreds of people with great ideas who have never made a dime. They needed great effort, as well.

It is not true that if you build a better mousetrap, the world will beat a path to your door. In fact, building a better mousetrap is only a beginning. You've got to find financing for your mousetrap company, produce, market, and ship those mousetraps, and fight with the patent office over your mousetrap patent. Then you'll have to figure out how to respond when a competitor brings in cheaper foreign imitations. Some days you'll wish you'd never invented a better mousetrap!

Great faith. Great doubt. Great effort.

Others will question your chances of success. With great faith, you'll never be shaken. With great doubt, you'll also be prepared. With great effort, you will triumph. ■

Index

A

Accountant, 222. *See also* Bookkeeping; Internal Revenue Service (IRS); Tax

Administrative assistance, 12, 13, 92, 191–92, 238

Advertising, 104, 111–12, 119–20

    ethics, 254

    mailing list, 109, 115–16, 234

    newsletter, 109

    newspaper, 20

    sales sheet, 121

    website, 135–36

    word-of-mouth, 109–10, 234

    See also Marketing; Media relations; Public relations

Advertising products, specialty, 104, 109, 117–18

Advisors, 9, 179–80, 236

Advisory committee, 180, 181–82. *See also* Board of Directors

Associates, professional, 97–98, 176.

    See also "Virtual company"

Associations, professional, 109, 139–40

Attire, business, 131, 133–34

Authority, delegating, 32, 79–80, 152, 177–78, 187–88, 192, 200, 201–2. *See also* Employees: managing

B

BADD Boss Syndrome, 203–4

Balance sheet, 209–10, 224

Banks

    as source of financing, 215–16, 217–18

Billing. *See* Invoicing

Board of Directors, 180, 181–82, 219.

    See also Advisory committee

Bookkeeping, 95, 222. *See also* Accountant; Internal Revenue Service (IRS); Tax

Boss, being a, 173–206, 251, 252, 253.

    See also Employees; Management

Business

    closing, 7–8, 82, 87–88

    failures, 7–8, 25–26, 73–74

    first, 19–20

    implementation, 33–42

    motivation for starting, 5–6, 11

    risk, 9–10, 12, 251

    sale of, 81–82, 87–88

    start-up, 3, 19, 24, 25–26, 28, 147–48, 214

    time commitment, 8

    training-wheel, 19–20

    type, 5

    See also Failure, business; Start-up, business

Business cards, 14, 104, 107–8, 124, 132

Business idea, 21–32, 24, 26

    evaluating, 27–28, 31–32

Business plan, 93–94, 95, 183, 234

Business statement, fictitious, 240

Buy/sell agreement, 183

C

Capital, venture, 49, 69, 86, 181, 219, 220

Cash flow, 218, 232, 251

Cell phone, 230, 233. *See also* Telephone service

Change, 43–52, 91, 96

    to be competitive, 67

    preparing for, 45–46

Charitable giving, 77–78. *See also* Community involvement

Closing a business, 7–8, 82, 87–88. *See also* Failure, business

Cold calls, 163–64

Commitment, 39–40, 42, 48

Community involvement, 77–78, 110, 254

Company. *See* Business; Name, of business

Competencies, core, 70, 86

Competition, 23, 30, 63–64, 65–66, 69–70, 232

    analysis of, 65

    differentiation from, 67

    Internet, 65–66

    with large companies, 65, 67–68

    new, 87

    on price alone, 234

    products changing the basis of, 70

Complacency, avoiding, 45–46, 62

Complaints, customer, 169–70, 233, 234, 238.

    See also Customer relations; Customer service

Computers
    data backup, 248
    efficient use of, 92
    passwords, 79–80
    templates for repeat tasks, 237
Consulting, 7, 9, 19, 75
Contingencies, 31. *See also* Emergencies
Contractor, independent, 245
    tax issues regarding, 239, 241–42
Control
    of own business, 3–4, 11–12
    giving up, 32
Corporate accounts, landing, 159–60
Corporate competitors, 65, 67–68
Corporate structure, 222, 239, 240
Costs, 13, 79
    of delivering services, 31
    of delivering products, 72
    opportunity, 47
    reducing, 13, 74, 161–62, 209, 223, 229–30, 232
    of virtual staff, 245
Courage, 17–18
Credit
    history, 218
    line of, 214, 217, 232
Credit cards, 214, 221, 225–26, 230, 233
Customer relations, 136, 151–52, 154, 161–62, 165–66, 167–68, 169–70, 171, 232, 233, 234, 253. *See also* Complaints, customer; Customer service
Customers, 26, 141–72, 176
    advice from, 180
    complaints, 169–70, 233, 234, 238
    corporate, 159–60
    defining, 143–46
    difficult, 165–66
    first, 147–48
    follow-up with, 234
    inertia, 63–64, 65
    informed, 63
    loss of, natural, 87
    low-price shoppers, 73
    loyalty of, 74, 151–52, 233
    loyalty to, 252
    needs, 23, 143-46
    new, 16, 103, 253
    overdependence on one, 61, 233, 251
    refusing, 161–62, 167–68, 234
    remote, 245–46
Customer service, 62, 68, 74, 110,151–52, 169–70. *See also* Complaints, customer; Customer relations

D

Data backup, 248
Decision making, 11, 16, 39-40, 42, 235–36
    abandoning a project, 47
    fear of, 235
    See also Planning; Strategy
Demand, consumer, 23, 72
Direct mail, 104, 116
Distribution, product, 23, 233, 251
Diversification, 55–56, 62, 233
Dogs, at the office, 6, 195
Doing Business As (DBA) statement, 240
Domain name, 14, 106
Dress, business, 131, 133–34
Dun & Bradstreet
    credit history, 218
    report on competitors, 66

E

Economic vulnerability, 61–62
Efficiency. *See* Time management
Effort, 5–6, 8, 91, 256–58
Elevator pitch, 124, 125–26, 233
Email, 14, 115, 237, 238, 246
Emergencies, 79–80, 247–48
Employee buy-out, 82
Employees, 5–6, 39, 46, 92, 176
    advice from, 180
    delegating authority to, 32, 79–80, 152, 177 78, 187–88, 192, 200, 201–2
    diversity, 198
    evaluation of, 200
    excellence, 68
    flexibility, 46
    managing, 177–78, 187–88, 193–94, 196–97, 199–200, 203–5, 251, 252, 253
    mistakes, 188
    motivation, 88, 200

pay, 73, 195, 197
and pets, 6, 195
and planning, 46
recruitment, 195–96
remote, 245–46
rewards, 194, 195, 200, 205
training, 68, 178, 199
virtual staff, 189, 245–46
Employer Identification Number (EIN), 240
Entrepreneur,
    associations, 176
    creative, 3
    and fear, 15–18
    money consciousness, 11
    motivation, 3–4, 5–6, 11–12, 28
    personality, 9–10
    recognition of, 13
    serial, 19
    status, 13–14
    thinking like an, 1–20
    types, 9–10
Entrepreneurship, 2
    failure in, 7-8
    like sports, 17–18, 39
    time commitment, 8
Environmental responsibility, 253, 254
Equipment, 223–24
Estate planning for business, 79–80
Estimates, submitting, 161–62
Ethics, 234, 253–54
Exit strategy, 81–82
Expenses. *See* Costs
Experience, business, 26, 49–50, 60

F

Failure, business, 7–8, 25–26, 73–74
    avoiding, 42, 45–46, 48
    dwelling on, 51–52
    fear of, 15–18
    growth too fast, 69
    learning from, 47, 49–50, 51–52
    See also Closing a business
Faith, 256–57, 251, 256–58
Family
    advice from, 180
    effect of business on, 47

financial support of, 27
takeover of business, 82
time for, 5, 99, 234
working with, 176, 185–86, 190, 220
Fear, 15–18, 257
    of change, 46
    of decision making, 235
Federal Employer Identification Number (FEIN), 240
Federal Tax Identification Number, 222, 240
Fees, 184
    extra, 75–76
    setting professional, 83
Financial management, 11, 95, 207–30, 218, 232, 251
Financial planning, 27, 211–12
Financial terminology, 208
Financing, 207–30, 213–14
    angel investor, 215, 220
    bank, 215–16, 217–18
    collateral, 216
    credit cards, 214, 221
    venture capitalist, 49, 69, 86, 181, 219, 220
    See also Investors; Loans
Firing, legal issues, 239
Flexibility, 39-40
    in employees, 46
Focus, 31–32, 55–58, 86, 191, 203–4
Free products and services, 72, 75–76, 78, 147, 232, 233
Friends
    effect of business on, 47
    working with, 184, 220

G

Get rich quick schemes, 92, 209, 251
Goals, 2, 3, 40–42, 93, 95, 234
    achievable, 35–36
    personal vs. business, 27–28
    quantifying, 93
    vs. tasks, 37–38
Goodwill, 77-78, 110, 252, 253–54
Growth, iv, 69, 77–78, 85–100,
    benefits of, 87–88
    funding, 86
    Rhonda's Rules for, 86
    strategies for, 89–90, 232

H

Health, personal, 238, 249–50, 252
Hiring, 46, 195–96, 199
    first employee, 191
    legal issues, 239
Hobby vs. business, 24, 27, 29–30
Holidays, 249–50, 252
Home office, 14, 243–44
    hours, 234
    and pets, 6, 195
    vs. rented offices, 99
Human resources. *See* Employees; Management: of
    employees

I

Image, business, 123–40, 97-98, 105–6, 109–110,
    111–12, l35–36. *See also* Charitable giving;
    Community involvement; Goodwill
Implementation of business concept, 33–42
Incorporation, 7, 240
Innovation, 3, 23, 55, 49, 74
    disadvantages of, 25, 26
Insurance, 80, 230, 247
Interests, personal, and business, 24, 27, 28, 29–30,
    58, 88, 251
Internal Revenue Service (IRS), 27, 239, 241.
    See also Accountant; Bookkeeping; Tax
Internet business, iv, 26, 31–32, 135
    as competition, 63
Internet service, 233, 243
Investors, 10, 81, 175, 179–80, 213, 219–20
    angel, 215, 220
    friends and family, 220
    legal issues, 239
    venture capitalist, 49, 69, 86, 181, 219, 220
Invoicing, 158, 222, 237
    non-payment, 234

L

Leadership, 39, 173–206. *See also* Management
Leasing vs. buying, 223–24
Legal issues, 181, 183, 190, 239–40, 254
    documents, 26
    estate planning for business, 79–80
    and hiring, 239

and investors, 219
trademarks, 106
transfer of ownership, 81–82
License, business, 239, 240
License, resale, 240
Limited Liability Company, 222, 239, 240
Loans, 86, 215–16
    legal issues, 239
    SBA, 218
    term, 214, 217
    See also Financing; Investors

M

Mailbox, business, 244
Mailing list, 109, 115–16, 234
Management
    of employees, 177–78, 187–88, 193–94, 196–
    97, 199–200, 203–5
    of finances, 210
    See also Authority, delegating
Market
    creation, 90
    existing, 25
    expansion, 90
    new, 25, 90
    niche, 20, 23, 26, 59–60, 73–74
    research, 86
    target, 86, 91
Marketing, 101–22, 76, 77–78, 95, 147–49, 157–
    60, 232, 233, 237
    direct, 20
    elevator pitch, 124, 125–26, 233
    inexpensive, 68
    joint, 97
    planning, 103, 232
    sampling, 72, 78
    techniques, 104
    See also Advertising; Networking; Sales
Marketing channels
    established, 20
    overdependence on few, 61–62, 86, 251
Media relations, 113–14. *See also* Advertising; Public
    relations
Mentoring, 78
Mission statement, 56, 58
Mistakes, handling, 188, 235, 251

Money, 5, 207–30
    consciousness, as entrepreneur, 11
    discomfort with discussing, 209
    management, 11, 95, 210, 218, 232, 251
Morale, 13–14
Motivation, to run a business, 3–4, 5–6, 11–12, 28

N

Name, of business, 14, 105–6, 239
Networking, 20, 104, 107–8, 109–10, 124, 125–34,
    233. *See also* Marketing
Niche market, 20, 23, 26, 59–60, 73–74
    sustainability of, 59–60

O

Office
    atmosphere, 5–6, 195–96
    hours, 234
    procedures, 237, 238
    set-up, 224, 233
    space in home, 14, 243–44
Operations, importance of, 25, 251
    procedures, 237
Opportunities, response to, 45
    and strategy, 57
Overhead, 19, 20, 99, 232
Ownership, 86
transfer of, 81–82

P

Partnerships, 26, 81–82, 175, 183, 222, 239, 240
Payroll, 222
Pets
    business advice from, 252
    at the office, 6, 195
Perseverance, 48, 69, 257–58, 251, 252
Planning, 2, 31, 36, 42, 92, 96
    business plan, annual, 93–94, 95, 183, 234
    employee involvement in, 46
    exit strategy, 81–82
    and financials, 211
    marketing, 103, 232
    for owner's absence or death, 79–80
    retirement, 87–88, 222
    vacations, 250, 252

See also Decision making; Strategy
Planning Shop, The (www.PlanningShop.com), ii,
    61, 93, 109, 140, 145
Presentations, making, 129–32
    PowerPoint, 130, 132
Pricing, 71–74, 232, 234
    increases, 72
    reductions, 78
    underpricing, 73
Priorities, setting, 37–38, 45, 55–56, 237
Procrastination, 15, 236
Products,
    adding new, 91, 149–50
    consumable, 150, 152
    development, 95, 143–46
    distribution, 23, 233, 251
    environmentally responsible, 253
    free of charge, 147, 232, 233
    goal-directed design (Alan Cooper), 145-46
    improved, 23
    integration, 23
    line extension, 90
    new, 23
    pricing, 71–72, 92
    proven, 20
    quality, 254
    sampling, 72
Professional associations, 109, 139–40
Professional development, 68, 95, 178, 199, 232
Profitability, 4, 62, 86, 93, 218, 232
    narrow margins, 73
    See also Revenues, increasing
Profit sharing, 197
Promotion. *See* Advertising; Marketing; Media
    relations; Public relations
Proposal writing, 157–58
Public relations, 104, 113–14. *See also* Advertising;
    Media relations

R

Record keeping, 222, 238, 239
Referrals, 76, 104, 110, 234
Remote customers, 245–46
Remote employees, 245–46
Retail, 9, 67–68
Retirement planning, 87–88, 222

Revenues, increasing, 91–92. *See also* Profitability
Rhonda's Rules, 25, 31, 161, 172, 211
Risk, 9–10, 12, 17–18, 73, 251
    low, business, 19

S

Sale, of business, 81–82, 87–88
Sales, 141–72, 90, 91
    cold calls, 163–64
    preparation for, 155
    structure, simple, 20
    techniques, 153–56, 171–72
    See also Marketing
Sales channels. *See* Marketing channels
Salesperson, 9, 10, 153–54, 238
Sales sheet, 121
Sales tax, 227-28, 240
Self-employment, 5
    vs. being an employee, 11–12, 13, 15–16, 99
    morale, 13–14
    status, 13
Self-promotion. *See* Networking
Services,
    adding new, 90, 91, 97, 149–50
    continual, 150
    development, 95
    free of charge, 75–76, 147, 232, 233
    improved, 23
    integration, 23
    new, 23
    pricing, 71
    proven, 20
    quality, 254
Shares, issuing, 82
Shipping, 230
Skills, personal and business, 28, 29–30
Social Security Number, 222, 240
Sole proprietorship, 7, 222, 239, 240
Specialization, 59–60, 62
Sports
    business lessons from, 251
    like entrepreneurship, 17–18, 39, 50
    figures and employee types, 198
Start-up, business, 3, 19, 24, 25–26, 28, 147–48, 214
    fear of, 15–18
    legal issues, 239

    motivation for, 11
    preparation for, 8
    training-wheel business, 19–20
    transition to, 11–12
State Identification Number, 240
Strategy, 16, 37–38, 53–84, 86, 96, 251
    changes in, 39-40
    developing, 57–58
    for growth, 89–90
    See also Decision making; Planning
Stress, 238, 249–50, 252
Subcontracting, 152, 158
Success, business, 2, 7–8, 19–20, 26, 65, 69–70, 232, 251, 256–58
    fear of, 15
    from failure, 49–50
    See also Failure, business
Survival rates, business, 8

T

Tax, 222, 254
    and buying equipment, 224
    deduction for home office, 244
    estate planning for business, 79–80
    and independent contractors, 241
    and investors, 219
    and leasing, 223
    returns, 7
        Federal Tax Identification Number, 7
        Schedule C, 7
    sales, 227–28
    See also Accountant; Bookkeeping; Internal Revenue Service (IRS)
Technology, 31
    and strategy, 57
    See also Computers
Technology, new, companies, 69
Telecommunications, 14, 115, 229, 230, 233, 237, 238, 243, 246
Telephone service, 14, 229, 230, 233, 243
Time management, 37–38, 237–38
Trade associations, 176, 237
Trademarks, 106
Trade shows, 20, 104, 110
Training, 68, 95, 178, 199, 232
Trustworthiness, 72, 253–54

U

Unemployment, 11
Upselling, 149–50

V

Vacations, 249–50, 252
Value, perceived, 75–76
Venture capital, 49, 69, 86, 181, 219, 220
"Virtual company," 97, 245–46. *See also* Associates,
    professional
Virtual staff, 189, 245–46
Vision, 3–4, 21–32, 95
    transition to plan, 35–36, 42
Vulnerability, economic, 61–62

W

Websites, 92, 98, 104, 135, 137–38
Workaholism, 5–6

Acknowledgments

For twenty years I have had the good fortune to be my own boss. But this wouldn't have happened without the advice, assistance, and inspiration of many others.

I am particularly grateful to the people who work with me every day: the staff of The Planning Shop. They make certain that we reach our goal of publishing books that enable entrepreneurs to build successful businesses and live their dreams.

In particular, I'd like to thank Arthur Wait, who is the brain—and eye—behind the look and feel of all The Planning Shop's products. His design sensibility adds value to everything we do. Arthur also serves as our CIO, and his tech knowledge keeps us on the cutting edge of publishing technology.

We jestingly refer to Deborah Kaye as the "glue" that holds The Planning Shop together, but it's no joke. Deborah makes certain that the company runs efficiently. And since she took over as head of our Academic Marketing Department, The Planning Shop's books have been adopted by over 400 colleges and universities.

Mireille Majoor, our Editorial Project Manager, oversees the writers, researchers, proofreaders, and indexers, as well as all the commas, semicolons, and em dashes at The Planning Shop. Mireille has had to read every sentence in this—and every one of our books—many times, yet she manages to maintain her positive outlook and sense of humor.

Dorienne Goodmanson is the newest addition to our team and is already proving to be invaluable.

We also have a talented and dedicated group of writers and researchers who help The Planning Shop fulfill its mission and extend its reach.

Much of the content for this book grew out of the column *Successful Business Strategies,* which I have written for Gannett News Service since 1992. It has truly been a pleasure working with my editors there, especially Craig Schwed, who is both a gentleman and a gentle man. He is every inch the professional and a joy to work with, and his advice has helped make my column more effective. And I'd like to express my gratitude to Mark Rohner, who first hired me for Gannett, and to Gary Schulz, who got me the interview.

Since 1992 I've also written a column for the *Costco Connection,* the monthly magazine of Costco. It's been a pleasure working with Tim Talevich, Anita Thompson, and Dave Fuller, and I'd like to thank them, for being so great to work with and for producing such an outstanding publication.

Over the years, I've had a number of good friends whom I've been able to call for advice and last-minute column inspiration including Cathy Goldstein; Edward Pollack; Kenneth Allen; Jennifer Arthur; my siblings, Janice Hill, Arnie Abrams, and Karen Colbert; and my niece Adeena Colbert.

I was particularly fortunate to have an incredible mentor—the late Eugene Kleiner. Eugene was not only a brilliant venture capitalist, businessman, and engineer, he was a wonderful human being and great friend.

Of course, work wouldn't be the same without a dog around the office, so I'd like to thank the dogs who have been by my side, or at my feet, the entire time I have run my businesses: Teddy and Cosmo.

Finally, I'd like to express my gratitude to my readers and clients, who have shared with me their concerns and questions, revealed their dreams and goals, and every day remind me of the vitality, creativity, and dedication of today's entrepreneurs.

Grow Your Business with The Planning Shop!

We offer a full complement of books and tools to help you build your business *successfully*.

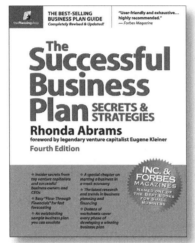

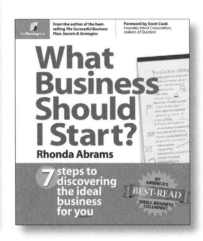

Ask your bookseller about these titles or visit www.PlanningShop.com